THE AGE OF GLASS

THE AGE OF GLASS

A Cultural History of Glass in Modern and Contemporary Architecture

Stephen Eskilson

Bloomsbury Academic
An imprint of Bloomsbury Publishing Plc

B L O O M S B U R Y
LONDON · OXFORD · NEW YORK · NEW DELHI · SYDNEY

Bloomsbury Academic
An imprint of Bloomsbury Publishing Plc

50 Bedford Square	1385 Broadway
London	New York
WC1B 3DP	NY 10018
UK	USA

www.bloomsbury.com

BLOOMSBURY and the Diana logo are trademarks of Bloomsbury Publishing Plc

First published 2018

© Stephen Eskilson, 2018

Stephen Eskilson has asserted his right under the Copyright, Designs and Patents Act, 1988, to be identified as Author of this work.

All rights reserved. No part of this publication may be reproduced or transmitted in any form or by any means, electronic or mechanical, including photocopying, recording, or any information storage or retrieval system, without prior permission in writing from the publishers.

No responsibility for loss caused to any individual or organization acting on or refraining from action as a result of the material in this publication can be accepted by Bloomsbury or the author.

British Library Cataloguing-in-Publication Data
A catalogue record for this book is available from the British Library.

ISBN:	HB:	978-1-4742-7836-2
	PB:	978-1-4742-7835-5
	ePDF:	978-1-4742-7837-9
	ePub:	978-1-4742-7838-6

Library of Congress Cataloging-in-Publication Data
Names: Eskilson, Stephen, 1964- author.
Title: The age of glass : a cultural history of glass in modern and contemporary architecture / Stephen Eskilson.
Description: New York : Bloomsbury Academic, 2018. | Includes bibliographical references and index.
Identifiers: LCCN 2017028111 (print) | LCCN 2017028960 (ebook) | ISBN 9781474278379 (ePDF) | ISBN 9781474278386 (ePub) | ISBN 9781474278362 (hardback : alk. paper) | ISBN 9781474278355 (pbk. : alk. paper)
Subjects: LCSH: Glass construction–History–20th century. | Glass construction–History–21st century. | Architecture and society–History–20th century. | Architecture and society–History–21st century.
Classification: LCC NA4140 (ebook) | LCC NA4140.E85 2018 (print) | DDC 721/.04496–dc23
LC record available at https://lccn.loc.gov/2017028111

Cover design by Eleanor Rose
Cover image: One World Observatory, New York, United States, photo by Khara Woods on Unsplash

Typeset by Integra Software Services Pvt. Ltd.
Printed and bound in India

To find out more about our authors and books visit www.bloomsbury.com. Here you will find extracts, author interviews, details of forthcoming events and the option to sign up for our newsletters.

CONTENTS

List of Figures vi
Preface xi
Acknowledgments xiv

1 The dawning of the age of glass 1
2 Stained glass and modernity 27
3 Daylight rules the modern building 59
4 Glass visions 89
5 Structural glass 121
6 Shade 161
7 The politics of glass 193

Notes 209
Index 217

LIST OF FIGURES

1.1 Robert Smythson, Hardwick Hall, 1597   5

1.2 Joseph Paxton, Crystal Palace, 1851   8

1.3 Follett Oster, Crystal Fountain at Crystal Palace, 1851   10

1.4 Eighteenth-century English Shop Front   14

1.5 JW Benson Store, 1866   16

1.6 Holmes & Sons Machinery Store, Norwich, 1863   17

1.7 Galerie D'Orleans, Palais-Royale, Paris, 1825   20

1.8 Louis-Auguste Boileau, Bon Marche Store, 1876   26

2.1 "Art Glass Church Windows" Foster-Munger Company, 1902   33

2.2 John La Farge, example of opalescent glass, c. 1890   35

2.3 Louis C. Tiffany, Tiffany Chapel, 1893   37

2.4 Ker-Xavier Roussel, Design for Tiffany Window, 1895   40

2.5 Martin Roche, Cathedral Hall, University Club, Chicago, 1908   41

2.6 Frank Lloyd Wright, Design for Luxfer Prism tile, 1897   43

2.7	Frank Lloyd Wright, Robie House Window, 1904	45
2.8	Frank Lloyd Wright, Coonley Playhouse Stained Glass, 1912	47
2.9	Theo van Doesburg, Composition IV, Alkmaar, 1917	50
2.10	Josef Albers, "City" stained glass, 1928	53
2.11	Le Corbusier, Light Wall at Ronchamp, 1954	56
2.12	David Adjaye, Stephen Lawrence Center, 2007	58
3.1	William Jenney, Home Insurance Building, 1885	61
3.2	Chicago Window on Charles Atwood, Reliance Building, 1895	67
3.3	Holabird & Roche, Champlain Building, 1894	68
3.4	Holabird & Roche, Gage Group, 1899	75
3.5	Charles Atwood, Reliance Building, 1895	76
3.6	Burnham & Root, Rookery, 1888	80
3.7	Luxfer Prism advertisement, c.1911	81
3.8	Le Corbusier, Villa La Roche, 1923	84
4.1	Bruno Taut, Glashaus, 1914	97
4.2	Bruno Taut, Glashaus, 1914	98
4.3	Walter Gropius, Faguswerke, 1914	101
4.4	Peter Ellis, Oriel Chambers, 1864	103
4.5	William Polk, Hallidie Building, 1918	104

4.6   Walter Gropius, Bauhaus Dessau Workshop Elevation, 1925 106

4.7   Philip Goodwin/Edward Durell Stone, MoMA Building, 1939 111

4.8   Skidmore, Owings, and Merrill, Lever House, 1952 113

4.9   Ludwig Mies van der Rohe, 860–880 Lake Shore Drive, 1951 115

4.10 Ludwig Mies van der Rohe, Seagram Building, 1958 116

4.11 Le Corbusier et al., UN Secretariat, 1949 118

5.1   Jacobs & Sons, Advertisement for Vault Lighting, 1890s 126

5.2   Gustave Falconnier, Glass Bricks, 1890s 127

5.3   Stephane Tarnier, Baby Incubator, 1890 128

5.4   Pierre Chareau, Maison Verre, 1932 130

5.5   Le Corbusier, City of Refuge, 1933 133

5.6   Vitrolite Advertisement, 1933 136

5.7   Owen Williams, Daily Express Building, 1933, Getty 139

5.8   Owens-Illinois Glass House at A Century of Progress, 1933 141

5.9   Alexander M. Pringle, Manhattan Laundry, 1936 143

5.10 Shin Takamatsu, Kirin Plaza, 1987 149

5.11 Renzo Piano, Maison Hermes, 2001 150

5.12 FAM, Atocha Station Memorial, 2007 151

5.13 Norman Foster, Willis, Faber, 1975 153

5.14 Toyo Ito, Sendai Mediatheque, 2000 154

5.15 Bohlin Cywinski Jackson, Apple Cube, Mark I, 2006 156

5.16 Jean-Marie Duthilleul, The Gare de Strasbourg, 2006 158

5.17 SANAA, The Toledo Museum of Art Glass Pavilion, 2006 159

6.1 George Nimmons, Sears Pavilion, A Century of Progress, 1933 165

6.2 George Nimmons, Sears Englewood Store, 1934 166

6.3 SANAA, Dior Omotesando, 2004 168

6.4 Le Corbusier, City of Refuge, South Façade, 1933 171

6.5 Peter Belluschi, Portland Bank, 1948 175

6.6 Oscar Niemeyer et al., Ministry of Education, 1943 177

6.7 Lucio Costa, Parque Guinle, 1954 178

6.8 Jean Nouvel, Institut de le Monde Arabe, 1981 182

6.9 Jean Nouvel, Doha Tower, 2012 183

6.10 Norman Foster, Commerzbank, 1997 186

6.11 Renzo Piano, Debis Tower, 1998 187

7.1 Philip Johnson, Glass House, 1949 197

LIST OF FIGURES   ix

7.2 Norman Foster, Reichstag, 1999 201

7.3 I. M. Pei, Grande Pyramide Louvre, 1989 203

7.4 Norman Foster, London City Hall, 2002 204

7.5 Legat Partners, Waukegan City Hall, 2004 204

7.6 John Portman, Westin Bonaventure, 1976 206

PREFACE

Where to begin? Industrialists surveying the ongoing age of glass have sought to pinpoint their favored substance's origin, adding layers of history, nostalgia, and even romance to their product line. For this reason in 1856, Henry Chance, a partner in the eponymous firm that had provided the glass for London's Crystal Palace, ruminated in a lecture about the roots of window glass: "Pompeii, awakened from a slumber of seventeen hundred years, has proved the existence of window glass in the days of the early emperors. In a small chamber, attached to the bathing room of a private dwelling-house, excavated about the year 1763, was found, 'a window, which, ... still held, when it was found, four panes of glass.'"[1] The drawn-out, staccato rhythm of this revelation must have added drama to this lecture on early manufacture. Likewise, in the twentieth century, the corporate authors of *Glass History Manufacture and Its Universal Application* began with a chapter called "The Romance of Glass," which includes this origin story: "Many thousands of years before the Christian Era this romance began. It is older far than Pliny's tale of the Tyrian mariners who, he recounts, landed in some Mediterranean harbor to cook themselves food, and to prop their kettles over the fire used lumps of natron ... 'tis a plausible fancy: true or not, what matter?"[2] 'Tis also true this particular version of the story ends rather less romantically, with a detailed description of the products made available as of 1923 by the Pittsburgh Plate Glass Company.

This book captures the cultural and technological ascension of glass in modern and contemporary architecture. Wedded to the idea that glass is a culturally elastic material with immense symbolic resonance, it traces a series of interwoven threads regarding what glass means and how it has produced and dispersed meaning over the past two centuries. While not immersed in the minutiae of glass technology, it covers the highlights of the industrialization of glass that began centuries ago and continues through to today. Outside of the technological story, there is the role of glass in the stylistic and ideological development of architecture that needs to be considered as well. As glass has crept quietly, if inexorably, into a position of great architectural prominence, we need to sort through some of the events that have gotten us here and examine what the future might bring.

The following text is not proffered as a comprehensive history of glass in architecture; rather, it attempts to engage episodically with some of that history's most defining moments while offering new interpretations of past buildings and the texts that helped to define them. Methodologically diverse, the narrative mixes theoretical analyses and conventional historical takes with close readings of specific buildings. Chapter 1 opens up the discussion, laying the groundwork in regard to the pioneering technological and cultural changes that emerged early in the industrial age of glass. From humble shops to the dazzling Paris arcades, glass quickly became a mediator of many aspects of urban space. Additionally, we get our first glimpse of the Crystal Palace, a building that will haunt and inspire future generations of architects.

While much of the work on glass history has focused on transparent sheet glass, in fact one of the most prominent manifestations of urban glazing came in the form of its stained variant. The nineteenth century was a metaphorical sea of stained glass, as the Romantic revival of medieval culture combined with new decorative trends to create strong consumer demand for this quintessentially modern industrial product. Stained glass also played a large role in the developing aesthetics of twentieth-century designers such as Frank Lloyd Wright and Theo van Doesburg, both of whom formulated their own approaches to architecture through experiments with the medium.

Until the electrical light and power industry matured after 1900, windows and the entrance of daylight into buildings were the prime concern of many architects. Chapter 3 begins with a reevaluation of the birth of skyscrapers in late-nineteenth-century Chicago, arguing that the horizontal form of the "Chicago Window" has been wrongly displaced from the core of the emerging modern aesthetic. This section is partnered with an examination of Le Corbusier's later fascination with horizontal windows and their effect on views and interior illumination.

No issue has done more to define the status of glass in the twentieth century than the apparent conflict between the functionalist and the expressionist view of the material that came to the fore early in the century. Chapter 4 attempts to reconcile these two supposed poles, and detail how this situation came about in both a historiographic and material fashion. In terms of cultural visibility, the glass curtain wall—an obsession of the architects who formulated the modern style—has been burdened with considerable symbolic importance, and its trajectory from utopian dream to banal reality helps to shed further light on the conceptual formation of glass architecture.

Part of the dream of glass architecture since the beginning of the industrial age has been structures created out of glass alone. Glass walls, roofs, and towers shimmering in the sun have provoked many aspirational projects over the years, and Chapter 5 investigates structural glass and its gradual evolution over the past century. Sometimes glass walls served as a comforting incubator or signifier of cleanliness, at other times it symbolized wealth and glamour. In contrast, some structural glass started out with much promise but has been consigned to the alleys and basements of history. It is only in the last few decades that the dream of structural glass has become much more of a reality, as new technology has allowed for a wave of innovative buildings.

From the time of the first hothouses for tropical plants, architects have recognized the thermal and hydrologic problems created by great swaths of glass. As the material has proliferated over the skins of countless buildings, various scientific advances have helped to mitigate the effects of glass, while architects have struggled to counteract or block out the sun. With the dawning realization of the extent of glass architecture's energy inefficiency beginning in the 1970s, sustainability strategies have come to the fore and green building now dominates the discussion. Can technology save glass architecture from its own astounding success?

Chapter 7 concludes the narrative by delving into some of the key moments when glass architecture has intersected with powerful political currents. Be it the transparency of democratic policy or the crystalline hardness of fascist ideology, glass has proven to be a slippery material that has been enlisted to support multiple contradictory belief systems. This chapter also offers a provocative new interpretation of Philip Johnson's Glass House and its relationship to the architecture of the Third Reich.

ACKNOWLEDGMENTS

I would like to thank my long-time editor and friend, Lee Ripley, with whom I first discussed this work. She introduced me to James Thompson, my insightful editor at Bloomsbury Academic. Also at Bloomsbury, Claire Constable and Sophie Tann provided continual editorial assistance. The staff at the Ryerson & Burnham Libraries of the Art Institute of Chicago, especially Autumn Mather, provided valuable research assistance. At Eastern Illinois University, this project bridged the tenures of two Art Department Chairs, David Griffin and Chris Kahler, both of whom were quite supportive of the project. My family, Jordi and our boys, David, Gavi, and Jack, are a constant source of love.

1 THE DAWNING OF THE AGE OF GLASS

Glass technology

As with so many other materials vital to modern architecture, the technological history of glass begins with a series of breakthroughs that shifted glass manufacture away from its artisanal roots into the urban world of mass production. In the early industrial age, glass served architecture mainly as a utilitarian product: to enclose windows from the elements and admit light while preserving a view outside. For glazing windows there were two technologies in play, blown glass and cast plate glass. Blown glass was itself separated into two processes: one producing crown glass, the other, cylinder glass. Crown, cylinder, and plate: simple enough terminologies except insomuch as many substitute names have been used depending on the country and the era. Just to give one example, blown glass made by the cylinder process was called alternatively "broad," "spread," or "sheet" glass in nineteenth-century London and "window glass" or "drawn glass" in twentieth-century New York. Mindful of these vagaries in terminology, the industrial history of windows begins with a worker endeavoring to manipulate the molten, liquid mass of silica, lime, sodium oxide, and sodium carbonate that form the raw materials of most architectural glass.

While the original invention of blown crown glass dates back more than a millennium, its story in modern Europe begins in the 1600s in France.[1] Called Normandy glass by Francophones, crown glass is created by a blower who repeatedly dips his blowing pipe into the liquid glass, gradually building up a glob of syrupy fire. This mass is continually rotated and pressed against a flat surface until it takes on a shape like that of an oddly proportioned vase; next, it is detached from the blowing pipe and attached to a new rod that is used to spin it in the heat of a fire so that centrifugal force will transform the three-dimensional shape into a flat disk. After the glass "flashed" into a flat shape, it, like all glass, went in an annealing oven that governed the transition from hot, pliable molten material to hard, brittle cool glass. Finally, the disks of glass had to be cut into orthogonal patterns to make the squares and rectangles suitable for glazing. While the largest disks might reach a diameter of 6 feet and produce a pane of 34 × 16 inches, in practice most crown glass was smaller. Crown glass had one advantage over other processes: its brilliant sheen. Partly because of this luminous quality, crown glass was popular in England until the end of the nineteenth century, although it had been eclipsed by cylinder glass elsewhere in Europe well before then.

The foremost blown glass of the industrial revolution, cylinder glass, was produced through an even more arduous method. A worker would accumulate a mass of up to forty pounds of liquid glass that would be shaped into a compact cylinder; the cylinder would then be passed to a blower who stood on a platform and swung it mightily back and forth like a pendulum in order to stretch it out to the appropriate length. Successive cycles of blowing, swinging, and reheating produced a long tube of glass measuring several feet long and less than a foot in diameter. With the ends removed, this cylinder would next be cut lengthwise, often by a diamond, and then reheated and flattened, a process that led to cylinder glass lacking the lustrous sheen of crown glass, the latter never having had its surface despoiled. Cylinder sheets also reverted to a slightly bowed shape that had to be accounted for in construction. Annealed and cut, the cylinder process produced a large quantity of useful, if imperfect, sheets that were widely available in larger sizes than those produced through the crown process. For example, the glass for the Crystal Palace was "blown to cut" to a size of 49 × 30 inches, these sheets were subsequently cut down into three panes measuring 49 × 10 inches. By the middle of the nineteenth century, cylinder glass was available in a combination of six grades and six weights (thicknesses), for a total of thirty-six different offerings. The highest grade cost about triple the price of the coarsest. These advantages in size and variety made cylinder glass the preferred material for larger nineteenth-century projects such as railroad stations and greenhouses.

Cast plate glass, which overtook cylinder glass as an industrial staple around 1880 and later became the basis for twentieth-century glass technology, was also introduced in France at the dawn of the industrial revolution. In that process, molten glass is poured onto a flat casting table and then rolled out like cookie dough. After the annealing is complete, the real work begins, as the cast plate must be gradually ground down and then polished into transparency. A plate that started out a half inch thick would finish the production line at less than half that measurement. The labor involved in grinding and polishing was immense, and plate glass only became an economically viable product as that procedure was gradually mechanized beginning after 1800. By the end of the Victorian era, cylinder and plate glass were both widely manufactured, with plate glass serving as the higher end product for larger windows that also needed to be flawless. Overall, the emphasis of glass manufacture was always to make it cheaper, clearer, and larger, and there are myriad technological improvements over the years that advanced all three of these processes—concerning, for example, furnace construction or the substitution of compressed air for workers' lungs—that may be of interest to the glassmaking enthusiast but are outside the realm of the current study.

Glass as commodity

As a parallel to this technological transition of glass from artisanal product to industrial material, there was a series of economic adjustments made at the dawn of the age of glass. As glass gradually became more widespread in pre-industrial Europe, it came to the attention of governments looking to raise revenue via consumption taxes on "luxury" goods. In England, two taxes on glass were instituted as early as the 1690s: one on windows and another on glass itself. While the glass tax was quickly repealed, the window tax, which was originally intended as essentially a property tax indexed by windows, remained an important source of revenue throughout the eighteenth century. Easy to determine and collect, the window tax was raised six times during its tenure. This progressive tax applied only to houses, and featured an exemption over the years ranging from the first seven to ten windows so that smaller homes avoided the tax. However, urban tenements were subject to the tax in aggregate, so the poor often lived in squalid housing with boarded-up windows. It was thus for public health reasons that this "tax on light and air" was finally repealed in 1851 after a chorus of experts and activists successfully publicized the role fresh air played in combatting typhus epidemics and the like.

In 1746, the glass excise tax had been reinstituted based on weight, a factor that sustained the crown glass industry because that material was significantly lighter than cylinder glass. The glass tax had a mixed impact on English producers—at times it more than doubled the cost of production—because it increased prices but also served as a partial tariff that stifled the competition arising from the glass factories of Belgium and France, both of which had instituted their own version of the English taxes. However, the English tax had become so onerous by the 1840s—when it was so high that British glass dealers would actually import glass from the continent and then resell it as an export—that its repeal was taken up by the prime minister himself, Sir Robert Peel. "I shall make no preliminary observation, but mention it at once—it is the article of glass. (hear, hear!)"[2] Sir Peel argued that less expensive glass would not only give Britain "command of a commodity" but also improve the heat retention of the majority of homes not subject to the window tax as they would be able to afford double-glazed windows: "Nothing prevents the passage of heat so much as glass." Sir Peel's 1845 repeal did initiate a brief boom in glass manufacture in England, although rapid oversupply ("Glass-houses sprang up like mushrooms"[3]) led to a major bust. Still, it is clear that the industry as a whole prospered because of the repeal, and once the "exciseman was released from his attendance at the glass-house,"[4] the technological advances in English glass manufacturing, especially in cast plate, accelerated. There was yet one more English glass tax that lives on in historical infamy; it was instituted for the American colonies as part of the Townshend Act of 1767. Considered a prime driver of the discontent that fomented the American Revolution, the Townshend Act was mostly repealed (except for the tax on tea) in 1770.

The end result of the glass and window taxes in Britain (Ireland was mostly exempt) was that the substance became one of the most overt symbols of personal wealth. However, the onset of this type of conspicuous fenestration has traditionally been associated with the 1597 completion of Hardwick Hall a full century before the institution of the glass taxes (figure 1.1). Designed by the architect Robert Smythson for Elizabeth Talbot, the countess of Shrewsbury, the mansion's most visible feature has long been enshrined in the children's rhyming couplet, "Hardwick Hall, more glass than wall." The south elevation is simply staggering, hundreds of lustrous crown glass panes forming towering windows. The hierarchy of social class is even more transparent, as the higher floors that housed Bess of Hardwick's main social spaces—she was the second richest woman in England after Elizabeth I—feature the tallest windows. Constructed of

FIGURE 1.1 Robert Smythson, Hardwick Hall, 1597.

twice as many panes on the vertical axis as those on the ground floor, these twenty-five-foot-tall sheaths of glass fixed into lead cames fronted a long gallery. The gallery featured a string of fireplaces, so Smythson also has the dubious distinction of having designed a *sui generis* example of thermal inefficiency; a cold day saw the chimneys of Hardwick Hall drawing cold air through the drafty windows and circulating it again to the outside.

Greenhouse to Crystal Palace

Perhaps even more than the windows of a manor house, the all-encompassing glass skins of nineteenth-century greenhouses stunned viewers with their display of wealth and cultivated learning. These iron and glass conservatories—that are so often cited as the progenitors of modern design—came about originally in the 1700s not to spark architectural advancement but for reason of science and status. The eighteenth century's spirit of Enlightenment fueled the collection of empirical facts almost as an end in itself; the sense developed that everything on the globe was knowable and could be mastered by Europeans. In the emblematic *Encyclopédie* edited by Denis Diderot and Jean le Rond d'Alembert, the frontispiece (1772) by Charles-Nicolas

Cochin pictures a slew of allegorical figures related to learning; in one of the middle rows one finds botany grouped somewhat eccentrically along with agriculture, chemistry, and optics. The *Encyclopédie* makes mention of early glasshouses, calling them "verrieres, small greenhouses made from planks and covered at the top and in front with glazed panels which close up neatly. They are opened out over beds for growing pineapples and tender plants. These casings are commonly used in England and may also be seen in the Jardin du Roi in Paris." Using this passive solar technology, horticultural enthusiasts collected and nurtured thousands of plants from around the world that would otherwise never survive in temperate climes: palms, water lilies, and citrus fruits—the French term *orangerie* of course refers to a greenhouse dedicated to the latter—to name but a few of the exotic flora that appeared amidst the clammy damp of northern Europe. The greenhouse opened up a new world to conquer; as the hothouse designer John Loudon put it, "Artificial climates … gives man so proud a command over Nature."[5]

The gradual transition from greenhouse to glasshouse has been ably documented by John Dix, who has plotted out the technological progression that accelerated in the nineteenth century as different combinations of glass, wood, and iron sprung up on the country estates of European lords and ladies.[6] A surefire marker of social stature, the cultivation of exotic plants had a cachet in society outside of the financial realm, becoming a noted area of connoisseurship akin to the cultivation of the arts. Additionally, hot house plants signified the romantic atmosphere of far-flung travel. Simple comfort was in play as well; anyone who has retreated to a fragrant, humid, 27 degree centigrade greenhouse amidst a cold, dry winter's day savors the experience.

Although much of the greenhouse evolution story rests upon the creation of innovative structural and heating systems based on trial and error, it is the shimmering walls of glass that eventually come to define the type. While early hothouse structures often featured masonry walls punctuated with thousands of small "bulls eye" panes—the distorted section of a crown glass disc where the blowing pipe had been detached during manufacture—later iterations saw the wall dissolve as glass spread across the exterior like an invasive species of vine. Take, for example, the Bicton Gardens Palm House at Devon, completed before 1850 by some combination of the rival designers John Loudon and W. and D. Bailey. While perhaps the invention of the curvilinear sash bar deserves much of the credit for the accomplishment, it is the tesserae of glass that most impacts the visitor to the estate of Lord Rolle. The Palm House also played a part in the early implementation of structural glass, as the panes there are not simply infill but play a stiffening role on the skin.

Arguably the most important collaboration in the history of greenhouse construction was that between Joseph Paxton, a lowborn laborer at London's Horticultural Society, and William Cavendish, Duke of Devonshire. The pair met in the 1820s because of their mutual interest in plants, and the Duke soon made Paxton the lead designer and engineer of the various botanical endeavors at his Chatsworth estate. There, Paxton oversaw a magical world that included the Great Stove Conservatory (demolished 1920), one of the largest of its kind. Important to his subsequent work on the Crystal Palace, Paxton used Chatsworth as a sort of engineering laboratory where he experimented with new structural systems such as the ridge and furrow roof he used on both the Great Conservatory and the Victoria Regia water-lily pavilion of 1850. At the same time, Paxton developed a taste for standardized materials and so he built up relationships with industrial suppliers of iron and glass; significantly he started buying large quantities of blown cylinder sheets from Chance Brothers in the 1830s. It was a propitious time to connect with Chance, because in 1830 the firm had established a relationship with the French glassworks of Georg Bontemps located at Choisy-le-Roi; Bontemps oversaw a complete overhaul of Chance's cylinder glass operation that vastly improved the size, quantity, and quality of the product. For the Great Conservatory—the largest glazed building in Europe at 277 × 123 feet—Chance provided Paxton with 56,000 sheets of glass measuring 49 × 10 inches, much larger than would have been possible using the prevailing crown glass.[7]

Paxton's labors for the Duke of Devonshire—as well as the status wrought by the Duke's patronage—would eventually lead this greenhouse engineer to the design of the fabled Crystal Palace (figure 1.2). The Crystal Palace was built to house the Great Exhibition of the Works of Industry of all Nations, a grand display of over 100,000 manufactured objects, half from the British Empire and half from elsewhere around the world. Partly a response to the similar, but much smaller, exhibition of industrial goods held in Paris in 1844, the Great Exhibition is generally recognized as an iconic moment in the economic rivalry between the major European powers that marked the Victorian age. Sponsored by the Queen's husband Prince Albert, the Great Exhibition showcased a motley collection of just about everything: art objects—some of great beauty but many of dubious quality—shared the space with immense printing

FIGURE 1.2 Joseph Paxton, Crystal Palace, 1851.

presses and loads of American firearms. As Queen Victoria wrote in her diary, the Great Exhibition held "every conceivable invention." The glazed walls and roof of the Crystal Palace was not the only glass on display, as stained glass filled one large exhibition space and was also featured in Augustus W. Pugin's Medieval Court (See Chapter 2).

Curiously, the stage was set for Paxton's design of the Crystal Palace by the formation of perhaps the most inept Building Committee of all time. In March 1850, with less than fourteen months remaining until the exhibition's scheduled opening, the dolorous Building Committee began soliciting design proposals. This competition resulted in 248 proposals, all of which were promptly rejected. The Committee then offered up its own collaborative design, a completely impracticable and uninspired mass of bricks (mind you, this was to be a temporary building). It is only then in June that Paxton enters the fray, and within a matter of weeks has used his connections to publicize and prepare for the construction of the Crystal Palace.

The story of the construction of the Crystal Palace is generally a recitation of statistics: constructed in seventeen weeks; 4,000 tons of iron; twenty-four miles of gutters; 300,000 panes of cylinder glass measuring 49 × 10 inches, 76 custom-made glazing wagons; over 18,000 panes installed in just one week, etc. The resulting structure also stakes a claim to fame based on its massiveness: 562 meters long by 124 meters wide; transept at 32 meters high in order to house a small grove of mature elm trees; 33 million cubic feet of space; 17 acres of roof. The message here, as everywhere, is that the Crystal Palace was really big. What is often left out of the discussion is the fact that it was big but ungainly, lacking the gorgeous proportions and finely wrought details found on the greenhouses of private estates. Despite this flaw, the sheer size of the structure in Hyde Park repositioned glass that had started as a signifier of private wealth into a signifier of public, national identity replete with democratic overtones.

What made the erection of the Crystal Palace possible in such a short amount of time was Paxton's control of the supply chain—using the telegraph to communicate with his main suppliers in Birmingham—and his use of standardized parts that could be prefabricated in order to create 24 × 24 inch building units. This standardization also applied to the glazing, as the vertical walls were filled in with manufactured window units measuring fourteen by seven and a half feet. However, on the lower level many of the window units were blocked with wooden panels in order to provide background walls for the exhibits. These innovative techniques are the basis for its reputation as a precursor of the modern movement.

The Great Exhibition opened on May 1, 1851. Despite at times suffering from the extreme heat in the interior (see Chapter 6), over six million visitors attended the show in the Crystal Palace. But the walls and roofs of the pavilion were not necessarily the most notable use of glass, for at the nexus of the exhibition—a prime meeting point for visitors found at the crossing—shimmered a 27-foot-high fountain manufactured by Abraham Follett Osler (figure 1.3). A maker of crystal glass objects, mainly chandeliers, Osler had first come to the attention of the British elite when he displayed a set of glass candlesticks commissioned for the tomb at Mecca in 1847. At the Great Exhibition, his four-ton crystal fountain towered above the assembled throngs, "perhaps the most striking object in the Exhibition; the lightness and beauty, as well as the perfect novelty of its design, have rendered it the theme of admiration with all visitors." Tinted a slight pink, the ornate Osler fountain was carved to resemble a Gothic spire, giving it a spectral quality at odds with the clear light of Paxton's glass skin.

The contrasting glass of Paxton's Crystal Palace and Osler's fountain in a way announces two themes that will dominate the interpretation of this material for decades to come: functionalism and expressionism. The Crystal Palace itself has remained a key part of the backstory to the functionalist interpretation of modern architecture. Siegfried Giedion wrote it many times and perhaps stated it best.

FIGURE 1.3 Follett Oster, Crystal Fountain at Crystal Palace, 1851.

The possibilities dormant in modern industrial civilization have never since, to my knowledge, been so clearly expressed. It was recognized at the time that this combination of wood, glass, and iron—incidentally a combination resulting in an admirably practical exhibition technique—had evoked a new kind of imagination which sprang directly from the spirit of the age.[8]

Giedion famously had no love for expressionist elements in architecture, dismissing them as an aberration that undercut what he saw as the rational, pragmatic concerns of the modern movement. Along these lines, the historicist, expressive design of Osler's fountain was not part of the story he was trying to tell. Of course, condemning Giedion for espousing a strong narrative of functionalist development is engaging in a fight with a straw man, as the weakness of this position has been well-trammeled in the architectural literature of recent decades. The functionalist/expressionist dualism has always been a hierarchical one through which modernist aesthetics were validated after having come through the crucible of weighty emotion. Still, the lasting impact of the binary interpretation is hard to completely dismiss as there is some substance therein.

Glass is a slippery, elastic material in terms of its signification and so the rationalist Zeitgeist identified by Giedion at the Crystal Palace was also counter-interpreted as inspiration for subsequent legions of visionaries such as Paul Scheerbart and Bruno Taut. What is important today is that functionalist and expressionist points of view are recognized as dialogically intertwined—not oppositional—and over the course of modern architecture post–Crystal Palace these two terms will dissolve one into another. In many ways going forward the memory of the Crystal Palace represented a paradox like that of the American skyscraper described so artfully by Thomas van Leeuwen; look too long at the glass and you can see anything you need to see.[9]

In terms of architectural influence, perhaps it should be remembered that the Crystal Palace for most people was not architecture at all, but rather part of a subset of building large, transitory structures that economically met a specific, pressing need. In a parallel to the case made in the twentieth century for the 1890s Chicago skyscrapers as harbingers of modernity, the Crystal Palace arguably has been given too much recognition based on a certain type of hindsight. Probably John Ruskin was right; it was not architecture, just a "magnified conservatory." It is much too easy to denigrate Ruskin and other critics like Pugin as paleo-conservatives unable and unwilling to see into the future (after all, they did both go insane). But really, did the Crystal Palace have much going for it architecturally other than its size and spectacle? Perhaps it was not a forerunner of the modern architectural ideal but rather an ungainly work of engineering that should instead be remembered for signifying the shallowness of consumer culture. Ruskin wrote cogently in 1854 when the Crystal Palace reopened in Sydenham, "Our taste ... is dazzled by the lustre of a few rows of panes of glass; and the first principles of architectural sublimity ... are found all the while to have consisted merely in sparkling and in space."[10]

The nickname for Paxton's structure, the Crystal Palace, was a riff on a phrase that had appeared in 1850 in *Punch*, where the pavilion was anticipated as a "palace of very crystal." There is a strong suggestion of the supernatural in the name; cheap, industrial cylinder glass has been semiotically transmuted into effervescent crystal. For this reason, the great greenhouse has been interpreted by the Marxist inclined as forming the kernel of commodity fetishism, whereby manufactured objects become magical things that are the focus of consumer desire."[11] With their "use-value" suppressed, the sign value of conspicuous consumption comes to the fore. Historian Thomas Richards has opined, "The Crystal Palace was a monument to consumption, the first of its kind, a place where the combined mythologies of consumerism [first] appeared in concentrated form."[12] Along these lines, the Crystal Palace also stands as a formative example of that other great monument to nineteenth-century consumption, the department store.

Shop windows

It is impossible to imagine the department store without thinking of glass. Display windows, show cases, skylights: all of these formed a key part of the architectural environment first promulgated in 1852 at merchant Arthur Bourcicaut's Au Bon Marché. But the department store did not self-generate *sui generis*; before engaging with that apotheosis of conspicuous glass display, it is worth taking a look back at how glass had gradually entered the visual lexicon of merchandising. One of the first mentions in print of the shop window comes from Daniel Defoe, noted author of the ur-castaway novel *Robinson Crusoe* whose varied interests and endeavors ranged from novelist to merchant to spy. Throughout his life Defoe published prolifically on an eclectic range of topics, and he sought in 1726 to explain the current state of the retail trade in general goods. The handbook *The Complete English Tradesman* was written in the manner of a guidebook aimed at aspiring merchants seeking "a collection of useful instructions" and who would uphold the "dignity and honour of trade in England."[13]

In *The Complete English Tradesman*, Defoe recognizes the beginnings of a new phenomenon, the shop window display of goods through glass intended to stimulate the desires of passersby.

> It is true that a fine shew of goods will bring customers; and it is not a new custom, but a very old one, that a new shop very well furnished goes a great way to bringing a trade; ... but that a fine shew of shelves and glass windows should bring customers, that was never made a rule in trade "till now."[14]

Defoe goes on to bemoan this new commitment to overhead, warning the aspiring shopkeeper that the need to glaze his windows will eat into capital that could be spent on stocking goods. Defoe suggests that this fashion for display will be renounced in the future and that it "will hardly be believed in ages to come" that a hypothetical pastry shop required multiple transparent (he uses the term "looking-glass plates") sash windows, the panes measuring 12 × 16 inches. In time-honored English fashion, Defoe blames what he sees as the frivolous decoration of shop fronts on "the French Humour," noting that "when we do mimick [*sic*] the French, we generally do it to our hurt." For Defoe, glass is clearly a luxury good that should not play a role in commerce. He keeps swimming against the tide through to the conclusion of the book, insisting repeatedly that customers will always seek out a plain shop with good service over one with glazed pretensions.

It is important to recognize how most material histories of consumerism—display windows, architecture, etc.—remain wedded to the belief that it all began in the middle of the nineteenth century with cheap glass, the Crystal Palace, Karl Marx, and the department store. Maybe there will be a passing mention of the early nineteenth-century Paris arcades ("progenitor of the mall!" see below), but the eighteenth century gets written out of modernity once again. Disregarding Defoe's tales of pricey windows and the obvious development of window shopping as a cultural activity, historians have portrayed the eighteenth-century shop as a dingy, dark space that the consumer is likely to flee as soon as possible. However, at least in the upscale urban market, quite the opposite was true and many shops greeted the customer with a profusion of glass. For example, the records of the London goldsmith Martha Braithwaite from 1746 show that her retail environment featured 45 linear feet of glass cases, plus large shop windows at the front.[15] Innovations in projecting display windows from this era included the "cabinet window," an early type of bowed glass enclosure with curved corner panes. While the glazed area of the storefront may be quite large, measuring at times 10 × 10 feet square, the glass is of course made up of small panes of 12 × 16 inches separated by glazing bars such as those windows described by Defoe, and in England often benefitting from the added luster of crown glass. In eighteenth-century shops, the high expense of glass was utilized as a public sign of the financial strength of the establishment, announcing to passersby that this was a stable, high-end concern (figure 1.4). For any

FIGURE 1.4 Eighteenth-century English Shop Front, Picture by C. Constable.

shop able to afford a glass frontage there was the additional advantage of shutting out the filthy, bustling city streets—most without proper sidewalks—while allowing for display and the entrance of natural light. In this manner, glass in the eighteenth century served a major function in the gradual class-based stratification of shopping, signaling affluence in a way that has been carried through to the twenty-first century as witnessed in, for example, the overwhelming glass experience of a contemporary Apple store.

It was truly the eighteenth century that witnessed the transformation of the "tradesman into a merchant," as one Yorkshire reader complained in a letter to the editor of the *Tradesman, or Commercial Magazine* in 1809. This "merchant" had retired after a long career of gradually being saddled with all of the new marketing responsibilities and display needs of the ascendant age of glass. The letter culminated with a description of a friend's trip to visit a London pharmacy on Cheapside owned by the friend's son, a visit that clearly left both writer and friend appalled at the folly of the young: "no longer able to discern the neat but unadorned shop which formerly bespoke the habits of its dweller, which was now entirely changed; the windows were such as Gulliver would describe as a glass cage in Brognibag, each pane being no less than plate glass a yard square."[16] The analogy with Gulliver's sojourn to a land of giants is an apt one, as walls of glass panes separated by a frame of glazing bars were indeed becoming the norm in urban shops by the early 1800s; the shopkeepers caged in their boxes dedicated to commerce.

The simplest story of the nineteenth-century shopfront is one of size, as decade after decade the panes of glass expanded across the facade. By the 1860s, panes as large as 3 × 7 feet were not uncommon; in order to maximize the glass area, various experiments in joining sheets of glass with diminished glazing bars were tried. These intrusive separations, especially the horizontal ones that broke the passerby's view of the display (vertical bars could generally be incorporated into colonnettes or the like), gradually disappeared. For example, the J. W. Benson store (1866, figure 1.5) on Bond Street in London featured a semicircular pane sitting on top of a rectangular plate: there is only a minimal line at the attachment point, probably a bead of caulk or a small piece of fascia. The result is a dramatic swath of fenestration. Note the classicizing style of the facade; throughout the nineteenth century, large glass windows do not seem to be identified as part of any given architectural style. Survey the eclectic range of European shopfronts and one will find a sea of glass

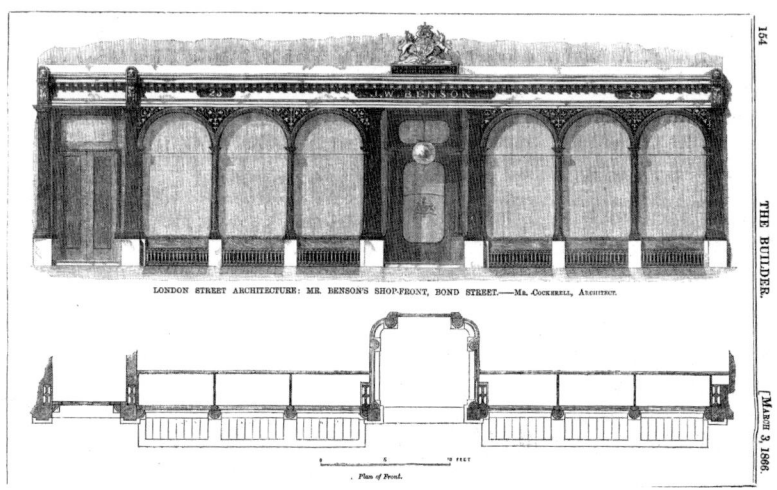

FIGURE 1.5 J. W. Benson store, 1866, Public Domain.

everywhere, as anonymous as the hinge on a door. Glass functioned as a utilitarian element appropriate for any and all types of architecture but was itself simply filling the void created by the design of the window opening. In contrast, for example, to the self-aggrandizing curtain wall of the next century, the shop window of the nineteenth—however tall and wide—is rendered in many ways invisible to the viewer. As the decades wore on, however, one of the formative aesthetic conflicts of modern architecture developed between classical masonry window treatments and glass; the uneasy détente seen on the storefront of J. W. Benson would gradually fray. Frank Lloyd Wright looked back from the 1920s and opined that glass had been the "curse of the classic," and "it has probably done more to show the classicist up as ridiculous than any other single factor."[17]

When the window glass did assert itself as more than infill, there were few architectural touchstones that could define it stylistically. For this reason, in England, pretty much any building in which the fenestration visually overwhelmed the architecture would be characterized as a "Crystal Palace." Such was the case for the two-story showroom of Holmes & Son in Norwich (1863, figure 1.6), in which the wall of glass, while still contained by an "architectural" frame of sturdy masonry blocks, rules the frontage. The glazing bars are quite thin and unobtrusive. A sign placed above the door explicitly states

16   THE AGE OF GLASS

FIGURE 1.6 Holmes & Sons machinery store, Norwich, 1863, Picture by Stuart McPherson.

the connection to the Great Exhibition, "Crystal House Inspired by the Great Exhibition at Crystal Palace." Remember, though, that few saw the Crystal Palace as representative of architecture per se in the 1860s; rather it was a novelty, a stunt. In this way, the elaborate windows of the showroom functioned more as a huge billboard than as an element of architecture. Because Holmes & Sons was a machinery dealer, to a certain degree the building represents an early symbolic connection in a private space between industry and glass.

Notably, the shop window overall had the effect of diminishing the stature of glass is the minds of many architects. If huge swaths of glass like those at Hardwick Hall showed the material symbolizing the heights of conspicuous consumption, in the shop window of the *petit bourgeois* glass got its social comeuppance. Pugin and Ruskin, as self-appointed defenders of elite taste, raged against the buildings that lined the commercial streets of London. In his *True Principles of Pointed or Christian Architecture*, Pugin railed against "mock stone columns (that) are fixed over a front of plate glass to exhibit the astonishing bargains, while low ticketed goods are hung out over the trophies of war." Pugin felt that shop glass crassly cheapened the refined art of architecture, reducing the structure to a plaintive come on.

As historian Julia Scalzo has shown, part of the disdain for shop windows was driven by the professional ambitions of architects. Seeking to enhance the stature of the practice, architects sought to create a strong distinction between their own work and what they saw as the tawdry imitations of commercial builders.[18] With the vast amount of storefronts designed by the latter group, large windows became tainted as something of a calling card of the type of mass-produced vernacular structure that "professional" architects held in contempt.

Another widely held nineteenth-century negative view of shop display windows stands in direct contradiction to the eventual interpretation preferred by the "functionalists" of the modern movement; Victorian architects at times criticized the insubstantial, fragile look of a large fenestrated wall. In the converse argument to the concept that the curtain wall honestly announces the strength of the underlying structural beam, it was argued that, in fact, a sheet of glass should not be made to appear as if it is holding up the wall as it is a dishonest illusion that may project a frightening sense of instability. Thus, the uncertain status of glass in the nineteenth century shows that it was far from being a narrative of one success after another—Arcades to Crystal Palace to Department Stores to the Bauhaus—and glass had a way to go in order to be accepted as a substantial part of architectural practice.

The arcades project

As noted above, dark dirty streets, a multitude of horses, unsavory characters, and a dearth of sidewalks were some of the major impediments to window shopping consumers around 1800. In response, merchants in Paris banded together and used glass to create their own little shopping utopias immune to the elements: the famed "passages" or arcades. It is generally accepted that the first arcade—a pedestrian street that is enveloped by surrounding buildings and roofed to keep out the elements—appeared at the Palais Royal in Paris in 1789, as revolution swept across France. It is this dating that has always given the arcades, sometimes called "Galleries" in French if they were more socially or architecturally substantial than average, their modern identity; the suggestion lurks that they represent a material transition from the aristocratic galleries of the palaces of the ancient regime toward the chaotic democracy of the shopping mall. This transition was most manifest in the arcades at the

Palais Royal, an aristocratic residence across from the Louvre originally built for the Cardinal Richelieu that was developed into a commercial enterprise by the Duc de Chartres in the 1780s. Eventually, a wooden roofed, skylighted collection of shops, the so-called Galerie de Bois, opened amidst the stone colonades. Renowned as a site where shopping, politics, conversation, and vice all came together in a motley stew, the Palais Royal fomented a trend that did not really come into fruition until after the fall of Napoleon and the onset of a period of relative prosperity during the Restoration.

It was the success of architect Francois Debret's Passage d'Opéra (1822–25) that sparked the subsequent construction of hundreds of arcades in Paris. Featuring a beguiling array of over seventy fashionable shops, eateries, and amusements lining two separate alleys, the Passage d'Opéra became a must-see destination for Parisians and tourists alike (nineteenth-century guidebooks are replete with exhortations to wander the famous Paris arcades). Quite narrow in proportion, eager shoppers were sheltered by a steeply pitched glass roof of small glass panes and a web of glazing bars. As was the case in many of these narrow spaces, the glazing was by no means part of the consumer spectacle, as one would have to crane their neck in order to catch a glimpse of the roof. Rather, the glass worked essentially behind the scenes, scarcely visible as it served the utilitarian function of letting in the sun and (mostly) keeping out the rain.

During the arcade boom of the 1820s, the old, wooden Galeries de Bois at the Palais Royal were replaced by one of the most stunning glazed interior spaces in Europe, the Galerie d'Orléans. A project financed by the Duc d'Orléans—later King Louis Phillippe—the Galerie d'Orléans featured a vast open space over sixty yards long that was surmounted by a glass barrel vault (figure 1.7). As noted by a German guide, "The glass alleys which we have seen in the past years, as much as they impressed us, are gloomy cellars or poor attic rooms compared to this. It is a large enchanted chamber."[19] In contrast to the narrow alleys of the Passage d'Opéra, at the Galerie d'Orléans the tunnel of glass that surmounted the shops commanded everyone's attention, and it set the template for the ever more spacious arcades that arose later in the century such as Milan's Galleria Vittorio Emanuele II that opened in 1877.

The Galerie d'Orléans was not immune to the greatest scourge of nineteenth-century glass roofs: water. As insatiable as the tides, hydrologic attacks from the air and the sky were a constant source of torment for the architects and engineers who designed and maintained

FIGURE 1.7 Galerie D'Orleans, Palais-Royale, Paris, 1825.

these structures. Excessive condensation could become such a problem that some glass-roofed structures featured internal gutters. Glass clamped to iron would never create a lasting seal, and all manner of caulks tried and failed as their elasticity waned. Structural solutions such as overlapping panes also gave little respite when the heavens opened up. Not so much of an issue in a greenhouse or a train shed, the puddles that grew in many arcades—also in the Crystal Palace for that matter—were at best a nuisance, and abrogated the social contract whereby consumers traded cash for comfort.

Numbering 300 at their height, the amount of Paris arcades began to diminish as early as the 1850s, as Haussmann's grand boulevards tore through the neighborhoods. Better sidewalks, cleaner streets, department stores, underground transportation, fire codes: all these chipped away at the remnants of the arcades. By 1925, when the Passage d'Opéra was finally demolished, the arcades had become such a bygone phenomenon that Louis Aragon could cite them as an inspiration for Dada and Surrealist thought. After the First World War, Aragon, Tristan Tzara, and Andre Breton had in fact gathered there in order to escape what they considered to be the fraudulent bohemia of Montmartre and Montparnasse.

In the latter half of the twentieth century, the twenty or thirty remaining passages had become nothing more than a historical afterthought, worthy of an anecdote concerning the "first shopping malls" but otherwise ignored. Most all had been torn down while the remaining few were dilapidated and unfashionable. In a quirk of fate, the arcades were saved from complete ruin by the most unlikely of circumstances, the publication of Walter Benjamin's *Passagen-Werk* in 1982. Written in a mix of French and German, this weighty tome—almost 1,000 pages—first fully appeared in English under the better-known title *Arcades Project* in 1999, although sections of the text had been printed decades earlier. Benjamin, a German Jewish author and intellectual, had died in 1940 by his own hand on the Spanish frontier while trying to escape Nazi-occupied France. The unfinished *Arcades Project* was a sprawling montage of ideas—filled with quotations and fragmented glimpses of urban life—through which Benjamin tried to interpret the origins of modernity. The book has had enormous influence in recent decades for many reasons, including Benjamin's rejection of totalizing master theories in favor of a rhizomatic accumulation of heterogeneous thoughts. For this reason the *Arcades Project*, which the author himself described as "the theater of all my struggles and all my ideas," can be daunting in both its complexity and its expected knowledge base rooted in Marx, Freud, and Surrealism.

Benjamin's recounting of the cultural implications of the Paris arcades are what begins perhaps the most famous section of his text, an essay subtitled "Paris—Capital of the Nineteenth Century." For Benjamin, the Paris arcade was the core material fact that facilitated the rise of consumer culture. Approached dialectically, the glazed roofs and glittering shop windows were a significant material part of what he called the "phantasmagoria" that shaped urban bourgeois consciousness. The arcade was the province of distinct new social types, most notably the *flâneur* first described by Charles Baudelaire; he is an ambling, fashionable voyeur whom Benjamin viewed as "a spy for the capitalists, on assignment in the realm of consumers." The spectacle of glass helped to shape the viewer's mind, to infuse in them that intoxicating state of desire that enabled them to partake of a society rooted in consumption. (For Benjamin, glass became a dominant, as opposed to ancillary, architectural material only in the twentieth century.) Regardless of the depths of one's intellectual engagement with the *Arcades Project*, on a simpler, albeit twisted, level, Benjamin's opus made the remaining arcades cool again. Today, there is a new type of radical-chic *flâneur* haunting the handful of remaining arcades, a

Benjamin acolyte reviewing the footsteps of their hero before catching the metro to Père Lachaise.

Glass utopias

The Paris Arcades and Benjamin's work also intersected with one of the first manifestations of what eventually developed into a major trend in glass architecture: the utopia of glass. While more closely identified with early twentieth-century building, the pioneering "utopian socialists" of the nineteenth century were among the first to put modern glass architecture into the realm of the visionary. Of course, utopian architectural speculation has its own prehistory, and much of the nineteenth-century work was likely inspired by an even earlier generation—Étienne-Louis Boullée and Claude-Nicolas Ledoux come to mind—that, however, lacked iron and glass.

Charles Fourier was in many ways foremost among influential French utopians of the nineteenth century. Like many thinkers considered to be proto-Marxists in hindsight, Fourier envisioned a society where capitalist wealth was distributed more widely and evenly than has generally been the case. Beginning with the publication of his *Théorie des Quatre Mouvements et des Destinées Générales* in 1808, Fourier—enabled by a sizable inheritance—continued for decades to expound upon his ideal of a society organized into small, agricultural communal groups. The element of escapism in designing an antidote to urban life that requires everyone to move into rural areas is self-evident. Hard to follow at times, Fourier called for humanity to embrace a cosmic order based on the passions, an underlying life force that will lead to a collective attainment of harmony. Architecturally speaking, groups of Fourierists (1,620 per microsociety: this relates to Fourier's theory of personality types) would be housed in communal quarters the author called *phalansteries*. In imagining a new type of architecture that would enhance the new social order, Fourier determined that all of the various outbuildings of the *phalanstery* should be united by a long, glass-roofed street gallery. As Benjamin observed in "Paris—Capital of the Nineteenth Century," "In the arcades, Fourier had seen the architectonic canon for the Phalanstery." While Benjamin marveled at Fourier's "reactionary transformation" of the arcades into rural domestic utopias, it is notable how Fourier first introduced the forward-thinking idea of glass roofs creating a womb-like biosphere, a self-contained utopia that uses glass as both a barrier and a window. Fourier described the space, using the grand gallery of the Louvre as a reference, as featuring a run of windows along one entire side. Wrote Fourier, "Once a man has seen the street-galleries of a Phalanx, he will look upon the most elegant civilized palace as a place of exile, a residence worthy of fools who, after three thousand years of architectural studies, have not yet learned how to build themselves healthy and comfortable lodgings."[20] Aside from quashing the risk of pleurisy, Fourier also enthused about how the street gallery will allow for a level of physical comfort on a day-to-day basis: his tendency to drone on about weather seems positively English of him.

While Fourier was inspired by the arcades, it is also clear that the inverse was true, as many nineteenth-century architects cited Fourier as a visionary whose ideas they hoped to bring into reality. Such was the case with the Belgian architect Jean-Pierre Cluysenaar, designer of one of the most spectacular of arcades, the Galleries St. Hubert in Brussels. Still extant, the Galleries St. Hubert opened in 1847 after only a year of construction, a feat that anticipated the more celebrated process overseen by Paxton three years later. More than a collection of shops, the Galleries St. Hubert was a massive indoor city (213 meters long, 18 meters high, and 8 meter wide), an urban *phalanstery* where the whole of Brussels could seemingly gather at one time. With spaces as wide as the streets of Brussels and a roof that soared effortlessly until it seemed to meld with the sky, it is easy to imagine how it would seem that Fourier's dreams of a harmonious community could become a reality. Like so many dreams from the nineteenth century, through the Galleries St. Hubert Fourier's vision becomes a reality through commerce. The historian Johann Geist has reminded readers that the arcades were a place of movement; writing in reference to the Galleries St. Hubert, he noted, "The glass vault is furthermore the initial stage of a systematic development of a space of transition and movement, a kind of space which originates in the arcade, continues in the railway station, and ends in the subway tubes."[21] In this manner the glass roofs of the arcades signified the speed and rhythm of modern life long before these themes were clearly formulated in the popular consciousness.

The other legendary utopian of the nineteenth century with an impact on glass architecture was the French aristocrat Henri de Saint-Simon. Like Fourier, Saint-Simon's writings can be obtuse, but a clear theme develops of a vision for a society guided by science and industry. Featuring some elements of a meritocracy mixed with capitalism and socialism, Saint-

Simon foresaw a world where technology would solve any and all societal problems. While, like Fourier, he advocated decentralization and a breakup of large imperial powers, Saint-Simon did not proffer a future of escapist, rural harmony, but instead a community where an elite class of beneficent businessmen and scientists worked together for all. After his death in 1825, the so-called Saint-Simonians promulgated his views, advocating for a more just economic order, increased rights for women, and demilitarization. While Saint-Simon's vision for architecture was less specific than that of Fourier, many nineteenth-century architects such as Christophe-Eugène Flachat and Hector Horeau cited his espousal of modern technology as a guiding principle for their work.

Hector Horeau was one of the few consistent proponents of iron and glass architecture throughout his career. Responding to Saint-Simon's characterization of new technology as a savior for humanity, Horeau stressed how his visionary—meaning unbuilt—projects could help remake society for the better. In terms of completed works, the two winter gardens he designed in the 1840s—the first in Lyon, the second in Paris—represent both a Fourierist embrace of mild artificial climates as well as a Saint-Simonian belief in the power of industrial materials. The massive Jardin d'Hiver in Paris, a clear influence on the Crystal Palace, is representative of a whole class of building projects from this era that existed somewhere in between utopia and reality. Inspired by visionaries, the winter gardens offered a small piece of utopia to the general public, without any of the social engineering that was the main import of the original thinkers. Alas, reality often quickly reestablished its place, as was the case with Horeau's winter garden, which, because of investor fraud and the high value of land at its location near the Champs Elysées, was demolished in 1860 to make way for the future.

Another glassed-in urban space project that captured the public's imagination was Joseph Paxton's Great Victorian Way, a scheme that he unsuccessfully pitched to a parliamentary committee in 1855. Building on the fame garnered by his design of the Crystal Palace, Paxton advocated a ten-mile-long circle loop around London. This glass-roofed structure, 72 feet wide and over 100 feet high, would solve the city's transportation problems—it featured a street and a subway line—while also including space for miles of shops and residences. Unsurprisingly, the great cost of the plan proved its undoing, without there ever being serious attention paid to the practical questions surrounding such an ambitious, speculative plan. The Great Victorian Way, like the winter gardens in Paris, represented a kind of middle ground between the visionary spaces imagined by the utopians and the new, more practical structures of the industrial age. At its heart, the Great Victorian Way was essentially an extended arcade, and represented the logical extrapolation of that engaging shopping experience.

Department stores

In the latter half of the nineteenth century, while the Paris passages were being gradually dismantled, and the Great Victorian Way was never built, consumers were flocking to that other emporium of glass, the department store. Benjamin called them "temples consecrated to the intoxication of great cities," and as a focus of the shopping experience in urban centers, this new type of structure proffered all of the delights of consumerism while encasing the shopper in a cocoon of glass. As mentioned above, the era of the department store is conventionally thought to have begun with Aristide Boucicaut's ascension in 1863 to sole proprietor of the general goods store called Bon Marché, where he had been a part-owner since 1852. As a retail goods magnate, Boucicaut functioned rather like Gutenberg did in the world of printing; he did not necessarily invent anything original in terms of marketing strategies, distribution, or the like but he did put all of the existing ideas to work in order to form a new business. In fact, the most important contribution Boucicaut made to retailing was the commissioning of the first large, purpose-built store (figure 1.8). Eventually covering almost an entire city block, the Bon Marché building was begun in 1869. Mainly credited to Louis Auguste Boileau, over its eighteen-year construction process other architects including Gustave Eiffel, Jean-Alexandre Laplanche, and Boileau's son Louis Charles made important contributions to the design.

At Bon Marché and other Paris department stores—Both Au Printemps and La Samaritaine were founded in the 1860s and greatly expanded their stores beginning in the 1880s; Galeries Lafayette was founded in 1896—glass performed both basic utilitarian and more complex theatrical functions. In terms of the former function, large exterior windows provided natural light as these gigantic buildings relied on the sun more than the gas jet or electric bulb until the early twentieth century (see Chapter 6 for a discussion of how natural light eventually became a liability in department stores). In order to get sunlight into the

FIGURE 1.8 Louis Auguste Boileau, Bon Marche Store, 1876.

depths of the interior, sweeping glass and iron light courts provided both illumination and a striking social space, one that created a spectacular focus similar to that of the grand staircase at Charles Garnier's recently opened opera. While these open courts were long ago banished because of fire codes, Jean Nouvel's 1996 Berlin branch of Galeries Lafayette serves in many ways as an homage to the original wave of glazed department store architecture. Nouvel's syncopated assemblage of conic light wells pierce the building repeatedly, opening up vistas through which today's consumers can look but cannot pass through.

All of the nineteenth-century department stores also used glass symbolically in order to invoke a sense of technological forwardness and to foment a visual relationship with other strikingly modern structures such as train stations and exhibition buildings. As notable department store historian Meredith Clausen has asserted, "they evoked a sense of progress and were heavily loaded with associations of modernity and technological advances, representing the antithesis of the dark, dingy, cramped quarters of the 19th century."[22] Yes and no. The department stores clearly represented a crescendo in terms of the employment of glass in a nineteenth-century consumer environment; however, Clausen depicts the pre–department store era as a foil: one that sounds suspiciously like a Renaissance historian's view of the "dark" ages. As I hope this chapter has shown, there was little that was dark and dingy about the retailing spaces in place long before Bon Marché and the like walked on stage and stole the spotlight.

2 STAINED GLASS AND MODERNITY

Although stained glass has played a major role in modern architecture, perhaps no other utilization of glass during the era is as maligned and misunderstood. In the conventional wisdom of the twenty-first century, no material more embodies the ornamental past that modern architecture was designed to combat and diminish. For later modernists, stained glass was ornament and ornament obscures form. Modern architecture depended literally and symbolically on the new industrially produced sheet of transparent plate glass, not the handmade, historically freighted, and often opaque filters of color. This stigma became so great that architects such as Le Corbusier even designed stained glass while denying it was stained glass (see below). Books and collections devoted to modern design ignore its existence; to cite one example, the official catalog of the quite comprehensive Norwest Collection of "modernist design 1880–1940" is devoid of architectural stained glass.[1] This chapter offers a counterargument to this familiar narrative, asserting that modern architects employed stained glass as a core element of their emerging aesthetic. That being said, it is necessary to first trace how stained glass came to thrive in that most industrial of centuries, the nineteenth, despite, or because of, its seemingly retrograde aesthetic.

The stained glass revival

Despite its accelerating prominence in the formative years of modern architecture, stained glass has been consistently defined as evidence of the Victorian age's inability to address the material needs of mass culture and urban life. Many commentators today seem convinced that stained glass in the nineteenth century represented a dying vestige of a medieval art, when in fact the opposite was true and a critical mass of cutting-edge architectural reformers invested in and promoted the newly revived practice. Many of these designers were focused not on stained glass' historical lineage, but on making new works that expressed contemporary feelings.

It is indeed true that the stained glass boom of the 1800s represented a paradox, playing a leading role in industrial culture while appearing to be fleeing from it. Along these lines, Victorian stained glass arose partly as a manifestation of the Romantic period, that indistinct cloud of emotionally laden works of literature, music, and the visual arts that offered an escape from the realities of urban experience. More than a set of works, Romanticism was a state of mind, an approach to culture that highlighted melancholic subjective experience, sublimity rather than rationality. No work better expresses the paradoxical power of stained glass and the broader Gothic revival than William Wordsworth's 1845 sonnet *At Furness Abbey*. Located in Cumbria, Furness Abbey had been established in the twelfth century as a Cistercian monastery. After its abandonment and partial destruction during the Dissolution, the abbey's ruins were largely ignored until a resurgence of interest brought on by the Romantic movement. Because so many Romanticists delighted in evocative themes of decay and devolution, picturesque ruins such as those at Furness became a popular tourist attraction, a place to ponder existence and also have a pleasant picnic. Apparently spurred on by his wife's daytrip to the ruins, William Wordsworth wrote this sonnet on the impact the abbey has on nearby industrial laborers taking a break from laying railroad track. "They sit, they walk/Among the ruins, but no idle talk/Is heard; to grave demeanor all are bound." This meditative work has often been interpreted as representing a stinging contrast between the cold, secular modern age and the spirituality and harmony of a romanticized medieval past. Under this interpretation, medievalisms such as stained glass are revived as a defense against industry; but arguable the sonnet does not emphasize a chasm between the railroad worker and the abbey environs. Instead, the workers appreciate the scene, revel in its spiritual power, and then go back to furthering the age of steam. This was the case with a great deal of stained glass as well; it can be said to have harmonized with the industrial age rather than defied it.

Probably the most damning element of the Victorian revival to modern eyes was the manner in which architects linked the Gothic style to a reawakening of Christian culture. The greatest proponent of this belief was Augustus W. N. Pugin, who in many ways framed the discussion of the revival in England. Pugin, who converted to Catholicism soon after parliament passed the liberalizing Roman Catholic Relief Act in 1829, fought tirelessly to spread his belief that the Gothic represented not just a style but a set of moral principles. That being said, it is obvious that Pugin's religiosity has at times skewed the historical appreciation of his work. In point of fact, Pugin offered a presciently modernist view of stained glass and other architectural ornament. In the two lectures that formed the basis for his 1841 book *The True Principles of Pointed or Christian Architecture*, Pugin offered this fundamental maxim: "all ornament should consist of enrichment of the essential construction of the building." While it is in the Gothic style that Pugin saw this type of integrated building system, the idea itself is representative of the most forward-thinking architectural theory.

It is typical to see the Gothic revival as engineered by Pugin utilized as a foil in order to dramatize the strikingly protomodern aesthetic of Joseph Paxton's Crystal Palace at the Great Exhibition of the Works of Industry of all Nation in 1851. Who has read a text (of any sort) about the Crystal Palace and not seen Pugin listed as one of its primary detractors, usually quoting his succinct quip, that the building is a "glass monster"? While many have noted that Pugin oversaw one of the Great Exhibition's most spectacular successes, the Medieval Court, again that work is portrayed as at least oppositional if not completely out of touch with the industrial reality symbolized by the Crystal Palace. Is a Medieval Court really so out of touch with a building that featured a nave and transept?

In choosing decorative arts objects for the Medieval Court, Pugin had relied on his colleagues John Hardman Jr. and John Hardman Powell. Beginning in 1845, Hardman Jr. and his nephew Powell had been producing stained glass for use in various Pugin commissions. At the Medieval Court, Hardman Jr.'s stained glass formed just one part of the assemblage of medieval works that were highlighted by the massive crystal and brass chandelier from the Earl of Shrewsbury's estate at Alton Towers. Part of the problem with the manufactured "Pugin v. Paxton" opposition is that Pugin was displaying decorative arts out of context, in a large glass greenhouse, not as part of his systematic employment of Gothic architecture. If any comparison should be made, it would be between the Medieval Court and the other exhibits—not the exhibit hall—most of which appear equally retrograde in style and subject matter. One has only to peruse the souvenir images of the exhibits to realize that Pugin's work was perfectly in keeping with the overall abundance of richly decorated objects.

There are two significant details that contest the facile idea that Pugin's court represented artisanal handcraft while the Crystal Palace equaled industry. First, Pugin was by no means the only exhibitor of stained glass at the Great Exhibition. The Official Catalogue listed over twenty-five separate manufacturers under the category "stained and painted glass." These exhibitors included Chance Brothers Glass Works, the industrial supplier of the plate glass that sheathed the Crystal Palace. Chance Brothers displayed a series of lighthouse lenses based on the work of Fresnel along with "Painted windows: leaded work, with medallions and ornamental work of the early Gothic style, and in the style of the fourteenth century."[2] Clearly, stained glass was an important part of their business, a business that was synonymous with the industrial age. Similarly, "Glass Monster" quote aside, Pugin was by no means an enemy of industrial production. He never insisted upon medieval techniques in his various Gothic enterprises, and should never be grouped with, for example, the luddites who surrounded William Morris later in the century. Just like plate glass, the creation of which involved an enormous amount of hand labor, stained glass was another product that was manufactured as efficiently as possible.

Jasmine Allen has shown how stained glass during the Gothic revival in nineteenth-century England had strong ties to other elements of mass culture.[3] Where some viewers might see stained glass through romantic, medieval eyes, surely others made the connection between its colorful light and the glow of thoroughly modern novelties such as the magic lantern, the kaleidoscope, and the phantasmagoria. All of these theatrical instruments produced an atmosphere of colorful, kinetic light not unlike that of a space lit by stained glass. It is important to recognize that stained glass is not a static medium, but one whose iridescent emanations change with the passing daylight. Painted transparencies were another part of nineteenth-century popular culture that paralleled the revival in stained glass. Amateurs and professionals alike had access to the materials and instruction books that could allow one to try their hand at this endeavor. Through these types of popular art the medium of colored glass developed a broad, urban audience, one that saw stained glass as a single example out of a myriad group of entertainments. This situation was recognized by a character in Samuel Foote's 1774 play, the Cozeners, who promises to bring a guest to Kensington Gardens in order to see the "exhibitions, the stain'd glass, dwarf, giant, and Cox's museum."[4] Of course, in the minds of more serious stained glass enthusiasts, these idle pastimes were symptomatic of the depraved state of contemporary culture.

It should be noted that despite repeated instances where stained glass broke through into the modern consciousness, it was indeed a decorative refuge for those who felt that the medieval period represented an "age of faith" that had been lost and forgotten. All the major nineteenth-century architectural periodicals were replete with surveys of medieval glass supplemented by biblical quotations and exuding a sentimental longing for another age while condemning the present. In England, the most conspicuous antimodern group was the Ecclesiological Society, which was founded at Cambridge in 1839. The Ecclesiologists were committed to the revival of stained glass in its strictly medieval form, and also were strict proponents of the idea that the Gothic symbolized an ideal model for a moral, spiritual society. Thus, the medieval revival in one way or another—from Cathedral restoration to collegiate Gothic—remained a sturdy part of architectural practice well into the twentieth century. The American artist Caryl Coleman, writing in the *Architectural Record* of 1898, offered this summation of the Renaissance and post-Renaissance glass and culture, "looking to Grecian and Roman art for their criterion, and, as this spirit of paganism spread, the faith of the people was weakened, selfishness increased, ... There was no room for art of any kind, except as a factor in giving sensual pleasure to the 'best man,' and even this ended in France amidst the atheistic orgies of 1798."[5] What Coleman was overlooking in his despair at the soullessness of modern culture was that the industrialization of stained glass was dramatically expanding the art form's reach to the remaining faithful.

Industrial stained glass

In 1893, there were over 4,000 churches under construction in the United States. It was in these late nineteenth-century ecclesiastical buildings that stained glass truly broke through into mass culture. While in the United Kingdom and the continent, stained glass had in some ways steadfastly remained the special preserve of Catholicism and the Church of England, in the United States it eventually became democratized, a standard element of any and all religious buildings. Early American Protestants had rejected stained glass as an oppressive symbol of the Church of

England, favoring plain, clear windows. As the conflict with the British faded from memory after the War of 1812, stained glass started making its way into American Protestant churches. First on the scene were so-called quarry stained glass windows, which consisted of small pieces of colored glass arranged so as to create spare abstract patterns of colored light. By the middle of the century as the industrial production of glass accelerated in the United States, all manner of figural, historical styles were produced, soon sweeping the nation side by side with plate glass.

While a great deal of attention has been lavished on the fine, handcrafted stained glass of elite American artisans such as Louis Comfort Tiffany and John Lafarge (see below), it was the industrialization of stained glass manufacturing that had the greater impact on the visual environment. By the latter half of the nineteenth century, American glass manufacturers—as well as Chance Brothers in England—considered stained glass to be just one more product that they needed to produce in order to serve the industrial world. Some glass manufacturers even boasted that they kept costs down by employing the same workers to make stained glass windows as ran their plate glass machinery, thus allowing them to keep markups low as their labor force was constantly occupied and downtime was limited. In actuality, stained glass and plate glass were much alike at this time. The key product of modern stained glass manufacture was so-called cathedral glass, a one-eighth-inch sheet of colored plate that was the fundamental product of the industry. These sheets could then be cut and fixed into windows that were designed based on standard pattern books. The page illustrated here of "Art Glass Church Windows" is a typical example of a catalog from a building wholesaler (figure 2.1). Standard pricing ranged from 80c to $1.25 per square foot, with letters and emblems a few dollars extra, "Subject to discount." The Foster-Munger company was as banal a contractor supply firm as existed, one of thousands serving cities across the country. Founded in 1886 as a sash window, molding, and other millwork supply house, stained glass was added later as demand increased. Outside of the cities, mail-order houses offered to ship stained glass to even the most remote communities. In 1903, American stained glass producers formed their own trade group, the "National Ornamental Glass Manufacturers Association," which published catalogs and lobbied for the industry.

While most prominent in churches, stained glass became such a commonplace signal of religiosity that it even found its way into American synagogues, which were also being built at a rapid pace during this era.

FIGURE 2.1 "Art Glass Church Windows" Foster-Munger Company, Official 1902 Catalog. Trade Catalog and Product Sample Collection, Ryerson and Burnham Archives, The Art Institute of Chicago. Digital file # 200004_160226-009.

One of the first examples of a large stained glass window in a synagogue was seen in May 1850 in the new building for Congregation Anshi Chesed. Located in what was then the Little Germany neighborhood of New York City, the building's circular window featured an iconographic program based on the Ten Commandments. When the window was unveiled there was a fair amount of kvetching by a number of congregants, some of whom were uncomfortable with the innovation. A development that they saw as a turn away from tradition, these complaints represent probably the only time that stained glass was accused of being too modern during the nineteenth century. Interestingly, when decades later the migrations of Americans led to a number of formerly Jewish urban areas transitioning to African-American ones—and as a result synagogues turned into churches—the stained glass usually remained. Adler & Sullivan's 1891 Kehilath Anshe Ma'ariv is a case in point; when it became the Pilgrim Baptist Church in the 1920s, the Jewish iconography in the stained glass windows remained, reinterpreted in a now-Christian environment.

By 1900, stained glass was omnipresent in American buildings: as one purveyor crowed, "[We have] every description of stained glass for use in private houses, churches, public buildings, halls, stairways, etc."[6] In particular, it became an expected decoration in new construction in the domestic market. While the mansions of the industrialist class employed the likes of Tiffany and La Farge, even the most humble worker's cottage usually included a pane or two of stained glass. A typical wholesaler offered "house decorations, such as windows, doors, transoms, skylights, hall lamps, fire screens, etc." with an "unlimited variety of designs and magnificent color effects ... and moderate cost."[7] Adding a touch of color to the often drab, polluted urban byways, stained glass had reached its peak as an industrial product at the heart of the capitalist enterprise, a far cry indeed from the medieval collectives dreamed of by the Ecclesiologists and the like.

Tiffany and La Farge

While wholesalers such as Foster-Munger blanketed the United States with inexpensive stained glass fenestration, other producers concentrated on the carriage trade at the top of the market. During the last two decades of the nineteenth century, a strong rivalry developed between the two legends of high-end stained glass: John La Farge and Louis Comfort Tiffany. Both La Farge and Tiffany had trained as painters—La Farge with Thomas Couture—but eventually found their way into the decorative arts. Both also cultivated connections among the social elite, as La Farge's client list included Cornelius Vanderbilt, while Tiffany had been born into the upper class on account of his father, Charles L. Tiffany, a successful merchant and later jeweler to the rich. Around 1880, just as the stained glass boom accelerated, a dispute developed between the men over a pair of patents that each claimed some control over a then-revolutionary technology: opalescent glass. Opalescent glass, like its namesake the opal, is translucent or even opaque, and possesses a startling iridescence when its milky streaks are exposed to the light.

La Farge was the first to strike, filing a patent application in 1879 only weeks after first exhibiting an opalescent glass window. In his patent application for "improvements in colored-glass Windows," La Farge acknowledged that he had not invented this type of glass, but attempted to lay claim to some technical details that allowed it to be manufactured in inexpensive flat sheets suitable for glazing and to increase its range of effects (figure 2.2). In support of his application, La Farge wrote,

In my studies, both as architect and artist, I have aimed to overcome the objections commonly urged against colored-glass Windows and to give to them new qualities and properties of a pleasing nature, to thereby increase the use of colored-glass windows and give additional variety and beauty to public edifices and private dwellings; and by experiment I have discovered that opalescent and iridescent effects may, in an eminent degree, be obtained for windows by the employment of that class of glass known as opal glass.

Some months later, Tiffany filed his own patent applications featuring a different set of principles that would allow him to lay claim to the opalescent window. As was the case with La Farge's application, Tiffany did not purport to have invented the glass itself but rather sought to

FIGURE 2.2 John La Farge, example of opalescent glass, c. 1890, credit: Photo by James Steakley, CC BY-SA 3.0.

patent some technical details regarding its employment in windows; one patent involved a method of plating opalescent glass, while another dealt with a background chemical layer that would increase the glass' iridescent qualities. It is clear from their personal correspondence that this was something of a patent war—a stained glass version of the litigious disputes that play such a huge role in the digital industry today—and that failed discussions on a possible business alliance was at the core of the dispute. In subsequent years, La Farge wrote testily of his intention to sue Tiffany for breaching his intellectual property. In the end, none of their patents were ever enforced, probably because they dealt with small, obtuse details of the window-making process. Also, as no one had patented opalescent glass itself, so the greater part of the glass industry quickly geared up its production—in 1888 the vast Kokomo Opalescent Glassworks opened in Indiana—and the status of opalescent pioneer became one for vanity if not simply moot.

While rivals for a time, Tiffany's business acumen and family connections would in the 1890s allow him to totally eclipse La Farge as the premier American manufacturer of stained glass. One of Tiffany's greatest coups occurred at the legendary World's Columbian Exposition held in 1893 in Chicago. While the official exhibition contained no stained glass, Tiffany was able to borrow space leased to his father's jewelry business in the Manufactures and Liberal Arts building. There, the Tiffany Glass & Decorating Company exhibited stained glass in three separate spaces, the most stunning of which was the so-called Tiffany Chapel (figure 2.3). This vaguely Byzantine-inspired space provided a flood of color amidst the austerity of the White City. The glass at the Exposition had all the hallmarks of the Tiffany style; that is to say, each piece of glass was unique unto itself. Early in his career, Tiffany had noted that buyers prized the look of handicraft that only flaws in the glass could bring. For this reason, batches of glass were always manufactured in varying thicknesses and with different types of adulterations so that no two pieces were the same. In this lies the greatest contrast between stained glass and the plate glass of so much modern architecture; plate glass manufacturers devoted centuries to making the glass flawless: smoother, flatter, more transparent and more homogenous. Tiffany created value by playing off of that formula and making a product that stood out in its apparent individuality.

While ostensibly a religious space—reportedly male visitors would doff their hats in response to entering it—the Tiffany Chapel was in fact more akin to today's pop-up store, a place dedicated to commerce rather

FIGURE 2.3 Louis C. Tiffany, Tiffany Chapel, 1893, US Library of Congress/Public Domain.

than spirituality. The only deity served by Tiffany at the Exposition was Mammon; Tiffany's savvy marketing strategy should be given greater renown. As a complement to the exhibition, Tiffany published an essay in *The Forum* magazine of July 1893. In this case, the title of the essay in some ways said it all: "American Art Supreme in Colored Glass." In this essay, Tiffany offered the familiar argument from this era that American designers benefited from their lack of historical baggage and were therefore freer to experiment with stained glass versus their European counterparts. He cited the invention of opalescent glass and the adoption of the mosaic—as opposed to the painted—style as evidence behind this presumed American superiority. Tiffany also sought to distinguish his own work from that of the larger industry, noting without irony that "an intelligent exhibition would have aided greatly in crushing out the purely commercial spirit which too often invades this field." Winner of over 50 medals and a popular sensation, the Tiffany exhibit at the Columbian Exposition greatly expanded his reputation in the Midwest and even in Europe, where his glass famously came to the attention of one of the central merchants of the Art Nouveau, Siegfried Bing.

As Tiffany noted in his essay, there was no official display of stained glass at the Columbian Exposition. However, there were a handful of examples scattered throughout the grounds; one of the most compelling was the center pane of a triptych installed in the Woman's Building by the state of Massachusetts. Designed collaboratively by Elizabeth Parson, Edith Brown, and Ethel Brown, the window had been executed by the Boston glass firm of Ford & Brooks. The window utilizes an age-old allegorical strategy in order to support a progressive cause of the era: women's emancipation. In it a mother figure (representing enlightened Massachusetts) supports a young woman in a liberty cap who symbolizes the "Coming Woman of Liberty, Progress, and Light." Perhaps this window represented the first use of political stained glass in the modern sense.

It is important to recognize that Tiffany's windows had been exhibited in the Manufacturers section of the Columbian Exposition surrounded by industrial products, many complete with suggested prices. This is relevant to the fact that Tiffany had already been busy turning his art studio business into a major industry. When he opened his own factory at Corona, New York, in 1892, Tiffany was running a business that employed hundreds. His glassworks kept over 200 tons of glass on the premises, divided into some 5,000 colors. In 1894, when Bing surveyed the premises, he was astonished by the "army of craftsmen" dedicated to stained glass production. Impressed with Tiffany's creative and business acumen, Bing exhorted his fellow French decorative arts enthusiasts to embrace American strategies, eventually penning a long form essay titled "La culture artistique en Amérique" in 1896. Bing also had sought out a partnership with Tiffany, whereby Bing would provide French designs for stained glass windows; Tiffany would execute the windows and send them back to Bing for sale in Europe. For this project Bing approached the Nabis, a group of experimental abstract painters who had coalesced around the circle of Paul Gauguin. Self-styled spiritualists—the name comes from the Hebrew word for prophet—the Nabis' penchant for flat areas of brilliant color must have seemed a perfect match for the colored glass medium.

At this point in his career Bing was transitioning from his role as an Asian art dealer to becoming a patron and merchant of European works inspired by Asian, especially Japanese, aesthetics. This was to be the basis for revolutionary new art, hence the name Art Nouveau. When Bing exhibited the Nabi/Tiffany windows in 1895, he was pulling stained glass into the orbit of the most avant-garde artists in Paris. Few of these windows survive, but the design by Ker-Xavier Roussel is typical of the Nabis' work, creating tension between a seemingly banal scene of bourgeois family life and a mystically abstract style (figure 2.4). In exhibiting windows that drew upon such an edgy style, Bing opened up stained glass to the critical assessment of modern painting, as the designs were lauded by a few but derided by many as strange and unseemly. Perhaps because of lackluster interest from buyers, Bing kept most of the windows for years, and installed them in the first iteration of his *Salon de l'Art Nouveau* gallery. Bing's relationship with Tiffany was overall a great success, however, as he became the principal European agent for the American artist's other works, especially vases and objets d'art. Based on Bing's attempt to integrate stained glass and a modern sensibility, it would seem possible that the medium possessed a promising future. But this was not the case. By the 1920s Tiffany's business—and the entire stained glass era—would be beleaguered and bankrupt, even as stained glass continued to have a strong role in modern aesthetics up until the end.

The stained glass revival lasted almost 100 years, from the 1820s to the 1920s: most of the glass produced during that time for secular buildings consisted of accent pieces that were not necessarily integrated with the architecture. Windows by La Farge or Tiffany harmonized with a general tone of luxury, but were often installed in buildings irrespective of the architectural style. The major exception to this situation came from the Gothic revival, whereby the stained glass, of course, formed part of a holistic aesthetic approach. Buildings such as Martin Roche's thirteen-story University Club (Chicago, 1908)—the first gothic revival skyscraper—adopted stained glass as the most spectacular element of an

FIGURE 2.4 Ker-Xavier Roussel, Design for Tiffany Window, 1895, credit: © [2017] Artists Rights Society (ARS), New York.

overall medieval-esque design. The twelve large windows that dominated the building's most stunning space, a dining room known as Cathedral Hall that was architecturally based on London's Crosby Hall, featured iconography based both on individual colleges and universities and various branches of the arts and humanities (figure 2.5). The windows had been designed by Frederick Bartlett, a club member and artist of

FIGURE 2.5 Martin Roche, Cathedral Hall, University Club, Chicago, 1908, Picture by S. Eskilson.

notorious eclectic taste. In stark contrast to the transparent panes of the Chicago Window (see Chapter 3), Roche in this instance adopted the mantra of the contemporary critic who hoped that stained glass would "driv[e] the ugly plate-glass window out of existence." As an aside, the University Club's historians later recounted a story whereby Bartlett, in an attempt to pass the time while waiting for Tiffany to arrive from New York with window designs, showed his own ideas to the assembled board. According to this legend, Tiffany entered unnoticed to the back of the room and then announced that he was deferring to Bartlett, who had created "the most beautiful, most fitting, most remarkable stained glass windows done in modern times."

The Gothic revival idea of a collective, integrated design had been picked up and codified by William Morris as part of the broader Arts and Crafts movement. Melded in the late nineteenth century to the Wagnerian *Gesamtkunstwerke*, the unified aesthetic of the Gothic revival was also adopted by purveyors of both the Aesthetic movement in England and through the broader development of decorative art termed Art Nouveau. All these threads came together in the work of Edward Burne-Jones, a founding member of the Morris firm. Burne-Jones's stained glass was mainly produced for ecclesiastical buildings, representing the Gothic revival side of the business. But these windows are far from simple recreations of past art, as his languid, sensual figures exude the spectral power sought by dedicated aesthetes of the day. For example, the mid-1890s designs for Harris Manchester College Chapel at Oxford University demonstrate this hybrid type; while medieval in overall character, the pensive faces of the figures carry the distinct flavor of Pre-Raphaelite art. Overall, the stained glass produced by the Arts and Crafts reformers served as something of a negative example to the integration of the medium with modern architecture. Driven by disdain for the commercial stained glass industry and its production of stained glass as nothing more than another manufactured product, Burne-Jones, Morris et al. sought to reinforce the skilled craftsmanship of a bygone age and impractically insisted that windows be created under the supervision of a single skilled artisan.

Frank Lloyd Wright

Another stained glass designer strongly influenced by Arts and Crafts ideals but who was also open to the machine age, Frank Lloyd Wright, created some of the most conceptually innovative stained glass of the early twentieth century. Importantly, as a builder guided by a Louis Sullivanesque commitment to organic expression, Wright's windows had no independent existence outside of their architectural context. Over the years, much has been made of how Wright's designs were based on the rhythmic assemblage of geometric units that he learned as a child after his mother brought home the pattern books authored by the German education theorist Friedrich Froebel. According to Wright and his countless biographers, the architect's early childhood education using Froebel's exercises (Froebel, founder of the Kindergarten movement, called them "gifts") led Wright to an intuitive understanding of elementary morphologies. It should be noted that this oft-repeated tale bears all the hallmarks of Wright's notable vanity, as it garners him the status of a form-builder who developed unencumbered by historical precedent.

There is an alternative to the legend of Froebel; perhaps Wright learned best at a later stage, working with glass. The historian Otto Antonia Graf has asserted that Wright did not come to a mature understanding of his "formative geometries" until age thirty, at which point he designed a series of over forty compositions for the Luxfer Prism Company (figure 2.6). Recorded in a patent application of that year, these drawings for the surface of 4 × 4 feet glass blocks "set into motion the main sequence of the architect where every building has a specific place and function within the cosmic entirety."[8] Indeed, the patent application's description of the inscribed lines on one of the tiles is suggestive of its strength as a compositional seed for Wright's future work. "These ornamental lines take the form of circles, arcs of circles, squares, and the like, arranged

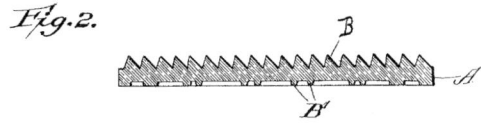

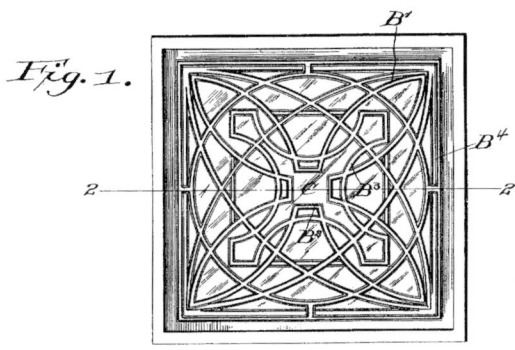

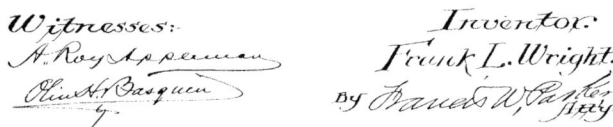

FIGURE 2.6 Frank Lloyd Wright, Design for Luxfer Prism tile, 1897, US Library of Congress/Public Domain, © [2018] Frank Lloyd Wright Foundation. All Rights Reserved. Licensed by ARS.

concentrically about the center C and interlacing or overlapping each other. The whole forms a grid-like sort of ornament." The central element of the design is of a stylized quadratic blossom overlaid on a circle; unlike Leonardo's *Vitruvian Man* the circle does not contain the flower, but rather a unique, interpenetrative dialog develops between the respective curvilinear forms. The tile described above (and illustrated here) was the only design actually produced by Luxfer, and it in fact became a staple of their business, providing Wright not only with inspiration but royalties as well.

Four years before the Luxfer work, in 1893, Wright had come upon a building that would have a strong influence on his structures and his stained glass windows alike. That was the Ho-o-den, or Phoenix Pavilion, sponsored by the Japanese government at the World's Columbian Exposition of 1893. A showcase of Japanese architecture and culture, the Phoenix Pavilion was the first exposure to actual built Asian structures for Wright and his contemporaries. The impact on Wright's subsequent work, particularly through its projecting eaves and open, flowing interior spaces, has been recognized for decades. Not as well-known is the manner in which the pavilion may have inspired Wright's future deployment of stained glass. The key element here was how the Phoenix Pavilion was decorated throughout with shoji screens and doors. Shoji screens, typically made up of a wooden frame infilled with translucent white paper, are utilized as semipermeable, light-emitting barriers in Japanese architecture; placed on the exterior as windows, they seem to have constituted the seed of Wright's conception of the stained glass assemblages he called "light screens."

Wright utilized stained glass windows as fluid, fugitive transitions between the interior and exterior of his early twentieth-century houses. These so-called Prairie houses, most constructed between 1900 and 1909, represented a maturing distillation of both the elemental geometric forms seen in the Luxfer drawings as well as the shoji-like window screens that mediate the relationship between inside and outside spaces. The Susan Lawrence Dana house (1904) in Springfield, Illinois, stands as a superlative example of Wright's conception of stained glass as a "light screen," a transitional membrane that divides interior and exterior spaces without completely separating them. This sense of a fluid relationship between building and landscape was at the center of Wright's aesthetic insomuch as the Prairie house style was based on an organic relationship with the surrounding world. Replete with glass, the Dana House has over 250 separate windows to accomplish this task.

Some of the most spectacular windows in the Dana House exhibit Wright's desire to screen, not block, the view from inside. Notably during an era when stained glass windows were usually translucent or functionally opaque, Wright's windows generally feature clear glass over half the surface. His stained glass windows therefore create a tension for the viewer between two and three dimensions as the rectilinear design formed by the cames and the opalescent glass calls attention to the flat surface while the clear glass encourages a view of the deep space outside.[9] Wright preferred brass and zinc for the cames for his windows, which allowed him to eliminate the superfluous structural pieces required by softer metals such as lead. These stiffer members also worked well for his rectilinear style and its patterned, lattice-like imagery (figure 2.7). Furthermore, there exists a balance between the abstract design of the windows and the realistic view of the natural world. Fittingly in the Dana House, Wright based a number of the windows on organic forms—a note on one of his drawings indicates it was the sumac blossom—so as to strengthen the bond between light screen and view. This is not to say that Wright sought for the motif of the windows and the world outside to be merged. The two-dimensional/three-dimensional and abstract/real contrast was at the heart of the design. Wright later wrote in an essay wherein he had just mentioned the Dana House glass: "Nothing is more

FIGURE 2.7 Frank Lloyd Wright, Robie House Window, 1904, US Library of Congress/Public Domain, © [2018] Frank Lloyd Wright Foundation. All Rights Reserved. Licensed by ARS.

annoying to me than any tendency toward realism of form in window-glass, to get mixed up with the view outside."[10] In all of his Prairie houses Wright was notoriously controlling about the interior decoration, and was quite adamant that his clients never install curtains that would destroy the effect of the light screen.

It is important to recognize that in most cases Wright worked out the designs for his windows at the end of the design process, often with the construction of the building well underway. This fact is suggestive of another way in which Wright's stained glass had a determining influence on his architectural compositions; as a designer who believed wholeheartedly in the artistic power of the *Gesamtkunstwerke*, Wright's window and structure designs are strongly interconnected. As his style evolved over the years, it appears that Wright would experiment with new forms in his windows and establish principles that he would later implement in architecture itself. In this way the windows of the last commission served as something of a proving ground for the architecture of the next ones. A good example of this phenomenon can be found in the windows for the Avery Coonley Playhouse of 1912, the first project after the European sojourn that had punctuated Wright's abandonment of both his family and his studio practice in 1909. Avery Coonley was a wealthy industrialist who lived on a large estate in Riverside, Illinois; Wright had designed the main house on the grounds in 1907. The name "Coonley Playhouse" is something of a misnomer as it was quite a large structure and housed a kindergarten run by Queene Ferry Coonley.

The stained glass on the building consisted of a large triptych set into the facade that was complemented by over twenty clerestory windows running around the perimeter of the open interior space (figure 2.8). The iconography of the Playhouse windows is child-centric—Wright once referred to it as a "kinder-symphony"—in that it was based on the forms of balloons, confetti, and flags at a parade. Stylistically, the Playhouse windows represent a pretty stark departure from Wright's earlier rectilinear designs at various prairie houses. There, symmetry had reigned; in the Playhouse windows a new dynamism was evident as asymmetry unleashed a kinetic element not seen before. Large stretches of translucent white, negative space—as clerestory windows the view was a nonissue and there is no clear glass—provide a counterpoint to the fresh, bright palette of bold colors that mark a sharp break with the earthy hues of the Prairie years. While the exact parameters of what

FIGURE 2.8 Frank Lloyd Wright, Coonley Playhouse Stained Glass, 1912, credit: Avery Coonley Residence Playhouse, Riverside, IL, 1912. Frank Lloyd Wright, architect. Historic Architecture and Landscape Image Collection, Ryerson and Burnham Archives, The Art Institute of Chicago. Digital file # 17833, credit: © [2018] Frank Lloyd Wright Foundation. All Rights Reserved. Licensed by ARS.

Wright had seen in Europe have never been established with certainty, it seems obvious that the architect had come across abstract modern painting while abroad. Here, the Coonley Playhouse windows were acting as an experimental laboratory much as the Luxfer prisms had years earlier. While some would say that it is indicative of correlation more than causation, the case can be made that the more complex, pinwheeling asymmetries of later Wright structures such as the Kauffmann House at Fallingwater represent the fruition of designs that he first worked out in glass.

Stained glass and Constructivism

The strategy whereby Wright worked out some of his aesthetic ideas in glass before applying them to architecture was equally true of one of the most influential European modern designers, Theo van Doesburg. Van Doesburg, a pseudonym of Christian Marie Emil Küpper, is most closely identified with the Dutch De Stijl collective and associated journal that he helped found in 1917, although his wide-ranging interests included Dada and Constructivism. After his discharge from the Dutch army in 1916, Van Doesburg immediately began work on fomenting a new, universal aesthetic that was attuned to both the ascetic impulse of his native land and the contemporary current of neo-Platonic spirituality that had been revived by artists during the First World War.

Captivated by what he had seen in the Wasmuth Portfolio (1910) that had publicized Wright's work to Europeans, Van Doesburg cultivated relationships with architects and saw De Stijl as an architectural movement from the very beginning; in 1916, he first collaborated with J. J. P. Oud, who was soon joined in the orbit of De Stijl by Jan Wils and Robert van 't Hoff. While De Stijl had little immediate, tangible impact on the built environment, in the long run the fundamental principles espoused by Van Doesburg had a lasting influence on modern architecture. De Stijl was focused on elemental geometric forms as they are perceived in two, three, or, somewhat mystically, even four dimensions. Three of De Stijl's principles—the orthogonal grid as a starting point, a dialogic relationship between positive and negatives spaces, and dynamic asymmetry to activate space—had immense sway on subsequent architecture. For Van Doesburg's part, he first worked through this aesthetic in colored glass.

Van Doesburg's first experience working with an architect was on the design of stained glass. In 1916, Oud commissioned him to design a work as part of the renovation of the Villa Allegonda in Katwijk. At this point Van Doesburg was transitioning from his earlier commitment to painting, and saw in stained glass a medium that could serve as a platform for his desire to create a style that would be a unifying cultural force. Far from seeing stained glass as some sort of medieval reference, for Van Doesburg it represented the most modern opportunity, a form of intermedia that could connect painting, architecture, and décor in a contemporary *Gesamtkunstwerke*. Through the framework of De Stijl, stained glass did not function as some sort of secondary, ornamental supplement, but was able to embody core aesthetic principles of architecture. The window at the Villa Allegonda, called *Composition II*, is able to express the rhythmic motion of the surf—the villa was on the North Sea coast—through the asymmetric composition of simple geometric shapes arranged in a rectilinear fashion. Still, at this point in his work in stained glass, Van

Doesburg had not yet broken away from natural motifs as the window represents a distilled abstraction that appears rather figural, and has not entered into the realm of the nonobjective.

De Stijl scholar Carel Blotkamp has identified a stained glass window from another home, this one for the De Lange family in Alkmaar, Holland, as signifying Van Doesburg's decisive stylistic leap into nonobjectivity. At Alkmaar, Van Doesburg was working at the behest of architect Wils in order to provide three windows for the main stairwell. Here, in a window known as *Composition IV* (1917, figure 2.9) for the first time Van Doesburg created glass that does not seem tied to representation, but instead embodied the syncopated rhythm of abstract geometric form. Blotkamp credits Van Doesburg's love of music as providing the catalyst for this breakthrough, which the historian defines as a language based on "repetition, mirror image, and rotation."[11] This so-called music model for abstract art has been applied far and wide in the study of this period, as artists and designers sought to distance their work from the handmaiden status of narrative illustration. Whatever its exact origins, Van Doesburg had established for himself a visual language that would provide the basis for his architectural musings for years to come.

After the war ended in 1918, Van Doesburg embarked upon a peripatetic period, traveling far and wide to spread the gospel of De Stijl while also dabbling in Dada and the like. In 1922, during a sojourn in Weimar, Germany, he met another Dutch architect, Cornelius van Eesteren, and together they produced a series of ambitious axonometric drawings that were intended to demonstrate no less than the essential language of modern architecture. These designs, known as "Contra-Constructions," investigated the spatial relationships at the core of building through a series of floating, flat planes. Clearly a further elaboration of the stylistic grammar—the grid, rotation, asymmetry, repetition—that had first appeared in his stained glass, in the Contra-Constructions Van Doesburg sought to translate his principles into three and four dimensions. Now melding his own axioms with the ideas of the various Constructivists with whom he was consorting at the time, Van Doesburg's ideal structure was never intended as an actual building, although the free-floating, intersecting planes were implemented later to a certain degree in the De Stijl model home designed by Gerrit Rietveld and known as the Schroeder House.

In 1924, having settled for a time in Paris where he had the year before exhibited the Contra-Constructions alongside a set of architectural

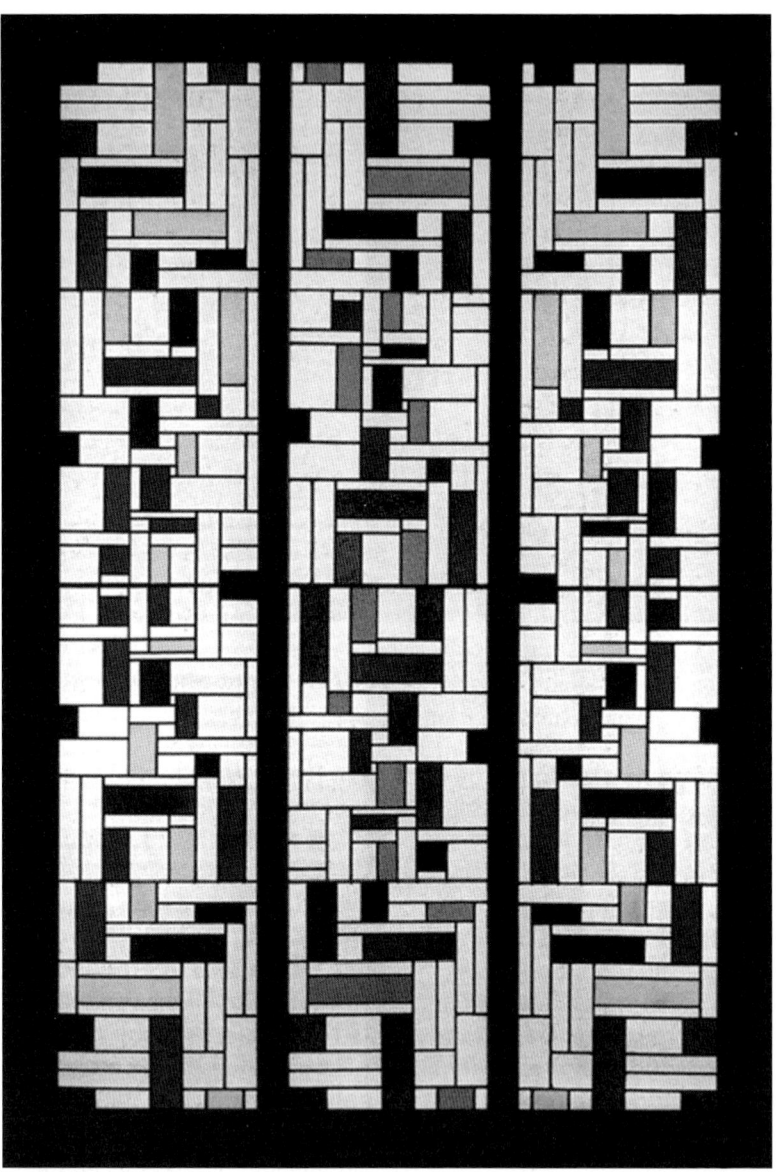

FIGURE 2.9 Theo van Doesburg, Composition IV, Alkmaar, 1917, credit: Theo van Doesburg 1883–1931, Stained-glass composition IV for the De Lange House, Alkmaar, 1917, Collection Kröller-Müller museum, Otterlo, the Netherlands, Transferred by the Dutch Government Buildings Agency 1980.

models, Van Doesburg published an architectural manifesto of sorts titled "Towards Plastic Architecture." This essay espouses the principles of open spaces defined by movable panels as opposed to fixed walls, and "the functional space is strictly divided into rectangular surfaces having no individuality of their own." These dicta resonate with the elemental language of his stained glass, yet, at this point Van Doesburg had moved on; the architecture must by definition have absorbed the lessons of stained glass into itself; in reference to the integration of art and building, Van Doesburg wrote, "Since the new architecture permits no images (such as paintings or sculptures as separate elements) its purpose of creating a harmonious whole with all essential means is evident from the outset." It is notable that Van Doesburg had turned away from stained glass at a time when the medium's popularity was declining across the board in Europe and the United States.

In 1919 amidst the aftermath of the First World War, the German architect Walter Gropius was made director of a combined fine art and design school in the city of Weimar. The so-called Bauhaus, or house of building, had a short lifespan—closed by the Nazis in 1933—but inestimable influence on both the 1920s avant-garde and the modern movement that coalesced after the Second World War. When Gropius founded the Bauhaus, it was only natural that stained glass would have a place at the table as it befit the school in at least three ways. First, Gropius touted this new institution as a place where all of the arts would be synthesized into a *Gesamtkunstwerke*, as envisioned in the famous Cathedral woodcut of Lionel Feininger; stained glass was one of the most prominent elements of medieval building and exemplary of the romanticized union of craft work that Gropius sought. Second, the strong expressionist leanings of influential faculty members such as Johannes Itten were open to stained glass in a modern context as emblematic of a new type of spiritual journey. Thirdly, and most easily overlooked, stained glass had become a standard part of architecture since the nineteenth century and was ubiquitous in the built environment of northern Europe.

The stained glass workshop was organized by Itten in the spring of 1920 with the backing of a local stained glass manufacturer named Ernst Kraus. While it was never home to many students and received little publicity, Itten did initially recruit at least one committed acolyte, the newly arrived, thirty-two-year-old former schoolteacher Josef Albers. It was Albers who really made the workshop succeed, first as its best student and, after 1922, as the journeyman master of craft, with the painter Paul Klee serving in the more exalted role of form master. Perhaps because of this personnel hierarchy, Albers seems to have viewed stained glass both as an element of architecture and a kind of experimental painting medium; he produced a number of commissions for architecture, both for Gropius and various commercial clients, but unfortunately all of these windows were destroyed in the conflagration that was to come.

Because Albers was one of the few early Bauhaus students who stayed until the end in 1933, his work in the stained glass studio charts the evolving conception of art at the school. Early windows such as *Rhenish Legend* (1921), an assemblage of brightly colored found glass that seeks to make a virtue out of a lean budget, are replete with the romantic titles and eccentric, whimsical stylings of an Itten or a Klee. It has a certain quirky charm and one can imagine it integrated into the fanciful expressionist buildings imagined by Itten or Paul Scheerbart. In 1922 Albers appears more settled, and his growing body of work includes windows for the Gropius-designed Sommerfeld and Otte houses in Berlin. These windows continue to feature clouds of color and jaunty, irregular forms and kaleidoscopic coloring.

In 1922, Van Doesburg settled for a time in Weimar, apparently with the hope of landing a position at the Bauhaus. This was not to be—historians believe that Gropius saw Van Doesburg's strong personality as a possible threat to his leadership—but Van Doesburg did organize a series of salons wherein he presented the ideals of De Stijl to an audience made up mainly of Bauhaus students and faculty. Van Doesburg's influence is usually seen as the main catalyst that fomented a transition in broad terms from an expressionist-oriented Bauhaus to one focused on Constructivist principles; the process gained momentum early in 1923, when the Hungarian artist Laszlo Moholy-Nagy was hired at the Bauhaus while eight weeks later Itten left the faculty because of his diminished role. Albers quickly adapted to this new milieu, and even collaborated with Moholy-Nagy on the institution of a new preliminary course, one that turned away from intuitive artmaking toward a staunch Constructivist analysis of the nature of materials. During this phase that encompassed the school's move to its new location in Dessau, Albers's stained glass work dramatically shifted in style. Gone are the poetic assemblages; now Albers utilized an industrial process, sandblasting, in order to make windows that resonated with the Constructivist principles of grid, rhythmic asymmetry, and interpenetrated positive and negative space.

City of 1928 represents the best of this new work (figure 2.10). Albers utilized a unique process whereby he started with opaque milky glass that he "flashed," or fused, with a veneer of colored glass, usually red. Next he would create a series of stencils that would allow him to sandblast parts of the red layer away in a precise, geometric layout, after which he would add additional designs in black by painting on the glass. The resulting compositions resonate both with De Stijl principles and the kinetic forms of the contemporary abstract films of Viking Eggeling and Hans Richter. Like so many stained glass designers, Albers left the field after the 1920s, presumably because despite the attempts of designers such as Van Doesburg and himself to keep the medium a part of contemporary architectural practice, the same decline that claimed Tiffany studios would prove inexorable.

In his later, American career, Albers became noted for his famous color studies called *Homage to the Square*, although he was also occasionally called upon to work in the architectural realm. His most stunning contribution in this latter regard was the huge, mural-like piece called *Manhattan* that Gropius commissioned in 1963 while he was architect of the Pan Am (now MetLife) building in New York City. This work on

FIGURE 2.10 Josef Albers, "City" stained glass, 1928, Photo Art Resource, credit: © [2017] Artists Rights Society (ARS), New York.

formica, not glass, resurrected the contrapuntal composition of *City*, and served as an iconic gateway piece that abstractly visualized the mass of people traveling through the concourse that connected the Pan Am building and Grand Central Station. *Manhattan* was removed during a renovation in 2000, and its asbestos backing has prevented it from being reinstalled at this time.

The struggle to stay relevant

While the overall stained glass boom ended in the 1920s, a few later developments are worthy of attention. In France, the decline was not quite so precipitous as elsewhere in Europe, and the Art Deco style inaugurated at the *Exposition des Arts Décoratifs at Industriels Moderne* of 1925 featured a large pavilion dedicated to the art form; thirty-seven stained glass manufacturers displayed windows as part of the "Glass Art and Industry" section. Likewise, the 1937 Paris exposition featured a great deal of colored glass in both the Art Deco and more conventional styles. However, soon the ascendant Constructivist aesthetic promulgated by De Stijl, the Bauhaus, et al. fomented a strong reaction against any architectural element such as stained glass that could be considered frivolous or ornamental.

While stained glass even in France gradually declined in the secular setting as the twentieth century passed its midpoint, one final creative surge reasserted its relevance in ecclesiastical structures. This phenomenon was largely spurred on by the artist, patron, and Dominican clergyman Pierre Couturier, one of the first artists to join the Art Sacré group. Founded in 1919 by a pair of artists including the symbolist painter Maurice Denis, the adherents of Ateliers d'art Sacré committed themselves to a revival of Catholic religious art. While the church and the secular French government had been in continual conflict for decades, the parties reached a rapprochement of sorts in 1924 that set the stage for the revival.

When Couturier began to assert himself in the 1940s as coeditor of the Ateliers' house journal *L'Art sacré*, he advocated the idea that artists should be chosen for religious commissions regardless of their personal beliefs. This argument directly contradicted Vatican policy, which had long insisted that artists themselves be observant Catholics. Nonetheless, in less than a decade, Couturier commissioned four different new Catholic edifices that included the work of non-Catholics and in some cases even non-Christians. The first building completed under the aegis of Couturier's artistic meritocracy was the church of *Notre-Dame de Toute Grâce du Plateau* in Assy (1946), a rather plain basilican type designed by Maurice Novarina. Couturier enlisted a host of School of Paris painters for its decorative elements, procuring a notable stained glass window by George Rouault (who actually was a spiritually minded Catholic) as the centerpiece. This church was followed by another Novarina basilica at Audincourt, *Sacré-Coeur* (1951), which had a wealth of windows devised by Fernand Leger, and the famous *Chapelle du Rosaire de Vence* (1951) that was designed and filled with stained glass by Henri Matisse. At Audincourt, Leger made use of the new stained glass material called *dalle de verre*, literally "slab of glass," whereby large chunks of thick glass (1 inch or more) were cut and hammered into crude shapes and then embedded into concrete. This process had the advantage of economy, as it required less skilled labor, while also introducing a raw, modern look that was well matched to concrete structures. Almost sixty years after Siegfried Bing had first enlisted modern painters to create works of stained glass, Couturier had succeeded where Bing had not, commissioning abstract works of color that captured the public's imagination in uniting one of the oldest mediums with the experimental abstractions of modernism.

Couturier died in 1954, but at that time one last monument to his vision was already well underway, Le Corbusier's *Chapelle Notre Dame du Haut* at Ronchamp (1954, figure 2.11). One of Le Corbusier's most renowned, expressive experiments in concrete, the Ronchamp chapel also should be recognized for its whimsical hand-painted stained glass. In particular, the south wall to the side of the main entrance is pierced by over twenty square and rectangular openings of different scales. This syncopated rhythm is furthered by the sculptural quality of the wall itself, a double shell several feet thick that creates tunneling, trapezoidal sashes most of which are narrow on the exterior shell where the glazing is located and then expand outward to light the interior. The glass itself has been painted with a light, expressionist touch, its geometric compositions enlivened with delicate, Paul Klee like passages and florid handwritten phrases.

Together the windows on the south wall seem to form a modernist homage to the luminous wall of the Gothic, while the deep sashes also recall the sculptural massing of a Romanesque church. That being

FIGURE 2.11 Le Corbusier, Chapelle Notre Dame du Haut, 1954, VIEW Pictures (UK), credit: © F.L.C. / ADAGP, Paris / Artists Rights Society (ARS), New York [2018].

said, by the 1950s progressive architects had truly taken Adolph Loos's famous words to heart, and the notion that these windows formed some sort of ornamental, historicist reference could be regarded as criminal to Le Corbusier and his circle. For this reason, Le Corbusier remained adamant that despite the fact that he had infilled the walls of a religious building with colored glass, the resulting fenestration did not form stained glass windows, but rather portholes that led to the sky as part of a heavenly metaphor. In regard to stained glass at Ronchamp, Le Corbusier wrote that he "regards this method of lighting as being too definitely attached to outdated architectural concepts, and to Romanesque and Gothic art in particular." One might think that he doth protest too much.

Of course, Le Corbusier's conflicted feelings about stained glass were right on point, and the medium was in fact soon to be teetering into oblivion in the face of the minimalist aesthetics appearing already on the horizon. Surely, stained glass is still made in the current era, most often for ecclesiastical buildings, but in our pluralist period bits and pieces may turn up anywhere, from Damien Hirst's Pharmacy installation (1992) to Marjan van Aubel's stained-glass solar cells (2015). Still, Le Corbusier's idea that the medium signifies "outdated architectural concepts" appears to have hardened over the ensuing decades, and much of the stained glass made today is created by artisans whose work is more likely to appear on Etsy than in the pages of *Architectural Record*.

While conventional stained glass appears moribund—although one could imagine a revival one day—the atmosphere of light, color, and/or pattern it produced has continually been invoked through new technologies. Today, silk screen and ceramic frit printers allow for a multitude of designs to appear on glass, sometimes as part of a sustainability strategy (see Chapter 6). For example, Rem Koolhaas's McCormick Tribune Campus Center at IIT (2003) features a fine example of a screen-printed photograph, in this case a close-up of Ludwig Mies van der Rohe which covers the main entrance doors. Screen printing can also be used to create trompe l'oeil effects, simulating the texture of wood or stone, while frit printers are lately able to reproduce full color photographs of any sort. A stunning example of the technology was built in Schijndel, Netherlands, in 2003. There, architects MVRDV created the Glass Farm, a trompe l'oeil building that appears to be a conventional farmhouse but is in fact a frit-printed photograph on top of a glass sheath. From the inside, viewers see a reverse of the image while standing in a chapel-like space surrounded by colored glass.

The newest imaging technology on glass involves "drop-on demand" ink jet printing that utilizes ultraviolet-cured ceramic inks. Perfected by the company Dip-Tech, these new durable inks have made high-resolution digital printing another spectacular, if expensive, reality. The AFIMALL in Moscow highlights the potential of this medium, as a Russian forest scene was printed on to over 2,000 panes of glass to create a magical natural vista amidst the hard urban reality of retail commerce. One could imagine that this technology will someday be used to create facsimiles of famous stained-glass monuments.

Some architects have used these new technologies to invoke a sense of the sacred that resonates with the origins of stained glass. Take, for

FIGURE 2.12 David Adjaye, Stephen Lawrence Center 2007.

example, David Adjaye's Stephen Lawrence Centre (2007, figure 2.12) in London, a social services building dedicated to the memory of Lawrence, an architecture-loving child who was murdered in a racist attack in 1993. The facade of the building features a luminous wall to the side of the entranceway, much like the composition of the facade at Ronchamp. Adjaye's wall is not sculptural, however, but rather a contemporary flat curtain of glass that has a rippled screen print on plastic film embedded between the layers of glass. The moiré pattern was based on a drawing by the artist Chris Ofili. Viewed during the daytime, the window recalls the grisaille stained glass of a bygone age, its pattern scattering the daylight as it falls into the building's atrium. Viewed from the outside at night with the interior lit, the wall of glass shimmers with the deep red of the painted atrium walls, glowing with the color of sacrifice.

3 DAYLIGHT RULES THE MODERN BUILDING

One of the essential components of early modern architecture was the windows that served as a gateway for natural light and ventilation. Because these elemental functions of the window were largely superseded by electric lighting in the early 1900s and air-conditioning in the 1930s, they have often been downplayed in terms of their centrality to the building arts. Also, these rudimentary functions have no glamour associated with them such as that associated with the curtain wall, and therefore languish in a purgatory of the banal. In point of fact, one could argue that windows were at the absolute center of the modern aesthetic, and the desire to open up interior spaces to the sun and atmosphere perhaps the most decisive functional element of modern design. Starting with the "Chicago Window" of the 1880s, glass that is perhaps the most literal manifestation of Louis Sullivan's truism that "form ever follows function," and cutting through Le Corbusier's ribbons of glass, there is a broad and deep engagement with windows that set the course of architecture for decades.

The first skyscrapers

There is a general consensus that one of the great eras of modern architecture occurred during the last quarter of the nineteenth century, when the first wave of skyscrapers—a term coined around 1890 to denote office buildings of between ten and twenty stories—appeared in the business districts of the United States, especially those of New York and Chicago. The sine qua non of these new buildings was the development of the iron and steel skeletal frame, which in later years would be proffered as the engineering, aesthetic, and ideological center of modern architecture.

The historiography of this development of the skeletal frame has been marked by two sustained controversies: one rather anecdotal and the other in recent years freighted with intellectual and ideological substance. While these two *disputa* center on the skeleton, not the windows, they are key to setting the stage for early modern glass.

The first disagreement centers on when and where the steel frame was introduced, and has focused on William Le Baron Jenney's *Home Insurance Building* of 1885 (figure 3.1). In April of 1885 before the building was occupied, a writer for the *Inland Architect* reported, "In one, the Home Insurance, the iron construction of the interior is carried out to the exterior walls, and every pier contains an iron post, which is secured on each story to the whole system of girder construction, and it thereby becomes an iron structure complete in itself, masked by an exterior brick wall."[1] Until his death in 1907, Jenney agreed with this assessment and asserted that he had invented the frame, nurturing his reputation as the revolutionary who had changed architecture forevermore. As the years wore on, some initial rough edges around the story were worn smooth, and it has been noted that Jenney's claim intensified despite the fact that his building was, arguably, just one of a group that experimented with the steel skeleton while hedging in places.[2] After all, the Home Insurance skeleton was immersed in fireproof masonry and not open for further inspection. In 1900 Jenney wrote one of many articles where he perhaps overstated the transformative nature of his building: "[i]t was an entirely new one, one may truly say, in every particular; and for the new building everything must be invented, particularly the system of construction."[3] Jenney's 1907 obituaries witnessed the fact that his claim had won out in the short run, as they celebrated the man by relaying his by-then oft-told tale complete with colorful anecdotes that make Jenney sound like Brunelleschi pitching his dome to the potentates of Florence. For example, from *The American Architect*, "The drawings were then prepared and the first design for a fireproof skeleton building was made and presented to the building committee of the Home Insurance Company for their acceptance. As business men, they naturally inquired, 'Where is there such a building?' The architect replied, 'Your building at Chicago will be the first.'"[4]

Over the ensuing years this war of skeletal primacy raged on, with one battle engaging the rivalry between Chicago and New York. The former has maintained its position either because of or in spite of empirical

FIGURE 3.1 William Jenney, Home Insurance Building, 1885, US Library of Congress/Public Domain.

assessments, but no one can doubt that Chicago provides a far better backstory that undoubtedly bolsters its claim. The legendary fire of 1871 provides the most colorful vignette, setting the stage for a phoenix-like rise on the shores of Lake Michigan. But just as important is the way in which the consensus character of the city—as a uncultured, hard-nosed mercenary business center—played so nicely into the narrative of plain-spoken rationalism that dominates the history of this era. It was actually a New Yorker, the culture writer and famed architectural historian Montgomery Schuyler, who first set this story into motion. Unwittingly abandoning his eastern hometown, in 1896 Schuyler argued in the New York–based *Architectural Record* that the character of Chicagoans had defined their architecture.

> I asked one of the successful architects of Chicago what would happen if the designer of a commercial building sacrificed the practical availableness of one or more of its stories to the assumed exigencies of architecture, as has often been done in New York, … "No, we never try those tricks on our business men. They are too wide awake."[5]

In later years structural purists went deep into the weeds on this subject, debating what precisely constitutes a fully framed building, especially as it relates to the relationship between iron or steel frame and masonry. Jenney's claim to precedence has remained under attack, as detractors pointed to the fact that some of the masonry was not supported by the skeleton of steel, but rather had been left to carry its own weight. It was mainly for this reason that in 1931 the Western Society of Engineers completed a comprehensive study that downgraded the Home Insurance structure from skeletal to hybrid. Really this was the least of the Jenney building's problems in 1931, as the study was conducted during the building's demolition, as engineers picked over the cadaver like it was one of Vesalius's sixteenth-century corpses fresh from the gallows. As Charles Waldheim has noted, since 1931, "The assertion that Jenney invented skeletal construction … has been refuted over and over again."[6] It is a good thing that this debate is simply academic, as the scholarly experts have been unable to upend the legend of Jenney and the Home Insurance Building. Headlined the *Guardian* in April 2015, "Chicago's Home Insurance Building may no longer be standing, but it utterly changed the way we design cities, in ways that were previously unthinkable."[7]

Putting aside the Home Insurance controversy for the moment, I want to draw attention not to which building was first but rather how that discussion has framed the debate over early modern commercial architecture. In a number of primary sources but especially in the subsequent flood of secondary historical writing, absolute primacy is given to the skeletal frame. There is obvious merit to this argument; the frame carries the load, opens up the interior spaces, allows for vertical growth, and provides a basis for aesthetic decisions. Glass is usually a side story, grouped along with mechanical systems, foundations, fireproofing, and elevators in a sort of second tier of necessary infrastructure. To a large degree the stunning plate glass surfaces that were so integral to the new architecture are transparent, invisible. The argument to be advanced below is that the cart has been put before the horse, and, under whatever interpretive rubric one wants to apply, it is the expression of the windows, not the skeletal frame, which should be remembered as the decisive factor in defining the birth of the skyscraper.

In recent decades a number of scholars have pointed to the obvious fact that daylight ruled Chicago construction in the late 1800s. What about gas lighting? It had very low candlepower, was messy, and often dangerous. Arc lights were hard to handle and also burned hot and dangerous. While the wave of buildings produced in the latter two decades of the nineteenth century were most often wired for electric light, that technology was inefficient and expensive until around the turn of the century.[8] Of course there was no city-wide power grid, so any power that was for sale was generated locally, as the transmission loss of DC current was substantial at the time. When there was electricity available, bulbs were expensive and burned out quickly. Architectural historian Thomas Leslie has done an admirable job in parsing out the technical details and myriad economic forces that helped mold the early skyscraper in Chicago.[9] Leslie has tracked how the most expansive Chicago curtain walls (a term utilized starting around 1895) appeared at a time when plate glass prices were at their lowest, while subsequent price increases as well as a dawning recognition of the thermal inefficiency of large swaths of single-pane plate glass combined with better electric light helped to catalyze a scaling down of modern fenestration in the early twentieth century. But not having the benefit of hindsight regarding the future of cheap, efficient electric light, architects of the 1880s and 1890s took for granted the fact that a building without ready access to daylight was unthinkable. Jenney himself is oft quoted making the self-evident proclamation that the steel skeleton's raison d'être was to increase the amount of space open for windows.

> In 1883 and 1884 when the problem of building a tall, well-lighted, fireproof office building ... was first presented to the writer by the Home Insurance Company ... The many windows for the lighting of the offices so reduced the piers between openings that they were insufficient in the lower stories to carry the load of walls and floors above.[10]

In later years Jenney's world had been turned on its head. He wrote it clearly enough in *Inland Architect* that the windows were the primary concern, the frame strictly a solution.

It was not just Jenney who recognized that the windows were at the core of the new commercial high building. Architectural writers such as Barr Ferree stated this fact quite plainly in 1894. "The design of the high building is a definite problem which may be expressed in a very few words. It is the arrangement of the largest number of windows of the greatest possible size in a limited space."[11] Hence the skeletal frame. Scholars making the case for windows' primacy in what one architect in 1896 called "the reign of glass and steel," often resort to invoking the *gravitas* of John Wellborn Root, who, only seven months before he died, had the decency to set out the deterministic nature of windows in his essay "A Great Architectural Problem."[12] This famed article discusses Root's ideas about the design and construction of large office buildings, and was published a few years after the successful completion of Burnham & Root's Rookery building (1886). The essay details the design decisions made upon commencing the planning of any urban office building. "Of course, the first radical question to suggest itself is that of light ... Experience has demonstrated that all spaces with the inclosure [*sic*] of four walls which are not well lighted by sunshine, or at least direct daylight, are in office buildings non-productive." Root then goes on to pragmatically set out the need for daylight, citing the then-standard formula that a ceiling height of 11 feet can be matched with a room depth of 24 feet, if "giving to the space to be lighted the largest possible windows." George Hill was one of many who published calculations about window size, recommending that an office of 15 feet deep feature a window of a minimum of 4 × 6 feet with the upper edge placed within a foot of the ceiling.[13] It is in this regard that the demands of Montgomery Schuyler's emblematic Chicago businessman and his speculative real estate deals come to the fore. Records from this era show that well-lit spaces commanded considerably higher rents, at times almost twice as high as those far from windows.[14] As a practical matter, building well-lit office space cost no more than building dark office space. Since any office more than 15 feet from a window was considered suboptimal and in some cases was simply not marketable at all, the question of adequate daylight was an overall deterministic one. The windows were the moneymaker, while the skeletal frame a mere means to an end—daylight.

It is important to recognize how American success in the manufacture of plate glass set the stage for the vast windows of Chicago office buildings. While plate glass production had been invented in France centuries before, it had only spread to the European glass manufacturing centers of Belgium and the United Kingdom in the nineteenth century. Over the decades, continuing technical improvements saw the manufacturing process, which was initially dependent on armies of laborers to perform the grinding and polishing necessary to eliminate distortions, improved by increasing mechanization. In the United States, up until the Civil War plate glass was mainly an expensive imported product. During the last quarter of the nineteenth century, however, American manufacturers in Pennsylvania and in the Midwestern states of Indiana and Missouri rapidly expanded the American glass industry and plate imports shrunk considerably. By 1886 the plate glass market in Chicago, a key distribution hub, consisted of almost 90 percent domestic glass. Plate glass quickly became a fungible commodity that was manipulated by shrewd speculators riding the industrial boom. For example, Chicago glass distributor extraordinaire George Kimball built his reputation partly on cunning, having famously cornered a large part of the domestic market in the spring of 1884 and profiting from a resultant spike in the national price.[15] Notwithstanding his erstwhile success, market forces in the long run led to gradually declining prices for plate glass, eventually reaching a multiyear bottom in the 1890s. Not just a speculator, Kimball was a central figure in the supply chain that brought plate glass to the builders of Chicago, and his provisioning for Jenney's Second Leiter Building in 1891 was celebrated as the largest single order for plate glass ever executed up until that time.[16]

The Chicago Window

"It must be remembered that in the architecture of large buildings in Chicago at the present day a radical departure has been made ... The walls are a mere veneer ... They are often of glass."[17] Despite the fact that from a functional and aesthetic standpoint the windows of a tall office building were a dominant element, the very nature of the material, the transparency of the large plate window, worked against it being recognized as the aesthetic center of early modern commercial architecture. When glass was recognized as an aesthetic element in the 1890s, it was often described as a void, a complement to solid materials. As architect J. W. Yost wrote in 1896,

> It so occurs that plate glass and steel construction are directly opposite in character, and yet both work toward the same end. The steel may be said to be the positive quantity, and the glass the negative quantity. The steel is the solid—the glass the void. The glass can fill the space which the more positive material does not care to occupy.[18]

Yost was on to something there; in a way he recounts what has been the fate of the most important design element to come out of Chicago construction, its eponymous window, always recognized, but largely dropped out of the architectural conversation and into the void.

The Chicago Window is both everywhere and nowhere in architectural history (figure 3.2). While scholarly titans trade vituperative screeds over the genesis of the skeletal frame, no one cares to ask when and where the Chicago Window made its initial appearance. It is always mentioned: browse the index of just about any modern architectural tome and you will see the listing for "Chicago Windows." Usually the term will be enclosed in quotes, a sort of subliminal grammatical convention that suggests the author is somehow less than sure about the substance of the reference. At the same time that Chicago Windows are clothed with uncertainty in the literature, related terms such as "Chicago School" or "Chicago Construction" are offered up on the same page without the diminishing force of quotations mark. (This is somewhat ironic especially as the former term is a well-documented shape shifter, having lost its original ties to the circle around Frank Lloyd Wright and reappeared as a synonym for early modern tall buildings.) Chicago Windows, from where did they come? At some point after 1890 they were just there.

FIGURE 3.2 Chicago Window on Charles Atwood, Reliance Building, 1895, US Library of Congress/Public Domain.

The Chicago Window is a functional solution that quietly ranks with the best. It consists of a tripartite design with two fairly typical double-hung operable windows flanking a large, usually squarish sheet of plate glass. The Chicago Window is notable for its strong horizontal orientation. The central pane provides light and views, while the side windows open for ventilation. This latter function was of enormous import considering how plate glass curtain walls could create unbearable interior conditions, bleeding heat in the winter, but more devastatingly, trapping workers in a veritable greenhouse during the hot, humid summer months.

As is the case with the origin of the skeletal frame, the actual "inventor" of the Chicago Window is hard to pin down, and undoubtedly its origins represent the collective work of a number of designers and engineers working to solve a practical problem. Unlike the issue of the frame, the rewards here are slight and the question of authorship is of even less historical significance as so little posthumous fame would be attached to the achievement. For the purposes of illustration Holabird & Roche's Champlain Building (1894, figure 3.3) can play the role of the Home Insurance Building, as it represents a likely candidate for demonstrating the first near-total utilization of the Chicago Window. This is not to say

FIGURE 3.3 Holabird & Roche, Champlain Building, 1894, US Library of Congress/Public Domain.

that the Champlain displayed the *first* Chicago Windows, only that like the case of the Home Insurance Building, rightly or wrongly it can serve as the basis for discussion. Earlier examples of prominent use of Chicago Windows abound. For instance, the familiar tripartite form had been utilized on Holabird & Roche's Venetian Building that was completed in 1892 three years before the Champlain. The Venetian's twelve-story narrow street facade featured Chicago Windows on seven of its middle levels, but none appeared on its longer axis. Likewise, Adler & Sullivan's Chicago Stock Exchange of 1893 alternated Chicago Windows with bay windows over both facades. The Champlain differs from these examples mainly in that above the street level its Chicago Windows were used exclusively, and did not have to share the light with any other type of fenestration.

Holabird & Roche, the firm that made the most use of the Chicago Window, was a partnership formed in 1883 by two former students of none other than Jenney: William Holabird and Martin Roche. These two named partners were joined by a third partner, E. A. Renwick, in 1896. Their estimable business, headquartered for some time in the southern extension of the Monadnock building that had itself been one of their earliest large commissions, was quickly to become one of Chicago's architectural juggernauts, responsible for hundreds of homes and commercial structures in and around the city.

Completed in 1895, Holabird & Roche's Champlain Building was generally unremarkable in its own day and today remains undistinguished in the literature. Centrally located in the Loop on the Northwest corner of Madison and State, at fifteen stories of white terra cotta crowned with a heavy cornice, it did not especially stand out amidst the waves of speculative commercial skyscrapers of the 1890s. Not the headquarters of any notable businesses, it had been commissioned as a general office building by Chicago Leasehold Trustees, an active real estate development partnership. Up until now, the Champlain has been noted only for being the first steel frame skyscraper to have been demolished, as it was razed in 1915 to make way for further major expansion of the Boston Store. This latter building, also by Holabird & Roche, still stands.

When the Champlain was first designed around 1892, it was clear that daylighting was a primary concern. The *Chicago Economist* reported via what was apparently a press release that the owners intended a building "affording the most abundant light to its occupants, and to that end as much glass as possible would be used. The windows will occupy the entire distance between the stories save the small amount of space required for the mullions."[19] The article goes on to state that the vast central window will consist of two plate glass panes stitched together with a narrow mullion for a total width of 22 feet. If these windows had, in fact, been built, such a span of glass would have been spectacular even in the 1890s, at the peak of the inexpensive plate glass boom. "On each side of this large plate will be a smaller window, say 2 or 3 feet wide, provided for the purpose of ventilation." Even with the narrowest mullions this tripartite window would have stretched somewhere over 26 feet. Importantly, this 1892 article represents one of the first times that the Chicago Window was described for the record.

When the Champlain was completed in 1895, the windows had been scaled down to a more realistic size. While still featuring ample glass, the 66 foot wide State Street side had been divided into four sections and featured around 56 feet of glass. The new design limited each Chicago Window to a width of 14 feet and a single central pane of at most 11, as opposed to the imagined twenty-two. One important aspect of the Chicago Window is its pronounced horizontal composition. In most buildings that feature it, the Chicago Window contests or even overwhelms the verticality of other elements in the structure. This is true of the Champlain Building despite its prominent vertical mullions and the fact that its overall proportions—it was a tall building on a narrow site—emphasize the vertical. This perceived horizontal emphasis in the Champlain was strongly noted by the architect and critic Peter Wight when he wrote an analysis of the skyscraper in 1899. Wight's essay was generally dismissive of what he saw as a stark, Monadnock-like austerity in the Champlain's surfaces, a critique to be expected considering Wight's own designs for a number of floridly ornamented, historicist structures dating back to the 1860s when he had worked in New York City. Regarding the Champlain, Wight was struck by the Chicago Windows. "It … is the first building in which Holabird & Roche adopted the plan of throwing the whole space between the main steel posts into single, wide windows, wider than their own height."[20] So perhaps the Champlain can stake a claim here as the original example of the Chicago Window writ large(?) Wight continued, "The vertical lines … are not opposed by horizontal lines of decoration, which had before been tried in Chicago, … but by the horizontal *masses* of the windows themselves." This last element Wight compared unfavorably to the "stilted effect" of D. H. Burnham and Company's 1896 Fisher Building that did not have Chicago Windows resulting in less pronounced horizontal emphasis. As will be discussed below, in later years as writers sought to overstate the verticality of the early modern Chicago skyscraper, the horizontality of the Chicago Window, obvious to all, was something that had to be suppressed.

Another aspect of the Chicago Window, its tripartite form, is suggestive of one other possible generative influence, that of the academic training and culture of so many architects in this era. An analogous situation is widely recognized as one of the most notable stylistic conventions of the early modern skyscraper in both Chicago and New York: the tripartite sectioning on the vertical axis. Montgomery Schuyler waxed poetically on this element in 1899, writing how architects had "grouped their stories capriciously and eccentrically" until the tripartite form was born.[21] Schuyler related this compositional device to Aristotle, the "father of criticism," who had instructed that "a work of art must have a beginning, a middle and an end." Of course, the tripartite composition is a mainstay of classicizing styles in architecture, and students at the Beaux-arts academy in Paris, a group which included a large number of even the most progressive American architects, were summarily inculcated in its merits. While William Holabird and Martin Roche had not themselves studied in Paris, they of course shared in the general acknowledgment of classical forms typical of this era. The early modern twist on this classical trope was the idea of applying such a proportional scheme to buildings whose height seemed to take them out of the classical realm. Here the practice came to be one based on invoking not the overall building but the single column of the ancients, through which base, shaft, and capital made for a harmonious structure that was holistically complete. The Champlain serves as a typical example; it is sectioned through ornament and color into a tripartite columnar form, the mullions serving like the fluting of a column.

It can be argued that the tripartite division of the Chicago Window is also responsive to a classical form, not the vertical column, of course, but the horizontal expanse of the venerable Palladian, or Serlian, window. While identified mainly with Renaissance architecture, and having gone in and out of fashion over the centuries, the Palladian window had become a beloved staple of the classical canon in Europe and the United States. While its proportions vary, one dominant version presents a large, squarish section flanked by two narrower rectangular shapes. Remove the central arched element in your mind's eye and you can see the exact proportions of many Chicago Windows. If Holabird & Roche are indeed the originators of the form, it would be perfectly logical because the firm often employed Palladian windows in its domestic design business. For example, Holabird & Roche's 1889 William B. Bogert house in the suburb of Evanston just north of Chicago highlights a prominent Palladian window on its attic story. In this case the arched portion of the window is completely separated from the tripartite base by a rather wide lintel, so that the three main rectilinear forms exactly share the design of the

Chicago Window. This is not to say that the Chicago Window was a conscious evocation of the Palladian form. But just maybe.

Sullivan and the Organic Window

In 1896, amidst the commercial architecture building boom in Chicago, Louis Sullivan first published his famous essay "The Tall Office Building Artistically Considered."[22] While much of Sullivan's writings veered so far into the metaphysical as to be rather conceptually opaque, this essay made a pretty clear case in favor of height being the determining characteristic of the skyscraper. "It must be tall, every inch of it tall." Furthermore, Sullivan asserted that the tripartite division of the skyscraper on the vertical axis was in accord with his sense of "naturalness and completeness." Sullivan's fundamental conceptual premise underlining these arguments is that "function" is an organic process dictated by natural law, as "life seeks and takes on its forms in an accord perfectly responsive to its needs." Rooted in the Transcendentalist writings of Ralph Waldo Emerson, here Sullivan makes a profoundly contrarian argument insomuch as he asserts that commercial architecture has the ability to express some sort of eternal truth.

In support of his assertions—the basis for "organic architecture"—Sullivan coined, and in the essay reiterated, his famous adage, "form ever follows function." Sullivan did not write much about glass in this essay, and what he did write was easily overlooked because it came fairly early in the piece, before his argument had really kicked into high gear. In this preliminary section, Sullivan had argued that everything in the tall office building follows from the scale of human activity in a comfortable room. The size of the room impacts the size of the window openings, and these, in turn, "form in an equally natural way the true basis of the artistic development of the exterior." In this manner, the windows form an elemental link in the natural order of construction. I would go farther and make the claim that the Chicago Window, which of course Sullivan was familiar with and had been a prominent part of the exterior of the Chicago Stock Exchange, would have more naturally fit Sullivan's argument, had he not been led astray in pursuit of loftiness and verticality. The Chicago Window came into being exactly as it should have according to the tenets of organic architecture; its form grew naturally out of the need to fulfill the most elemental functions of the building enclosure, providing light and air. Sullivan backed the wrong tripartite form in order to justify the primacy of the vertical, and in essence contradicted his central assertion that human activity naturally determines the form of the building: people in comfortable rooms in office buildings occupy horizontal space in pursuit of their activities and leave the vertical to the elevators. While Sullivan was one of the first, he was by no means the last to distort the essence of Chicago Construction by emphasizing verticality at the expense of horizontal glass.

In October of 1896, six months after Sullivan's article had appeared in *Lippincott's Magazine*, his erstwhile partner Dankmar Adler took the opportunity of a panel organized by the American Institute of Architects—called "Influence of steel construction and of plate glass upon the development of modern style"—to riff on Sullivan's dictum.[23] In his own essay Adler shortened the key four-word phrase into a "three-worded aphorism," quoting it as the now ever familiar "form follows function."[24] In this brief essay Adler argues that the new materials of steel and plate glass are in accord with the natural world and should be treated as capable of artistic expression just as much as the conventional elements of wood and stone. There is one curious aside to Adler's discussion of Sullivan's take on the skyscraper; in praising the beauty of modern construction materials—which he floridly calls "utterances of scientific prose"—Adler inexplicably lets contempt for plate glass bubble to the surface. "Let us then welcome the prosaic output of furnace and mill, and even the unpromising and garish sheet of plate glass." Adler's remark suggests that plate glass was still of an uncertain reputation, and in some sense he and other architects of the era saw it as a material tainted by the glare of the shop windows that lined the streets of so many cities.

Decades later, one of the first historians of the era, Siegfried Giedion, would make the case for the Chicago Window's organic roots. Amidst one of his classic, and now notorious, attempts to connect later modern architecture with that of Chicago—in this case juxtaposing Sullivan's Schlesinger & Meyer Store (1899–1904) with Walter Gropius' Project for the Tribune Tower competition (1922)—Giedion noted that the Gropius project featured tripartite Chicago Windows (the consonance between Chicago architecture and European modernism was first articulated in the early 1930s by curators at the Museum of Modern Art; see below). Insisting that Chicago Windows were unknown in Europe, Giedion argued that since both architects in Chicago and Gropius had arrived at the same solution independently, "the Chicago school really was 'permeated by the spirit of the age.'"[25] An organic manifestation if ever there was one. It should be noted that the Chicago Window served as crucial evidence right at the crescendo of this famous comparison, as the next sentence turns to the familiar trope of the 1893 World's Fair and its supposed suppression of the new style.

In 1899, the struggle between the organic functionalism of the horizontal window and Sullivan's love of artistry played out in the design of three buildings collectively known as the McCormick Buildings, or Gage group on Michigan Avenue in Chicago (figure 3.4). While Holabird & Roche won the contract for these three millinery establishments, the owner insisted that Sullivan design the facade for the northernmost, tallest structure (it was at first only slightly taller: four more floors were added at a later date). In subsequent decades, Sullivan's facade has been celebrated as a stunning example of his organically derived ornamental art. Later critics have denigrated the southern buildings in contrast to the fine architecture of Sullivan. This widely expressed sentiment echoes the conventional wisdom in Sullivan's day that structures like the southern Gage buildings were too severe, betraying art in the service of crass commerce. However, the case can be made that in pursuing an ornamental scheme, Sullivan in fact betrayed his own organic-functionalist principles. At least that is the way Holabird & Roche partner E. A. Renwick described it when he looked back on the project.

> One of our clients wanted Sullivan to design the façade of a building, but wanted us to do the inside and erect the building... Now we would have run the windows up just as far as they could go, for the light at the top carries farther. But against our judgment Sullivan insisted on putting four feet of ornamentation at the top of the windows ... The owner let him go ahead and the store was ruined for a good many years—until artificial light.[26]

This quote actually confuses, rather than clarifies, the design of the Gage building. It is clear from the archival record that Sullivan did not place a strip of "ornament" in place of the windows, but rather a ribbon of Luxfer brand prismatic glass, which had been invented in order to throw daylight deeper into the building. While scholars have treated the Renwick quote as indicating his distaste for Luxfer prisms, it does not

FIGURE 3.4 Holabird & Roche, Gage Group, 1899, US Library of Congress/ Public Domain.

make sense that such an experienced architect would refer to the prisms as "ornamentation" in a discussion of how to get more daylight into the building; that is exactly what the prisms accomplished and Holabird & Roche had utilized the prisms themselves in many structures. But perhaps Renwick understood that Sullivan intended the prisms both as a functional technology and a type of ornament. The Luxfer Company advocated this view of its products, and a contemporary observer noted

FIGURE 3.5 Charles Atwood, Reliance Building, 1895, US Library of Congress/Public Domain.

that "From the outside the prisms have rather the appearance of a screen wall than of a window."[27] While there is some debate as to how Sullivan understood the prisms, it is clear that they ate into the area devoted to plate glass. The two southern structures display Chicago Windows seamlessly offering combined views and ventilation, while the Sullivan structure features ungainly fenestration: larger spandrels, a strip of Luxfer prisms, and a row of small casement windows. If the Luxfer prisms were indeed intended as ornament, the result was an unfortunate, disharmonious blend of surfaces. In subsequent decades the prisms and casements were replaced with rows of double-hung windows, which actually offered some aesthetic improvement.

The horizontal

In the Gage Group, the horizontally oriented Chicago Windows and Sullivan's ribbons of glass and prisms were often ignored in favor of the prominent vertical element articulated by the steel frame. While early modern architecture in Chicago varies in its horizontal or vertical emphasis, a case can be made that the latter has been greatly exaggerated in subsequent decades at the expense of the former. Simply put, today it is a truism in architectural history that early skyscrapers strove for the vertical. Sullivan's Wainwright Building (St. Louis, 1891) and his aforementioned "form ever follows function" truism are usually cited as a basis for this common wisdom. The Wainwright building indeed has an overwhelming vertical design. Sullivan's 1896 article absolutely calls for "loftiness," although to a certain degree he is actually making the case for tripartite division not for verticality—but so be it. That being said, today it is not at all uncommon to read about a building whose presumed verticality is taken for granted even though it is not expressed by the structure itself.

Take, for example, the Reliance Building (1895), which was largely designed by Charles Atwood at the behest of D. H. Burnham and Co. Erected by the George Fuller construction company that played such a huge role in the early Chicago skyscraper, the Reliance represents something of a pinnacle of the Chicago Window, as its plate glass surfaces cover almost 80 percent of the two exterior facades (it is on a corner lot). These bands of ribbonlike windows along with their allied, bright white spandrels establish a staunch horizontal element. However, descriptions of the Reliance often feature phrases such as "emphatic vertical thrust" that are out of sync with reality. This tendency to see the vertical where it is not did not arise in the 1890s, but is a development tied to the resurgent interest in Chicago skyscrapers that was a striking factor in the formation of the modern aesthetic in the latter half of the twentieth century.

It has become a fashionable narrative to say that mid-century champions of modern architecture often turned to the late-nineteenth-century Chicago skyscraper as a way of anchoring the International Style in a stable American foundation, both ideologically and aesthetically.

In the United States, much of the now-questioned work had been done by Henry Russel-Hitchcock and Philip Johnson, who made their case to the New York public in two exhibitions, first in *Modern Architecture: International Exhibition* (often referred to as the "International Style" show because it introduced that term) of 1932 and then in the lesser-known *Early Modern Architecture Chicago: 1870-1910* of 1933. Parenthetically, it is quite likely that this notion of ideological formulation could use some revision itself. Hitchcock and Johnson by no means developed this argument themselves, as it had been anticipated by many members of the 1920s European avant-garde in a host of publications. To cite one example, Bruno Taut recounted in his 1929 book *Modern Architecture*, "[Louis Sullivan's] towering constructions in Chicago are entirely right, entirely modern in the contemporary sense. Clear construction, clear window areas, no absurdities to hide the structure of the building—it is all well arranged."[28]

While some may presume that Johnson and Hitchcock pioneered the illusory verticalism of the Chicago skyscraper, in fact this misplaced analysis cannot be placed on their doorstep. What has been overlooked in the many discussions of these exhibitions is the way in which the curators resoundingly endorsed the horizontal orientation of skyscrapers created by their fenestration as the underpinning of the International Style. In the catalog for the 1932 show (not to be confused with the book released by Hitchcock and Johnson that same year), Alfred Barr, the director of the MoMA and a full participant in the research and preparation of the show, noted that the International Style features both horizontal and vertical repetition. Then, in the process of describing how modern architects had abandoned the tripartite division of the facade he wrote, "[The modern architect] permits the horizontal floors of his skyscraper and the rows of windows in his school to repeat themselves boldly." Barr associates this quality with the regularity that formed one of the fundamental formal principles of the International Style.

The case could be made that the horizontal emphasis simply reflected the low rise proportions of most buildings in the 1932 exhibition. However, in the catalog for the 1933 exhibition on early Chicago skyscrapers, Hitchcock and Johnson were even more adamant in recognizing the horizontal window as the fundamental design element, and say little about the supposed vertical, lofty expression of the steel frame. In a brief introductory essay "Chronology of the Aesthetic Development of the Skyscraper," the curators asserted that a "frank emphasis on wide-windowed horizontality" was the basis for skyscraper design. The ensuing sketches of specific buildings refer repeatedly to the embrace of "wide-windowed design" (Adler & Sullivan, Schlesinger-Mayer, 1899–1904) and the "Logical horizontal type of skyscraper design" (Adler & Sullivan, Meyer Building, 1893). The entry on the latter structure further asserts that "the horizontal type of design provides more logical expression than the vertical treatment." The root of this "logical" expression is tied directly to daylight. The Reliance building is notable because its "wide fenestration provides better lighting than the great majority of present day office buildings." Perhaps this line of argument represented a pushback against the distinctly vertical compositions of contemporary Art Deco skyscrapers; buildings such as the Chrysler Building (New York, 1930) and Palmolive Building (Chicago, 1933) included an embrace of ornamental schemes that Johnson et al. disdained. The focus on the horizontal window may also reflect a sympathetic assessment of Le Corbusier, whose own ribbon windows played such a large role in forming the International Style (see below). However, it is also quite possible that Johnson et al. simply recognized the functional organicism of the Chicago Window design at a time before Miesian verticality came to dominate the discussion.

Courtyards and prisms

The glazed inner courtyard was another important strategy in the daylighting of early Chicago skyscrapers. Many buildings of the time displayed Richardsonian-inspired dark, heavy masonry on the exterior that seemed to suggest that the interior would be equally gloomy. Take, for example, Burnham & Root's Rookery building (1888, figure 3.6), which from the outside has a fortress-like quality despite its substantial fenestration. Step inside, however, and the visitor found a magical space suffused by the light of an enormous glazed canopy. In the 1890s this type of glittering interior space became a standard feature of larger Chicago buildings, many of which covered close to an entire city block so that light from the exterior windows could not reach the inner recesses of the structure. Meredith Clausen has shown how these light courts were likely inspired by the department stores of Paris, and has traced the coverage of these European spaces in American architectural periodicals while also noting John Wellborn Root's travels on the continent in the

FIGURE 3.6 Burnham & Root, Rookery Light Court, 1888.

1880s.[29] While light courts experienced a surge of interest in the 1890s, their future proved none too bright. Two issues quickly came to the fore: space and light. Insomuch as the quest for height in Chicago buildings represented a response to the skyrocketing cost of land in the central business district, light courts simply gave away valuable space. While the stunning interiors were surely worth an investment, a twelve-story building with an average-sized court measuring 60 × 60 feet was giving up upward of 40,000 square feet of leasable space once electric lights became standard fare. Likewise, in fire-conscious Chicago the threat of conflagration was always at the forefront of architectural thought. The wide open space of a light court could turn a small fire into an inferno. K. C. Clark observed in 1898, "It is a well-known fact that in case of fire no greater menace than these lights courts exist."[30]

"Architects! By Luxfer Prisms You Can Bring in Daylight Without the Use of Large Light Wells." The space-eating and fire-spreading character of light courts was repeatedly brought up by the Luxfer Prism Company (figure 3.7), whose managers saw the courts as one of their major competitors in the quest to bring daylight into spaces far from the exterior windows. Founded in Chicago in 1896—with the branded neologism "Luxfer" that was supposed to mean "to bear light" coined the following year—The Luxfer Prism Company proffered a high-tech

FIGURE 3.7 Luxfer Prism advertisement, c. 1911, Public Domain.

solution to the problem of daylighting deep, or partially underground, spaces. The company's product did not represent a startling new industrial breakthrough, but rather the pragmatic application of decades of lens technology combined with sophisticated marketing.[31] In a material sense, the product consisted of racks of 4 × 4 inch glass lenses cut with prismatic ribs that could be engineered—like eyeglasses—in order to focus their light at a certain depth within a building. Aside from the lenses themselves, the Luxfer Company produced an assortment of framing and canopy devices to hold the prism squares in place; in this way the bands of prisms could be employed either as the window itself or as an additional screen outboard of a window.

"More daylight! More daylight! Is the cry—from the man at the desk, from the salesman, from the great business houses that have goods to show."[32] As was the case with plate glass, the fundamental need fulfilled by Luxfer Prisms was to provide sufficient daylight at a time when gas or electric lighting was inefficient, dangerous, or unavailable. It is compelling to recognize the powerful force of hindsight: here was a company predicated on the idea that artificial light would prove forever out of reach, a company founded only a few years before electric light would make its products precariously obsolete. That being said, for its first few years the company did a brisk business despite the expensive nature of the product, as considerable upfront costs caused Luxfer to try to continually reassure potential customers that the initial expense would be offset by subsequent lower energy bills and increased productivity. These arguments appear to have worked for a time, as the company claimed over one thousand adopters during its first full year in business.

Because of either sincere belief or marketing skills, the Luxfer Company went beyond promoting the prisms as an engineering solution, and continually promoted the idea that they would have a profound influence on architectural aesthetics. "What effect on construction of the future are they likely to have? … to try and guess the numerous changes likely to be brought about by the architect having absolute control of natural light … would open too many suggestions to the mind." Of course, the sense of wonderment expressed there seems rather quaint and precious today, but in the 1890s the Luxfer Company was successful in garnering the attention of both Louis Sullivan (see above, Gage Building) and Frank Lloyd Wright. Wright's connection with Luxfer seems to be a simple case of proximity at work; in 1897 Luxfer's office in the Rookery building was located on the same floor as that of the young architect.

While the prisms never had a determining effect on architecture—Wright's or anyone else's—he did a few Luxfer blocks in a Sullivanesque mode and also played a role in one of its major marketing schemes, an 1898 contest to design a building that showcased the prisms. In announcing the contest through trade publications, Luxfer published two elevations of hypothetical entries that had been designed by Wright. His more radical *Design No. 1*, which features a facade completely fenestrated with the prisms, remains unconvincing today as it is all too clear that the translucent, not transparent, prisms would almost entirely obstruct views of the surroundings, enclosing the occupants in a claustrophobic fortress of glass. While both Wright's design and the overall contest failed to make much of a splash in 1898, Dietrich Neumann has shown how *Design No. 1* was later altered and employed by the architect in order to substantiate his claim of a seminal role in early modern architecture.

Le Corbusier and the ribbon window

While the creators of the Chicago Window can lay claim to the first promulgation of the horizontal aesthetic in modern fenestration, clearly the Swiss architect Charles-Édouard Jeanneret devised the most striking one. Jeanneret—who around 1920 adopted the nom de plume "Le Corbusier" that would eventually supplant his given name—came to architectural prominence through a circuitous path. His first thirty years were peripatetic ones, as he traveled extensively and received training in the arts without, however, much formal architectural schooling. In 1908, he worked briefly in the architectural studio of Auguste Perret, who is famed for his early and innovative deployment of reinforced concrete. Le Corbusier's career was not to blossom until after the end of the First World War, when he developed a fruitful artistic collaboration with the French painter Amédée Ozenfant. Le Corbusier and Ozenfant together formulated the art movement known as Purism, launching an aesthetic that synthesized Cubist abstraction with a classical sense of harmony rooted in whole, "pure" forms. This aesthetic, which combines forms of the modern machine age with those of antiquity, was one manifestation of the "retour de l'ordre," a cultural hunger for stability that was a response to the devastation of the Great War.

In 1920, Le Corbusier and Ozenfant together founded an avant-garde journal, *L'Esprit Nouveau*, through which Le Corbusier published his thoughts on architecture (Le Corbusier's manifesto-like ruminations were compiled and published as *Vers une Architecture* in 1923). This theoretical work was put into practice in 1922, when Le Corbusier opened an architectural practice with his cousin Pierre Jeanneret. While Le Corbusier had already developed a predilection for urban planning and mass housing, his built work at this time consisted almost exclusively of homes for the Parisian bourgeoisie. In 1923, the same year that he published *Vers une Architecture*, Le Corbusier was immersed in the design of the Villa La Roche (figure 3.8), one of an anticipated set of four Paris townhomes. Dr. Raoul La Roche was in some ways the ideal client for Le Corbusier: Swiss, single, rich, and devoted to his collection of contemporary art. La Roche intended the new home in the neighborhood of Auteuil to feature a gallery for his Cubist and Purist painting collection, works that had been purchased utilizing the guidance of Le Corbusier and Ozenfant (La Roche had also provided the funding for *L'Esprit Nouveau*). The Villa La Roche was intended to complement his collection by standing as an artwork in its own right.

The totality of Le Corbusier's design is not at issue here, but only one of its most distinctive elements, the *fenêtre de longueur*, or long window.

FIGURE 3.8 Le Corbusier, Villa La Roche, 1923, credit: Photo by Sun-Young Park © F.L.C./ADAGP, Paris/Artists Rights Society (ARS), New York [2018].

The long window exemplified Le Corbusier's concern with simple, universal forms, Purist-inspired units that could be flexibly utilized as the building blocks of a new architectural language. In its standard form the long window had exceptionally wide proportions, stretching 2.5 meters versus less than half a meter in height. Strung together, the long window could form a distinctive band or ribbon ("la fenêtre en bandeau") that cut across the exterior wall; in Le Corbusier's view, the long window met the functional demands of the modern age—daylight and views more than ventilation—while also representing an ideal type, a harmonious form of enduring beauty. Le Corbusier went so far as to apply for patents for the long window, which he did not see as part of his own idiosyncratic style but as a pure expression of the machine aesthetic that was bound to be universally adopted by builders. At the Villa La Roche, Tim Benton has shown how Le Corbusier worked through different formulations of the fenestration, for practical issues challenged Le Corbusier's vision for the structure. For example, La Roche first objected to the clerestory of ribbon windows placed high above the painting gallery, as one of them would allow direct sunlight to bake the pictures on a daily basis. Also, French privacy laws—called *Jours de souffrance*—placed restrictions on ground floor windows that would provide too much of a view of the neighboring property.[33]

In the 1920s as Le Corbusier worked through practical building problems and relationships with clients, he also continually published theoretical tracts on architecture. While he could meander at times, Le Corbusier was also prone to declarative statements about architecture, and for windows he wrote simply, "Windows serve to admit light … and to see outside."[34] Here the functional aspects of Le Corbusier's long window contrast with those of the Chicago Window. Both utilized the horizontal to maximize daylight, but the Chicago Window also provided for ventilation. Le Corbusier often downplayed or eliminated this latter aspect, as he believed strongly in various artificial ventilation systems of his own devising and seemed to hesitate in employing operable windows in his buildings. No doubt some would say this relates to his lifelong disdain for crowded city streets and his desire to shut out the urban experience. Le Corbusier espoused the panoramic views of the ribbon window, particularly in bucolic settings. The Chicago Window, in contrast, provided for replenishing the interior with outside air but owners were ambivalent about the views, as there was some thought that worker productivity would be impacted by the distractions of the passing scene.

There is another issue that unites the Chicago Window and Le Corbusier's long window: subsequent misinterpretation; in both cases, the windows have been depicted as secondary to the structural frame. Almost any reference to either type of window is bound to suggest that its architectural meaning lies strictly in how glass demonstrates that the wall is not load bearing, just a skin that keeps out the elements. While this is certainly accurate on one level, it represents an anachronistic Miesian point of view that was largely beside the point at the time of initial design and construction. In the Villa La Roche, for example, the structure is in many ways as invisible as it could be, a negative element that makes possible the positive force of the ribbon window, not vice versa. As Le Corbusier put it in his *Five Points Towards a New Architecture* (1926), "The whole history of architecture revolves exclusively around the wall apertures. Through use of the horizontal window reinforced concrete suddenly provides the possibility of maximum illumination."

In *Vers une Architecture*, Le Corbusier famously promoted the iconic products of modern engineering—ocean liners, airplanes, and automobiles—as offering a model of functional beauty. He contrasted the sleek forms of engineered machines with the ponderous historicisms of much of contemporary architecture. While attention has focused on Le Corbusier's analogy between architecture and the automobile, partly because of his use of the Citrohan nomenclature for his early experiments in mass housing, it is through the ocean liner analogy that he made his strongest points about windows. And not just any ocean liner. While Le Corbusier refers to a number of ships, he clearly relishes the beauty of Cunard's *Aquitania*, a vessel launched in 1913 that was renowned for its striking sheer line and elegant interiors. Nicknamed "Ship Beautiful," the Aquitania surely served as part of the inspiration for the long window. Below a photo of a first-class saloon that features a long horizontal opening, Le Corbusier wrote, "For architects: a wall all windows, a saloon full of light. What a contrast with the windows in our houses making holes in the walls and forming a patch of shade on either side." Here Le Corbusier stresses the central thesis of the long window, that it allows for an unbroken stream of daylight to bathe an interior.

The Aquitania also provided a functioning example of another of Le Corbusier's core principles, in this case the "architectural promenade." The promenade acted for Le Corbusier as a type of implied itinerary in his buildings, a literal promenade whereby the viewer moved through a series of linked spaces and enjoyed the resulting perspectives. Le Corbusier illustrated this element in *Vers une Architecture* with a picture of a long external corridor on the Aquitania that again featured a concomitant horizontal opening, a prototype ribbon window. "Architects note: the value of a 'long gallery' or promenade ... a fine grouping of construction elements, sanely exhibited and rationally assembled."[35] In his houses, the ribbon window took on the role of the ship's open vista, providing a continually moving panorama that contrasted with the static view from a vertical window punched into a wall.

On November 1, 1923, the Salon d'Automne opened in Paris. In the "Architecture and Town Planning" section, Le Corbusier exhibited a selection of projects showing his and his cousin's recent work, including a model of the Villa La Roche. Some weeks later the *Paris Journal* published an interview with August Perret in which he was fiercely critical of some aspects of Le Corbusier's work, and thus began the affair of the horizontal windows. Perret argued that the ribbon windows shown in designs like that of the Villa La Roche were not only poorly suited to admitting daylight into the interior, but represented a type of aestheticized formalism that Perret saw as rooted in the academic practice of the past. Stated Perret, "Half of the rooms must be completely without light, which is pushing it a bit far for the sake of originality." In this way Le Corbusier was portrayed as an apostate to the very functionalism that he himself espoused so completely. Of course, Perret had a point as ribbon windows have a somewhat compromised relationship with daylight. If placed at the height of a clerestory as in the gallery of the Villa La Roche, then they may function beautifully. On the other hand, if set in the midpoint of the wall, they are not aligned with the acute angle of the sun's rays and may admit only half-light.

Le Corbusier seemed to recognize this possible flaw insomuch as he responded defensively in print almost immediately; while countering all of Perret's criticisms he seemed most upset regarding the denigration of his singular long windows. "And now Perret's last insulting censure: my windows admit no light ... What on earth is he talking about? I endeavor to create bright room interiors ... The alleged fancy was directed solely by the desire to supply the inhabitants with the most basic necessities of life."[36] Later in the same tone Le Corbusier wrote, "My whole architecture is based on windows." Le Corbusier also has a strong position, as the vertical window that Perret insists should be retained can create a patchy pattern of daylight. Also, Le Corbusier's window should be understood through its ability to bolster the promenade, providing a dynamic view as well as daylight. After the initial dispute in 1923, Le Corbusier never stopped marshalling facts and responding implicitly to Perret's criticism. In his *Five Points*, Le Corbusier claimed, "Experiments have shown that a room thus lit has an eight times stronger illumination than the same room lit by vertical windows with the same window area." This attempt to invoke rather dubious evidence of uncertain origin suggests that at times Le Corbusier doth protest too much. In pursuit of daylight, within a few years Le Corbusier would be adding to his repertoire of windows the curtain wall of glass, a phenomenon with its own difficult history that is first explored in the next chapter.

4 GLASS VISIONS

In the early years of the twentieth century, no conceptual issue quite consumed the practice of architecture like the present and future possibilities of glass technology. Notably, during the heroic years of the modernist avant-garde the perception of glass wavered between anointing it as an expressionist, utopian vehicle or as a signifier of rational functionalism. The practical use of the term "functionalism" is intended here in its broadest sense as synonymous with much of the avant-garde European architecture of the 1920s, not as a narrow indicator of designers who eschew aesthetic issues. Here is an example of Walter Gropius using the term in English: "the modern architectural revolution demanded that details and refinements must be constituent parts of the building's structure and derived from functional considerations."[1] At the same time that this conceptual issue lingered, both streams valued glass as a promising technology with an almost limitless potential to upend traditional forms. While the expressionist/functionalist threads would be originally portrayed in the history of modernism (as it was written at mid-century) as constituting polar opposite points of view, more recent scholarship has focused on how multivalent visions for glass intersected dialogically over several decades. This chapter focuses on the purported schism between the visible glass of expressionism and the invisible membrane of the functionalists, while also surveying work that fell in between these apparent absolutes. Additionally, glass during this era gradually proved its ability to thrive as both skin and structure, forging new types of form and meaning that resonate through to the present.

Even today, any discussion of the functionalist/expressionist intersection is haunted by the specter of the Swiss architectural historian Sigfried Giedion. Founder with Le Corbusier of the *Congrès internationaux d'architecture moderne* (CIAM) in 1928, Giedion's uber-influential *Bauen en Frankreich* (1928) and *Space, Time and Architecture:*

The Growth of a New Tradition (1941) polemically depicted expressionism as a pernicious force that "infiltrated" architecture. A typical Giedion assertion mixed opinion with a projection of the inner life of his subject. For example, in *Space, Time and Architecture*, Giedion described Walter Gropius's state of mind at the founding of the Bauhaus thus, "Gropius was instinctively aware of the inadequacy of expressionism and the need to escape from it." This statement is immediately followed by a recounting of the instructors that Gropius had hired in 1919, all of whom had strong expressionist leanings; the contradiction imbedded in this situation goes unremarked except for the note that Johannes Itten—the absolute bête noire of Bauhaus functionalism—is said to have been hired upon the recommendation of Alma Mahler. In a book that is devoid of any discussion regarding women's role in the formulation of architectural modernism, it is striking how Giedion absolves Gropius of this hire, and instead suggests that a woman and outsider is to blame for that particular "infiltration." Of course, in 1941 when *Space, Time and Architecture* was published, Giedion owed his job at Harvard to Gropius and was perhaps just being a loyal employee. It should also be noted that Giedion's texts are more descriptive than prescriptive, and he elegantly articulated a version of the emergence of modern architecture that represented something of a consensus opinion among its practitioners.

One of the first cogent retorts to the suppression of the expressionist strain in modern glass architecture came via the English critic Reyner Banham, whose 1959 essay "The Glass Paradise" took on the discourse of functionalism, a discourse that Banham referred to as an exclusionary "legend."[2] Banham made the astute observation that most avant-garde architects seemed to project an obsessive, at times mystical, fascination with glass that did not neatly align with the pragmatic, functionalist formulation put forth by Arthur Korn, Gropius, and Giedion, et al. Banham argued that the functionalist view was too skeletal, and it omitted "the Futurists, Romantics, Expressionists, Elementarists, and pure aesthetes" that had played a significant role in conceiving the modern. In pursuit of this line of argument it was Banham who anointed Paul Scheerbart, author of *Glasarchitektur* (1914), as the new anti-hero of modern architecture, a scrappy science fiction writer who together with Bruno Taut had envisioned a utopia of glass. For Banham, the visionary thread expounded upon by Scheerbart had always been behind the inspiring glass inventions of the moderns—Banham opened the essay with a nod toward SOM's Lever House (1952)—but it had never been publicly acknowledged because its hint of radicalism and revolution did not fit the standard story that had brought the movement into the corporate mainstream. Over the decades since "The Glass Paradise" was published, numerous other architectural writers—notably Dennis Sharp and Rosemarie Haag Bletter—took up the cause of Scheerbart and sought to cement his place in the modern pantheon. Theirs has been a slippery task outside of specialized academic circles, as Scheerbart seems to be constantly rediscovered in the mainstream (a newly edited collection of his texts was released at the end of 2015) only to fade away again as the skeletal functionalist narrative continually sheds its flesh.

Of course, when Scheerbart wrote his *Glasarchitektur* soon after the onset of the twentieth century, a great deal of speculation about the meaning of glass in architecture had already been recorded. This was one omission on Banham's part; he had presented Scheerbart as more of a lone voice than had actually been the case. As nineteenth-century glass took on a larger role in architecture, discussions of it as both an inexpensive, efficient industrial medium and one able to sustain a mystical, dreamlike utopian environment had arisen repeatedly. The Crystal Palace and the work of architects under the spell of Charles Fourier and Henri de Saint-Simon are obvious examples. In fact, by the end of the nineteenth century, the significance of glass technology had become a staple point of discussion for architectural societies throughout Europe and the United States. A sense of the state of the question can be garnered by a close look at one such proceeding, that of the Illinois State Association of Architects that occurred in June of 1887.

This symposium, focused on the architectural potential of new materials, was chaired by none other than Daniel H. Burnham, who was joined on the panel by the less familiar practitioners Normand Patton and S. M. Randolph. Burnham began the discussion as one might expect from someone with a reputation for hard-headed pragmatism; he points out that glass is inexpensive and has excellent compressive strength, and therefore would be a suitable structural replacement for stone, terracotta, and even plaster. Furthermore, Burnham emphasizes that glass is adaptable to many modern needs, and opines that one day its dealers will offer "annealed glass of any size or quality, solid or hollow, plain or ornamented, opaque, translucent or transparent, dull or polished, and of any color."[3] This is all what one would expect of Burnham, an architect generally viewed as conventional, an arch classicist focused on pleasing clients not on original designs. But in the next moment Burnham suddenly starts channeling Paul Scheerbart *avant la lettre*, as the thought of all that colorful, structural glass seems to sway his imagination.

> Imagine a ruddy dwelling built of this, and seen under the rays of a setting sun, with its glowing walls, rich with the penetrating depth of jasper stone; with crests and turrets softly melting against the evening sky, so that one may well doubt where a crimson cloud leaves off and the roofline of the house begins.

It is clear from the record of the meeting that this vision was largely met with skepticism—although one attendee asserted that the tomb of President Ulysses Grant, a major architectural question of the day, be made of glass—and so Burnham pushed back at the others both on their lack of imagination and their ignorance of the state of the glass industry. Burnham eloquently defended the "crank" as a societal type who is able to break out of small-minded conventions. In this latter passage, Burnham sounded like a follower of Saint-Simonism, recounting plans for a private hospital made entirely of glass, and arguing that by every possible technological metric—cleanliness, lighting, fire-resistance, patient's mood enhancer, infection control—glass construction was superior to any other building method. Burnham's seemingly unorthodox penchant for utopian glass has remained buried in the past, while his subsequent reputation for White City classicism overshadows all of his opalescent speculations.

The other point here is that Burnham slaloms back and forth between assertions that would later be termed "functionalist" and "expressionist" without separating them into distinct architectural threads. A mystical glass house of color and a practical, efficient, modern hospital are for him all of one piece. For Burnham at least, the functionalist/expressionist binary does not exist; rather, there is a dynamic, fluid age of glass that is on the cusp of being realized. This I would argue is the most sensible way of approaching the glass culture of the twentieth century. It is impossible to separate the visionary and the practical into a binarism; as it was for Burnham, architects embraced glass precisely because it gave voice to a multitude of hopes and dreams for the present and the future.

In 1914, upon the publication of his manifesto *Glasarchitektur*, Paul Scheerbart became perhaps the most unlikely promoter of glass architecture. Often appearing on lists of prolific but unread authors, by 1914 Scheerbart had published hundreds of short stories, essays, and the like. Master of long-form rants, Scheerbart's credibility as a learned source has always been compromised by his lifelong devotion to the modern alchemy of perpetual motion machines. With so much of his work rooted in outlandish speculation about the future—take a look at "Rakkóx the Billionaire" (1901) for an example—it was in fact eminently reasonable that Scheerbart never rose far above the status of being a bohemian fixture in Berlin café society. In Daniel Burnham's terms, Scheerbart was a "crank," a person of great imagination and optimism about the future. To twenty-first-century minds, Saint-Simon, Scheerbart, and the like may appear naïve, as contemporary architects have largely lost their sense of earnest wonderment at the possibilities of a technologically enhanced future; where they saw towers of glass, we see climate change.

Glasarchitektur consists of 111 titled and numbered paragraphs—snippets of thought expressed in a few sentences—and reads more like a list of bullet points than a developed theme, each thought compartmentalized to a large extent. (In some ways this technical treatise should be read side-by-side with a contemporary work by Scheerbart titled *Grey Cloth and Ten Percent White*. The latter text weaves a wildly silly romantic melodrama—the architect hero seeks a wife who will wear only gray so as not to clash with his colorful architecture—into a futuristic vision of Chicago as a city built of glass.) The manifesto *Glasarchitektur* begins by using glass as a utopian metaphor for contemporary culture. Scheerbart states that culture is "closed," and that by transforming opaque masonry walls into glass that would let in the light of the sun and moon society can be brought to a "higher level." This is, of course, all quite vague and mysterious, but for the practical-minded reader Scheerbart almost immediately shifts gears: paragraph three makes the case for double-paned glass in order to solve the tremendous heat loss of glass structures. In this way the *Glasarchitektur* adventure begins and is sustained, by a flurry of ideas—some logical, others obtuse, many in between—that bombard the reader like bomblets of glass. A certain skepticism regarding Scheerbart's prophetic skills when it comes to glass technology is in order; like many visionaries he throws a multitude of contemporary ideas out there and it is really no surprise that some of them actually stuck.

It is noteworthy that Scheerbart lays claim to the exact same architectural roots that are used to define the functionalists: the Gothic style and the iron and glass greenhouse. In Giedion's work, for example, the Gothic and its nineteenth-century revival are cited as an important precedent for modernism because of its honest, logical structure as defined by contemporary critics such as John Ruskin and Eugene Viollet-le-Duc. Similarly, the greenhouses of the nineteenth century adapted this structural honesty to buildings constructed out of industrial technology. Tellingly, Scheerbart examined the same two sources but saw something completely different: mystical color and light. For one, he wrote quite plainly that "It ought to be stressed here that the whole of glass architecture stems from the Gothic cathedrals. Without them it would be unthinkable." When he lapses into romantic descriptions of colored light, Scheerbart positively sounds like he is channeling the words of the twelfth-century theologian Abbot Suger, the leader of the Royal Abbey Church of Saint-Denis who was renowned for his espousal of stained glass as a path to the contemplation of the mystical divine. Suger or Scheerbart: "the multicolored loveliness of the gems has called me away ... transporting me from material to immaterial things." And in terms of iron and glass structures, Scheerbart cites the botanical garden at Dahlem near Berlin as an example of an "imposing glass palace" that demonstrates how his desired glass world is already viable.

A key aspect of Scheerbart's vision—and the basis for his statement that the Gothic cathedral "is the prelude"—for the coming glass utopia is his insistence that the crystalline world of the future be festooned with color. This has always been an issue through which the glass binary was made material: functionalist glass is clear and invisible, while expressionist glass is colorfully translucent or opaque. This division is something that Scheerbart reinforced. For him, it is unequivocal that colored light has a soothing effect on the human psyche, and he references the fact that ancient cultures produced and admired the mystical eminences wrought by colored glass.[4] In contrast, in his thirteenth dictum, Scheerbart specifically denounces the *Sachstil*, or functional style, for being cold in its lack of color. "I should like to resist most vehemently the undecorated *Sachstil* for it is inartistic." Near the end of *Glasarchitektur* one short paragraph is headlined simply, "More colored light!", and truly that slogan might serve to summarize the entire book.

One obvious influence on Scheerbart's espousal of color and colored light was the then resurgent esoteric spiritual movement known as Theosophy. In 1875, when the Theosophical Society was founded in New York by Helena Blavatsky, it set off a new wave of mystical thought, and satellites to the New York organization were soon established around the world. The movement was fueled by the publication of Blavatsky's two-volume tome titled *The Secret Doctrine, the Synthesis of Science, Religion and Philosophy*, a text which offered a mélange of occult and spiritualist thought. When the young British clergyman's wife, Annie Besant, read and wrote a review of the book, it had an immediate impact on her view of the world. Besant became an acolyte of Blavatsky, and her interest in Theosophy led her to a global career as an activist and speaker. In 1905 Besant along with a colleague named C. W. Leadbeater published the book *Thought Forms*, a theosophical riff on selected Tibetan Buddhist teachings. In *Thought Forms*, Besant and Leadbeater asserted that emotional and spiritual states could be made visible through colorful abstract drawings. Scheerbart was known to be familiar with Theosophical writings, and his vision of a mystical utopia of colored glass resonates with the followers' spiritual hunger for emotional and societal harmony.

Of course, close parallels exist in the work of expressionist artists in other media, many of whom were also impacted by Theosophical speculation. Painters such as Wassily Kandinsky created virtual worlds made up of dynamically contrasting swaths of colored pigment; as part of his work in the *Der Blaue Reiter* group, after 1910 Kandinsky promulgated his treatise "On the Spiritual in Art," an essay that precedes and rivals Scheerbart's in its mix of muddled utopianism and technical suggestions. Kandinsky wrote of color creating a "spiritual vibration" in the viewer, and expounded upon the glowing sense of soulfulness that only polychromy could provide. It is notable that while Scheerbart's *Glasarchitektur* has been largely ignored by historians and is always gently mocked as the work of an eccentric, Kandinsky's bewildering tangle of thoughts on synaesthesia and the like has been given the status of an epic text of artistic mastery: published and republished throughout the twentieth century, millions of copies have been printed in a multitude of languages, befuddling generations of budding artists.

In Scheerbart's terms painting never would fit the bill, as the fundamental idea expressed in *Glasarchitektur* was that new technology had allowed for the renewal and expansion of the ancient human yearning for colored light. In this respect, the works of the so-called color music artists of the early twentieth century represent a strong parallel to the dreams of Scheerbart. While a large group of artists and engineers experimented with projection equipment that utilized electric light to create colorful abstract works at this time, the Danish immigrant to New York, Thomas Wilfred, went the furthest in building a career based on this new technological art. During the 1910s, Wilfred experimented in New York with his hand-built color organs (he called them "Claviluxes"), planning for the day when colored light projections would sweep away the art of the past and lead to a new age of peace and harmony. Wilfred had some architectural connections, having befriended architect Claude Bragdon with whom he started a theosophically minded group called the "Prometheans." One Wilfred project of the 1920s resonates specifically with the world imagined by Scheerbart, as the color music artist planned a "Clavilux Silent Visual Carillon" that would be placed atop a skyscraper. Scheerbart had written in *Glasarchitektur*, "Every effort must naturally be made to lend enchantment to towers by night. Under the rule of glass architecture, therefore, all towers must become towers of light".

It is interesting to ponder the intersection between Scheerbart and the corresponding stained glass industry that was experiencing its own major boom at the time. While Scheerbart states that the color environment created by Gothic stained glass windows was the basis for all of his thoughts on the subject, he almost entirely ignored the fact that colored light was being introduced into buildings everywhere and had been for decades. While he does make a cursory mention of Louis Comfort Tiffany—who "put colored clouds into glass"—Scheerbart ignores how prevalent colored light was in everyday life. Perhaps like the functionalists, stained glass for Scheerbart was tainted by its historical freight; conventional religion did not hold forth the same degree of exotic spiritualism offered by Scheerbart's heady brew of mystical Theosophy, paganism, and imported fragments of Eastern faiths. In a more secular vein, the fact that colored light existed without having created a new utopia just did not fit the vision he held for the future.

The theoretical speculations espoused by Scheerbart in *Glasarchitektur* were famously made material in the Glashaus, a pavilion designed by Bruno Taut in 1914 for the Deutscher Werkbund exhibition in Cologne (figure 4.1). Taut and Scheerbart were friends and erstwhile colleagues, and the Glashaus represents a collaboration of sorts as it was the one and only modern building that was constructed to maximize the Scheerbartian dream of color and light. The Glashaus is conceptually linked to the treatise, and Scheerbart famously contributed rhyming couplets that were inscribed at the base of the building: "Colored happiness/Only comes in a glass culture" and "Glass opens up a new age/Brick building only does harm" are exemplary. It is sometimes assumed that the Glashaus stood out as an anomaly in the context of an exhibition famous for its functionalist structures, especially Gropius's

FIGURE 4.1 Bruno Taut, Glashaus, 1914, credit: © Bildarchiv Foto Marburg.

model factory, but in fact expressionist aesthetics played a substantive role at the Werkbund exhibition. Notably, the painting show highlighted the work of Ernst Ludwig Kirchner and other members of Die Brücke, whose sometimes dark view of humanity represents a counterpoint to the ebullient optimism of Scheerbart's imagined utopia.

The Glashaus was built of reinforced concrete that was embellished with the glass products retailed by the Deutsches Luxfer Prismen Syndikat, a quasi-independent subsidiary of the Luxfer Prism Company of Chicago. Friedrich Keppler, director of the German Luxfer branch, sponsored the pavilion. The most dramatic element of the Glashaus was the crystalline, multicolored dome, which was striking from the outside and immersed the interior visitor to the dome room in an atmosphere of colored light. Under the dome room there was a stepped, rectangular space that featured a fountain and a kaleidoscope that projected color on to a screen (figure 4.2). Keppler had himself invented a new type of glass tile set in concrete that was sold under the name *Glaseisenbeton*. The Glashaus exhibited these new tiles in addition to the existing Luxfer prisms and basement lights; glass dome, glass walls, glass stairs, the

FIGURE 4.2 Bruno Taut, Fountain inside Glashaus, 1914, credit: © Bildarchiv Foto Marburg.

scintillating range of products complemented the mosaic-lined fountain and kaleidoscope.⁵ The kaleidoscope itself demonstrates a point of intersection between colored glass architecture and the artists of electric light abstractions such as Wilfred.

No temporary exhibition structure has been pored over by historians as much as the Glashaus. As the building that anchors the whole modern expressionist universe, it carries a heavy symbolic burden. This intense fascination has continued despite the fact that scholars have long recognized that the Glashaus is not really that unique. As a spectacular vanity of color and light, it has a clear ancestry that goes as far back as the Great Exhibition in 1851 when the Crystal Palace's transept was dominated by the soaring four-ton glass fountain designed by Abraham Follett Osler. After that first success, almost every major world exhibition leading up to 1914 featured some sort of color and light centerpiece. The 1893 Columbian Exposition, for example, had at minimum three comparable displays: the Moorish Palace filled with mirrors and a kaleidoscope; the display of Tiffany stained glass; and the pavilions designed to showcase the glass blocks invented by Gustav Falconnier. Significantly, Keppler, the sponsor of Taut's pavilion, had been living in Chicago in 1893 and was likely awakened to the impactful nature of such spectacles at the

Columbian Exposition.[6] One could make the case that the pendulum has swung too far and, after years of neglect, the "rediscovery" of Scheerbart and Taut in the latter half of the twentieth century has led to a situation where their significance is perhaps overstated. Hindsight shows that there was very little future in the pursuit of overt color and light expressionism, and the history of glass was going to lead elsewhere.

Curtain wall

In 1929, Arthur Korn published the first book to explicitly focus on modern glass architecture, *Glas im Bau und als Gebrauchsgegendstan* (later translated as *Glass in Modern Architecture*). Korn's book was mainly a pictorial survey, the only text consisting of captions and a brief introduction. In the latter, Korn argued that glass had historically been considered a secondary, subservient material, despite its aesthetic potential and stellar service as a mediator of other structural elements. Korn argued that this hierarchy was in the process of being overturned, and that glass was gradually assuming a more substantial role in architecture; this new status he connected mainly to the utilization of glass as building sheath. "The contribution of the present age is that now it is possible to have an independent wall of glass, a skin of glass around a building; no longer a solid wall with windows."[7] Of course, Korn is here championing that most iconic element of glass architecture, the glazed curtain wall.

Reference the glass curtain wall and one is more than likely to run into a reference to the Crystal Palace. Seemingly every discussion of contemporary architects who embrace the form such as Cesar Pelli invokes the ghost of Paxton's great greenhouse. It is important to recognize that there really is no strong DNA link between 1851 in London, and say, 1926 in Dessau; there was no incremental, evolutionary development from Paxton to Pelli or whomever. That is not to say that the curtain wall developed *sui generis*, but rather that the genealogy of glass architecture is more ragged and unkempt than is often presupposed. Also, the link bears testament to the enduring power of the Crystal Palace as a shining star in the glass cosmology, inspiring architects quite removed from its material presence. In its ethereal lightness, the glass skin embodies so much that defines modernity: technology, dematerialization, and perpetual youth. (Of course, a curtain wall need not be made of glass, but in the twentieth century that is the most common meaning.) The story of the development of the curtain wall is one of continual attempts to efface the structure, and the glass area grows as the mullions and spandrels are eventually buried beneath the skin.

It is important to recognize the evolving flat glass technology of the early twentieth century as continual technical achievements made possible new architectural forms. Transparent flat glass at the beginning of the century was made through two industrial processes. As described in Chapter 1, plate glass, the most expensive and flawless form of flat glass, was made through the process of pouring the molten material on to a casting table. This initial step was followed by extensive grinding and polishing that required a great deal of energy and a large labor force. Advancements in the 1920s included the creation of the "straight line conveyor ribbon," whereby a factory could anneal, grind, and polish a continual strip of plate glass on an assembly line. Still, while the economics of plate glass went through low-price periods, overall it remained a premium product until well into the 1960s. The chief competitor to plate was blown glass made by the antiquated cylinder process; new advances in technology including the use of compressed air—as opposed to workers' lungs—had kept cylinder glass viable as a mass-produced product. However, in the decades after 1900 three separate processes were devised that together displaced cylinder glass as the economical alternative to plate. This new manufacturing process created "drawn" glass through a variety of techniques all of which involved drawing the molten material upward and allowing gravity to stretch it into sheets. In the glass trade, drawn and cylinder glass were known by the term "window glass." The vertical draw process was first invented in Belgium by Emile Fourcault—hence "Fourcault glass"—and next developed by the American Irving Colburn, who after a bankruptcy sold his patents to the Libbey glass company. It was Colburn who made the analogy of seeing maple syrup clinging to a knife as the moment that led to his epiphany. Colburn was hired by Libbey to perfect the process, and his invention became the basis for the eventual Libbey-Owens-Ford Corporation that was one of the two largest glass producers in the United States. The other was Pittsburgh Plate Glass, whose engineers invented the third vertical draw method, called the Pittsburgh process. Overall, drawn glass was quite transparent but it also has patches of noticeable distortion that well-polished plate eliminates. During the first half of the twentieth century, glass skins could be sourced by either process, with cost and the local supply chain forming the decisive factors.

1914, the year of the *Deutscher Werbund* Exhibition and the onset of the First World War, is often cited as the annum that saw the first appearance of the curtain wall. Conventional wisdom has anointed as leading pioneer none other than Walter Gropius, who, because of his deep and lasting involvement in modern architecture—he connected to Peter Behrens, the Werkbund, the Arbeitsrat für Kunst, Taut's Crystal Chain, Bauhaus, Harvard University, TAC—serves mightily as the originator of the form. Most are agreed that some combination of his model factory at the Cologne exhibition and the *Faguswerke* at Alfeld (figure 4.3), a UNESCO World Heritage Site, introduced the type on the world stage (in his book, Korn includes a photo of only the former, temporary structure). Notwithstanding Gropius's obvious contributions, there is in fact some greater complexity to this issue. First, what specifically is a glass curtain wall? And, second, which one was truly built first? The former question is important because there are two definitions that often overlap; sometimes the term is used to refer to any facade that appears to be largely made

FIGURE 4.3 Walter Gropius, Faguswerke, 1914, credit: Landesmuseum für Kunst und Kulturgeschichte Oldenburg, CC BY-SA 3.0.

up of glass. Other architects insist on a stricter, technical definition, whereby the glass curtain has no supporting structure anywhere within the plane of the facade, and the glass wall is cantilevered away from the load-bearing elements of the building. In actuality, the curtain wall of the *Faguswerke* misses the mark by either definition, as generic glass walls had been around for decades and Gropius's curtain wall does utilize vertical masonry strips amidst the glass. The point here is not to quibble over priority, but to point out how the modern canon formed around powerful architects who dominated the conversation, effacing the work of many near-anonymous designers whose careers did not fit elegantly into the narrative. Two of these unknowns, both of whom worked in cities well off the beaten path of most architectural grand tours, could stake a formidable claim to the curtain wall.

Using the looser, more forgiving definition of a curtain wall, Peter Ellis, architect of the modest Liverpool office building known as Oriel Chambers (figure 4.4), seems to have hit upon the idea of maximizing the visible fenestration exactly fifty years before the *Faguswerke* was completed. Of course, the facade is by no means all glass and the cast iron structural frame of columns and girders enmeshed in brick walls is readily apparent. Still, the sheer amount of glass is remarkable, as Ellis filled each large opening in the structural grid with oriels—bay windows that project outward without carrying the wall forward—that maximize the amount of glass that fills the space. Simply put, there is much more glass than there is space to infill. Each oriel has a single operable casement window for ventilation, an obvious precursor to the Chicago Window discussed in the previous chapter. While its location and quirkiness undoubtedly partially led to Oriel Chambers' relative neglect in the history of architecture, the uneven career of its designer also must have had an impact. Knowledge about Ellis is scant, and, working at a time when the profession of architecture was nascent and uncertain, he seems to have also pursued civil engineering as an additional career. Never firmly enmeshed in the modern canon, today Oriel Chambers—like the *Faguswerke*—continues to quietly serve its original commercial function.

If searching for a curtain wall that meets the narrower, purist definition of a glass facade that is unencumbered by structural elements, one is likely to end up surveying a building known more for its obscurity than its transparency, this is the Hallidie Building in San Francisco, an unorthodox structure completed in 1918 for the regents of the University

FIGURE 4.4 Peter Ellis, Oriel Chambers, Liverpool, 1864, credit: CC BY-SA 3.0.

of California (figure 4.5). The Hallidie was designed by William Polk, an architect and real estate developer known for his prolific output during the rebuilding of the city after the earthquake of 1906. Polk designed over 100 buildings in the decade after the disaster, yet, despite this overwhelming contribution to the San Francisco urban fabric, Polk was the type of architect that has often been slighted as he was notable more for his business acumen than his artistry—Benjamin Marshall

FIGURE 4.5 William Polk, Hallidie Building, 1918.

in Chicago is another example of the type—and so he does not fit the stereotype of a pioneering modernist. Nonetheless, the Hallidie has it all: seven storys of glass seemingly hang in the air like a curtain from the cantilevered spandrel girders while the reinforced concrete structural columns lurk a full 3 feet behind the plane of the facade. Curiously, nothing in Polk's oeuvre before or after the Hallidie looks anything like it: there is no incremental path to trace to this personal breakthrough as Polk seemingly chose the form almost on a whim.[8]

What is so unique about the Hallidie curtain wall is the fact that it appeared completely unencumbered by the discourse of expressionism and functionalism. When queried about the building, Polk spoke of its economical construction and earthquake resistance, barely mentioning what he called the "true simplicity" of the exposed concrete frame. He was overall quite modest and circumspect about the curtain wall. "It should not be claimed for the Hallidie building that this experiment, however bold, is in any sense successful, but it is certainly an innovation, ... it is the first building constructed with an entire glass front."[9] Polk was an architect and developer who had no commitment to the emerging modern style or to any other style for that matter; he tended to resort to a type of default classicism for most of his buildings. This is obvious in the way that he—from a later Miesian perspective—undermined the curtain wall by including four large iron cornices, each elaborately ornamental and decorated with blue and gold. The rather garish color scheme invoked the uniforms of the university's sports teams, making the building a billboard of sorts. Thus, the Hallidie did not represent some sort of functionalist ideology or spiritual breakthrough; rather, it was just the result of a busy architect with a curious mind trying something new. The sheer banality of the curtain wall on the Hallidie stands in stark defiance to the layers of meaning and soulfulness that will be applied to that shimmering form by generations of deeper thinkers. In its banality lay its defeat, as the narrative of the curtain wall was starting to be written in the late 1920s, and in it the Hallidie would not find a place.

The form of the historical narrative surrounding the genesis of the glazed curtain wall today in many ways still follows the path laid out by Korn in *Glass in Modern Architecture*. In that book, the first architect mentioned in the "Introduction" is Walter Gropius, whose Dessau Bauhaus is cited along with "buildings by Mies van der Rohe." (Give him credit for being proactive, as Korn included his own design for a retail shop as the third example in that same sentence.) In terms of the photos that really drive the book, Korn reverses the order, featuring the familiar set of five of Mies's projects for glass architecture followed immediately by two double-page spreads of the Bauhaus buildings. Ignoring Gropius's prewar works, Korn sets the stage for the Bauhaus to have bestowed on it the mantle of first curtain wall (figure 4.6). Of course, the workshops wing at Dessau indeed featured a striking example of the form, stretching three storys high (10 meters) while extending around the corners to over 30 meters in length. The curtain wall was furnished to the Bauhaus by Nord-

FIGURE 4.6 Walter Gropius, Bauhaus Dessau workshop elevation, 1925.

Draht of Rostock, an industrial supplier. In 1929, Gropius penned a letter to the company that was used in its catalog: "The supports of the building are in the interior, so that the entire outer skin of the high facade was manufactured to 10 meters in height … the frame construction is cheap and efficient." The smallish panes of plate glass were held in place by a quite visible grid of narrow glazing bars, the latter somewhat reducing the shimmer of the continuous glazing. While Gropius often maintained that the workshop wall was "completely dissolved" by its use of glass, the fact remains that the grid of sash bars give it a sense of steel structure that is far from what this viewer would call dematerialized. The rather anomalous use of hundreds of small square panes was never addressed by Gropius as the conversation usually pivoted on the words "first curtain wall." While the original wall was destroyed in the Second World War it is clear from pictures and documents that expensive plate glass—as opposed to drawn window glass—was used on the workshop elevation; the question remains as to whether Gropius was making do with his manufacturer's technical abilities or had an aesthetic intent in making the metal almost as prominent as the plate glass. Perhaps for Gropius the grid represented an example of degree zero architecture, and the growing fixation with the curtain wall eventually suppressed that original design impulse. It also gave the workshops a striking visual similarity to more prosaic glass structures. A key aspect of Korn's understanding of the glass skin is his contention that its purpose is to expose the building's inner workings. "But in the situation now, the outside wall is no longer the first impression one gets of a building. It is the interior, the spaces in depth and the structural frame which delineates them, that one begins to notice through the glass wall."[10] One could argue that in this manner the curtain wall has retained some residue of its roots in simple shopkeeping; Gropius's glass wall serves like a giant display window, its multitude of sash bars giving the Bauhaus something of a homey, familiar feel, while drawing the eye and allowing a tantalizing glimpse of the merchandise therein. Later, canon-forming historians such as Siegfried Giedion essentially ignored the visually obstructive nature of the glass bars, choosing instead to overstate the merging of interior and exterior spaces that the wall had enabled.

Despite its immense power as an image, the curtain wall at the Dessau workshops also exemplifies the practical reasons why architects had for a century struggled with the form. Reports by students and faculty make it clear that the glazed wall was not enough of a barrier in most situations. Noise was a serious issue, as was the build-up of condensation on the glass. Of course, single pane glazing in a metal frame does little to keep out the cold, while warmer months made the interior a veritable hothouse.

As opposed to Polk and his Hallidie building—or the Boley Building in Kansas for that matter—the origins of which are largely unstudied, there is a matrix of sources and meanings that have imbued Gropius's work. The expressionist glass of Taut and Scheerbart is a clear factor. Gropius is known to have recommended Scheerbart's *Glasarchitektur* to colleagues. Also, taking on the pseudonym Mass, Gropius had notably partaken of Taut's short-lived epistolary *Die Gläserne Kette* (Crystal Chain) group in 1919. For that group Gropius had acted rather like an ambivalent teenager on a new social media platform, lurking in the background but never actively contributing. Whether this attitude represented a decisive break from expressionist longings is an open question. As the first few years at the Bauhaus had been dominated by similar mystical talk, it is hard to imagine that the erstwhile functionalism of Gropius was immune from the expressionist "infiltration." It would seem likely that Gropius to some degree had sublimated, rather than repressed, the expressionist impulse in his new building. Of course, many expressionists saw their own poetic, mystical alignments as something equivocal, and the association of utopian promises with a hoped-for reality of societal change was a given.

Along these lines, the writings of the critic Adolph Behne are exemplary of the fluid nature of expressionist politics. Behne, one of the founders of the Arbeitsrat für Kunst along with Taut and Gropius, wrote his own essay titled "Glasarchitektur" (1918) that showed he was capable of producing the evocative prose of Scheerbartian renewal: "Glass architecture rules out the dull vegetative state of jelly-fish like comfort in which all values become blunted and worn, and it substitutes a state of bright alertness, a daring activity, and the creation of ever fresher, ever more beautiful values."[11] Yet in other writings Behne disavowed the theme of romantic inner vision that characterized so much expressionist thought and instead started to adopt the notion of glass as symbolic of a rational, transparent society rebuilding after the war, led by "clear-headed" thinkers. This recognition by Behne of what could be called the "rational within expressionism" seems to chart the path taken by Gropius, who later wrote, "glass architecture, which was just a poetic utopia not long ago, now becomes reality without constraint."[12]

Also, what of Laszlo Moholy-Nagy? After meeting Gropius in Berlin, Moholy-Nagy came to the Bauhaus in 1923 fresh off his series of "Glass Architecture" paintings, abstract images that were rooted in the cosmic dreams of Kasimir Malevich's Suprematism. Of course, Moholy-Nagy himself staunchly rejected spiritualisms of any sort, providing yet another intellectual substrata concerning the analytical employment of modern materials that was well known to Gropius. Similarly, the legendary glass-walled proposals of Mies—partly inspired by his disappointment over his exclusion from Gropius's 1919 exhibition of architectural projects—also existed in a fluid space whereby they could be interpreted in multivalent ways, inner vision and practical planning subsumed within one another. Behne, Moholy-Nagy, Mies, and Gropius all make this gradual transition, whereby mystical spirituality is transubstantiated into rational analysis. The lingo changes more than the substance; as Taut put it in 1929, "this state of mind, known as 'Expressionism,' was abandoned by the best of them as far back as 1923."[13] This transitional situation was given material form by the Dessau buildings and especially its glittering curtain wall. When Gropius first opened the Bauhaus in 1919 he had written of how the new building would be built collectively and rise "like the crystal symbol of a coming new faith."[14] Looking back from 1935, in *The New Architecture and the Bauhaus*, Gropius altered his language but reiterated this original concept. Now the "New Building"—a term that seems to reflect the lexicon of Henry-Russell Hitchcock and his published employment of

"New Building" and "New Pioneers"—had brought Gropius's vision to life. "The band of fellow workers inspired by a common will and purpose I once dreamed of had become a reality." *Expressionismus* had become *sahlichkeit*.

In the 1920s it was common to embrace this seemingly conflicted conflation of expressionism and rationalism as perfectly natural. For example, the American critic Sheldon Cheney writing in 1930 saw the Bauhaus curtain as "developed on a creed of economy and practicality," but also promoted Gropius as an architect who could be grouped with "Wright and Bragdon, who never fail to see the spiritual significance behind material architecture, [and] have remarked on the appropriateness of the increased utilization of glass in this hour when man is between an ancient darkness and a new enlightenment."[15] Of course, Cheney's comfort with contradiction—not to mention his audacity in grouping the now-forgotten mystical expressionist Claude Bragdon with the hallowed persona of Frank Lloyd Wright—was not characteristic of the writers who would take up the cause of modern architecture in subsequent years. Giedion and Hitchcock were the future, and the stature of the Gropius curtain wall was less a function of where it was coming from than where it was going, as the nexus of power and influence that solidified its standing would only truly arise years after the Bauhaus closed in 1933.

Mid-century modern

While 1920s architects had often written of how the transparent glass wall could open up a view of the inner structure, the true triumph of the curtain wall arises in the 1950s when the field of glass comes to the fore and effaces its innards on behalf of a glittering surface. The nexus of power that made Gropius's Bauhaus curtain so significant was its newly apparent relationship to the glamorous mid-century towers that arose in major American cities, especially New York. Much has been written about this seemingly absurd paradox, whereby the experimental, politically leftist designs of the 1920s become the ultimate signifiers of American capitalism. In the 1950s, the iconography of the modern corporation shifts dramatically, from one that embraced static monumentality to a new desire to project efficiency through the lightness and flexibility of the recently christened International Style. Of course, architecture did not stand alone in furthering this endeavor, as the newly professionalized graphic design and branding industries also promulgated a style based on a reconfiguration of formerly transgressive aesthetics.

As Philip Johnson put it in the catalog for MoMA's 1932 *Modern Architecture International Exhibition*, "Engineering was at last not only joined closely with architecture but made its basis." Johnson probably did not really mean it as an absolute, but it is true that the rapid expansion in the employment of glass curtain walls on skyscrapers involved a wide range of technological advances. The papers of Mies van der Rohe, for example, show his studio often immersed in the problems of thermal expansion and contraction of glass and its surrounding framing; for example, the new use in curtain walls of certain types of steel, stainless steel, and aluminum alloys all involved different calculations regarding the glass to sash mediation. Plus, the same challenges that were faced by nineteenth-century architects continued apace: water infiltration, solar gain, and condensation were constantly on the minds of architects and engineers. As the completely sealed building became the norm in the late 1950s upon the improvement of artificial climate systems, the ability to create a firm, lasting bond became paramount. An entire treatise could be written on the incremental advances made in just one decade on the sealants and structural pieces that bonded the glass to the frame.

In terms of the glass itself, the use of tempered, or toughened glass—either drawn or plate—became a standard practice. The invention of tempered glass, whereby through either chemical or thermal processes the material is made five or even ten times stronger than conventional annealed glass, was extremely important to the rise of the mass curtain wall. The fact that tempered glass breaks into relatively blunt edged pebbles was a huge advantage, as the fear of shards of annealed glass raining down on passerby was a real one. As is often the case, the invention involved multiple experiments by a range of engineers; however, the Austrian-born American Rudolph Seiden received the first patent for tempered glass in 1935. While the era of the mass curtain wall of glass is usually defined in terms of Thomas Carlyle's "great man" articulation of history, it is important to recognize how an entire products industry rose to meet the needs of commercial builders. For example, when one ponders the iconic glass curtain wall on the twin residential towers at 860–880 Lake Shore Drive (1951) in Chicago they think only of Mies, not of the Universal Corporation, supplier and installer of over 3,000 Sealuxe Model 42-A Ventilating Picture Windows.

There is a curious disconnect between the accolades accorded to MoMA for laying the groundwork through its 1930s exhibitions for the postwar acceptance of modernist constructivism—rechristened the International Style—and the exclusion of the museum's own building from this ongoing narrative. Part of this exclusion probably resulted from the competing views of MoMA personalities such as the director Alfred Barr and architectural curator Johnson. Johnson and Barr wanted Mies, J. P. Oud, or Gropius: combine that with a famously contentious interview with Le Corbusier and you have the makings of a veritable 1930s *telenovela*. In the end, a compromise was reached that seemed to satisfy no one.

The eventual 1939 museum building by MoMA trustee Philip Goodwin and Edward Durrell Stone was the first structure that was purpose-built for the then-ten-year-old institution (figure 4.7). Its geometrically plotted planar facade's most striking feature was the translucent glass that stretched in front of the two main exhibition floors. This curtain wall was made up of over 150 panels of Thermolux glass, a popular product made by Libby-Owens-Ford, consisting of a layer of milky glass fibers sandwiched within two sheets of drawn glass. The double height grid of steel mullions

FIGURE 4.7 Philip Goodwin and Edward Durell Stone, MoMA Building, 1939.

enclosing squarish panes would seem to reference the Dessau Bauhaus, just as the two bands of horizontal windows above it seem something of an homage to Le Corbusier. Similarly, the porthole windows at the top reference Le Corbusier again, while the use of expensive white marble cladding suggests some knowledge of Mies and Lilly Reich's Barcelona or Tugendhat stylings. In this manner the curtain wall encapsulated the recent history of the avant-garde while also providing a practical solution to lighting the exhibition galleries therein. Marginally reflective on the south-facing exterior, on the interior the Thermolux curtain created a soft, diffuse spread of natural light without excessive glare, a match to the obscured electric light sources that were first being implemented at this time. Despite its achievements and some initial praise, the Goodwin and Stone building was consigned to oblivion in the postwar era; designed by Goodwin, a classicist, and Stone—renowned for his supposed betrayal of modernism decades later—and neglected by Johnson and Alfred Barr, the new MoMA lacked a partisan in the era of Gropius and Mies. Additionally, the MoMA building was vertically challenged in an era when a wave of towering curtain walls would soon overshadow its more modest dimensions.

Think of just the storied few: the United Nations Secretariat, 860–880 Lake Shore Drive, Lever House, the Seagram Building, Pepsi Cola headquarters—the 1950s witnessed the rise of that ultimate modernist icon, the glass box skyscraper. While generally viewed as encapsulating the refined minimalism of Miesian aesthetics, these buildings in fact functioned more like the billboard architecture of any benighted commercial strip. Park Avenue in New York in particular became dotted with huge virtual signs advertising liquor, soap, soda, and airlines. While Lewis Mumford called it "chastely free of advertising,"[16] he recognized how the then-bold decision to eliminate storefronts from the ground floor of Lever House served to reinforce the concentrated advertising message of the building itself.

While the glass curtain wall made its first postwar American appearance at the Secretariat, it was Skidmore, Owings, and Merrill's 1952 Lever House that best captured the architectural moment (figure 4.8). The first sealed glass building complete with three-zone artificial climate, the tower's 1,404 green-tinted plate glass windows matched to slightly darker glass spandrel panels created a seamless glimmering form floating above its base like an avant-garde dream. Outside of whatever residual mystical feeling could be conjured up by the individual viewer in sight of all that colored glass, this new kind of building substantiated the functionalist

FIGURE 4.8 Skidmore, Owings, and Merrill, Lever House, 1952.

mantra of efficiency, clarity, and truthfulness. Critic Aline Louchheim seemed to sense the suppressed expressionist vibe:

> Astonishingly, although the expression of structure is direct, the first impression of Lever House is "coloristic" and poetic. What saves these effects from being contrived, merely picturesque or anti-architectural, is the fact that we know and can always see (when we consciously or subconsciously seek that reassurance) that they are logically

dependent on the structural scheme of the building, visual effects neither denying, contradicting nor confusing the constructive facts.[17]

There is almost a Freudian sense of intrapsychical conflict as Louchheim's worldview is briefly shaken by the id of Lever House's colorful glass, only to be re-grounded by the voice of authority provided by the ego of structure. While the curtain wall was in fact to bring in a new era of color on exterior cladding, that aspect had become disassociated from the color-dreams of past decades. For example, a writer in *Architectural Forum* opined that bright, garish exterior color had resulted in "a honky-tonk atmosphere that tended to give the curtain wall a connotation of cheapness once reserved for porcelain-enameled gas stations and stainless steel diners."[18] It is notable that Reyner Banham wrote "The Glass Paradise" in 1959 at a time when American cities were replete with a new wave of colored glass yet architects no longer referenced expressionism. Additionally, articles reporting on this new class of building often reveled in the functional-mundane: the speed of the elevators, the miles of wiring, the tons of steel. For example, descriptions of Lever House consistently referred to the gondola system for cleaning the curtain wall as a marker of its technological promise. These dry, fact-laden discourses also eroded whatever sense of Scheerbart's crystal utopia still remained.

If the glass box skyscraper retained any element of expressionist magic, it was through its nighttime illumination, a factor that Mies seemed especially attuned to exploiting. As far back as 1921 and his project for the Friedrichstrasse skyscraper, Mies had drawn steel and glass skyscrapers in such a way that emphasized their evanescent qualities; the lighting for the 1921 Berlin drawing suggests that the building is glittering in twilight, and it features streaky highlights that seem to emanate from within the crystalline structure. When Mies finally was able to build twin towers of light in Chicago at 860–880 Lake Shore Drive, he enlisted the help of lighting consultant Richard Kelly to perfect the nighttime illumination (figure 4.9). With dual undergraduate degrees in both theatrical lighting and architecture, Kelly had uniquely positioned himself in the profession; he became the go-to consultant at a time when architects were moving away from the colorful, applied spectacle lighting of Art Deco *Lichtarchitektur*, and embracing more nuanced strategies whereby nighttime illumination was integrated with the functional lighting of the interior. Mies wanted his buildings to glow from within. At the 860–880 Lake Shore Drive Apartments, the key element of illumination was not

FIGURE 4.9 Ludwig Mies van der Rohe, 860–880 Lake Shore Drive, 1951, credit: © [2018] Artists Rights Society (ARS), New York/VG Bild-Kunst, Bonn.

the towers themselves but the smaller, ground floor lobby that is inset on all four sides and surrounded by a fence of pilotis. These glazed cubes—a forerunner of the now ubiquitous Apple stores—featured transparent sheet glass on the entrance side and translucent glass on the back, the latter masking the elevator bank and other utilitarian spaces. Kelly devised a system whereby the glass walls that form the core of the lobby would be evenly washed by theater-grade downlights so as to avoid any type of shadowed shapes appearing as could be created by a focused filament. He then matched this brightly glowing core with softer exterior light from devices set into the perimeter soffits of the building. In this manner, the buildings sing with theatrical emotion at night, an unexpected effect if one has viewed their rather dry, spartan exteriors while the sun was high.

A few years later at the Seagram Building, Mies again subcontracted the lighting design to Kelly, who extended the dramatic lighting of the 860–880 Lake Shore Drive core all the way to the top of the tower (figure 4.10). Again utilizing a system of perimeter downlighting, this time through a luminous ceiling that extended inward from the curtain wall for 20 feet, Kelly made the building's 122,000 square feet of

FIGURE 4.10 Ludwig Mies van der Rohe, Seagram Building, 1958 New York City, credit: © [2018] Artists Rights Society (ARS), New York/VG Bild-Kunst, Bonn.

pinkish-gray glass shimmer against the night sky. In order to set off the transition of the tower from the ground, he quadrupled the intensity of the lobby lighting vis-a-vis the upper floors, creating an effect whereby the weightless glass sheath seems to be rocketing into the sky like the Atlas missiles that defined the power of technology during the late 1950s. The lighting system was tied to a timer that would dim the lights in the evening after the workday in order to get the right level of illumination, glowing without producing glare. The effect was so successful that many write-ups of the building featured photographs of it illuminated at night, even if the main thrust of the text was on the bronze color of the cladding that at night became invisible. Despite Kelly's manifest contribution to the Seagram Building he himself remained in the shadows, as the *New York Times*, for example, did not credit him with the work. This assertion appeared in a front-page article of the paper in 1957: "The lighting system was conceived by Philip Johnson, architect, and Lightolier, inc."[19]

Looking back with almost seventy years of hindsight, it is remarkable how often the mid-century glass boxes were viewed more as a conclusion than a beginning. Many architectural writers viewed them not as a new, emerging trend but as a refinement to a finished project. A *New York Times* reporter opined of Lever House in 1952, "Culminating rather than pioneering a new style, Lever House reveals more handsomely and with greater clarity than any other building in New York its structure of a steel skeleton with a glass curtain wall."[20] Likewise—and somewhat in contradiction to an editor's heavy-handed title ("Newest Building in the New Style")—critic Louchheim (not yet Aline Saarinen) asserted that Lever House "carries to a new point of refinement the Le Corbusier Mies van der Rohe style of steel skeleton with glass curtain wall."[21] Mumford railed against the curtain wall when given the opportunity. While he was accepting of Lever Brothers—although rather snarky in stating that upon the opening of the building "People acted as if this was the eighth wonder of the world"—the esteemed critic seemed to have delighted in what he saw as the failure of the UN Secretariat the year before (figure 4.11). Because of its East/West orientation and the resulting glare, Mumford condemned the manner in which the architects, "using glass so exuberantly," had created a building "that functionally is often windowless on all four sides."[22] He goes on to quote Hitchcock, who had prognosticated, "The most significant influence of the Secretariat, will, I imagine, be to end the use of glass walls in skyscrapers." Of course, solar considerations aside, Hitchcock was off-base and the curtain wall was

FIGURE 4.11 Le Corbusier et al., UN Secretariat, 1949, credit: © F.L.C./ADAGP, Paris/Artists Rights Society (ARS), New York [2018].

in fact "well on the way to becoming the new American vernacular," as *Architectural Forum* reported in 1959.

There was one last key link in the technological change that would make the glass curtain wall ultimately triumphant: the invention of the float glass process by Pilkington Brothers during the 1950s. While the basic idea—pouring molten glass not on to a casting table but rather onto to a liquid metal substrate—had been experimented with for decades, Pilkington managed to solve a number of chemical and engineering challenges that had prevented the technology from becoming commercially viable. In the 1960s Pilkington licensed their process worldwide, and because of additional refinements that improved the product and lowered the cost, float gradually took over the market. By the 1970s, other companies had developed their own float-forming processes and the sheet and cast plate glass industry was rendered obsolete. Even today, when myriad innovations have improved glass technology, the float process remains the basis of industrial glass production. The availability of inexpensive, flawless sheets of glass helped to ensure the continuing proliferation of the curtain wall. And it was through its ubiquity that the glass curtain walled skyscraper quickly returned to its American roots in banality. Just forty years after the completion of the Hallidie Building, the hallowed house of glass was just a staple of building practice, a monotonous wallpaper unlikely to inspire dreams of the future.

5 STRUCTURAL GLASS

In 1914, Paul Scheerbart at his most poetic speculated on the future age of glass architecture. "It would be as if the earth were adorned with sparkling jewels and enamels. Such glory is unimaginable. All over the world it would be as splendid as in the gardens of the Arabian Nights. We should then have a paradise on earth."[1] As in the previous chapter, these statements from *Glasarchitektur* have usually been evaluated in the context of the European avant-garde architecture of the 1910s and 1920s. Because Scheerbart died in 1915, his collaboration with Bruno Taut from 1914 marks his closest connection with a figure from the modern narrative. As Taut spread the word of Scheerbartian aesthetics in subsequent years, he connected at one time or another with the major figures in the avant-garde, including, of course, Walter Gropius and Ludwig Mies van der Rohe. As those latter architects are closely associated with the promulgation of the glass curtain wall, Scheerbart's work has often been identified with that form. An examination of the glass curtain wall as it emerges between the wars suggests, however, that, despite some residual expressionist feeling, it does not really appear to do much in the way of fulfilling Scheerbart's dream. The Bauhaus studio building? It is unlikely to cause many viewers to invoke the Arabian Nights.

The obvious missing item in terms of the avant-garde employment of Scheerbart's work was the lack of prominence given to glass. While curtain walls sometimes assert themselves, the overarching feeling of Gropius and Mies et al. was that glass should be flawless and transparent, a clear, even invisible membrane that showcased the structural honesty of a building. For this reason, it would seem wise to look for Scheerbart's paradise arising elsewhere, outside the tight confines of the modernist story; in fact, the same years that witnessed the rise of avant-garde transparency also saw the building of glass worlds of crystalline structure, many adorned with color and light. It is in these buildings that utilized "structural glass" where that material truly comes to the fore: visible, not invisible. Therefore it is the designers of structural glass in the 1920s and 1930s who actually seemed determined to build as Scheerbart wanted, "with sparkling jewels and enamels." Multiple advances in glass block technology combined with a focus on polychrome effects to spur the creation of a multifarious group of glittering glass structures. Many of these buildings stand outside of the modern canon—awash as they are in the ornamental effects it repudiated—yet captured the general public's imagination. While Bruno Taut—who had used glass blocks in his *Glashaus*—essentially abandoned the premise of this work in subsequent years, a generation of architects proved determined to spread the gospel of glass in the years between the wars and beyond. As a corollary, Scheerbart had predicted that glass architecture after sunset would be "truly indescribable," and structural glass came into its own as the preferred medium for spectacular displays of architecture at night.

Like many seemingly straightforward terms in the architectural lexicon, the words "structural glass" can mean a variety of things depending on the context and the time period. In its most logical sense, structural glass refers to elements such as glass blocks that have the capacity to transmit loads, particularly the dead loads of a structure. While all glass withstands the live loads of wind or casual contact, a window pane even in an early curtain wall is nonstructural because the dead load is carried by the frame. So for this reason a glass block wall or paving system without metal frames is clearly structural, even though as an exterior skin the effect may be largely the same. But then it gets murkier; strong glass elements such as the Nevada tiles preferred by Le Corbusier are always set into supportive metal frames, but nonetheless are still called structural glass because they were designed to be more resilient than sheet glass; however, the distinction between a sheet glass and a glass tile curtain wall, for example, is marked mainly by the differences in transparency. Another accepted use of the term is to name the ornamental surface glass made popular by Art Deco architects and utilized as cladding, wainscoting, partitions, countertops, and the like. Because of differences in chemistry as well as the melting temperature and duration—called "fusing" in the industry—and the annealing process, Art Deco glasses such as Carrara had greater all-around strength that made them suitable for quasi-structural deployments.

Finally, the later decades of the twentieth century saw technological improvements that allowed for glass membranes to be supported by true structural glass fins, columns, and beams, so much so that Scheerbart's dream of crystalline structures has become more and more of a reality in the contemporary age.

Glass and hygiene

There was an issue that was not nearly so seductive as crystalline cities that nonetheless gained momentum in the nineteenth century and helped to fuel the dream of a glass future: the fact that crowded urban areas in the United States and Europe were essentially seas of human waste and filth. Beginning with the Great Sanitary Awakening in Britain, public health reformers in the 1800s had begun making the connection between epidemics—typhus and cholera most prominently—and an overall lack of sanitation. In hindsight, most of these theories were inaccurate, especially as the prevailing belief in "miasmic" infection through various types of sewer, or polluted air, generally won the day. While the germ theory of disease would not really gain traction until late in the nineteenth century, early successes, such as John Snow's identification of the dreadful Broad Street Pump in Soho in 1854, furthered the work of the so-called contagionists. Whatever ones scientific faction, contagionist or anti-contagionist (miasmic), the trend throughout the century moved toward greater expenditure on public services that could improve the quality of air and water while also implementing better garbage and sewage removal. Quality of life was at issue as well; anyone who has seen vintage photographs of city streets strewn with dead animals, trash, and broken glass can begin to imagine the pervasive reek, as it was said sailors could smell New York City from ten miles offshore. Because urban areas forced the wealthy and powerful to live in much closer quarters with the poor and neglected, there was strong political emphasis on sanitizing the urban world.

Architectural glass comes into the picture of promoting public health through the same type of ambiguous science that had created miasma theory; part conjecture, part self-evident common sense, but not a lot of empirical data. First and foremost, glass *looks* clean. In terms of the cultural shift against accommodating urban filth, nothing appeared more reassuringly pristine than a newly washed sheet of glass. Along these lines but outside of the architectural realm, one can imagine the sense of technological wonderment felt when the French obstetrician Stéphane Tarnier introduced his glass-walled incubator for the thermal support of premature infants in 1890, after having modified the original design that had utilized a wooden enclosure (figure 5.3). Glass provided confidence to parents that the system was clean and technologically advanced. As a corollary to this symbolic perception was the understanding—based on reasonable assumptions—that the hard, impermeable surface of glass could be sanitized more effectively than other porous materials. Especially for those followers of bacteriology, or germ theory of disease, this latter quality was paramount. Just as with the infant incubators, architectural glass has always captured people's imagination through a symbiotic combination of symbolic properties and actual material successes.

The other important role for glass as a combatant against filth and disease evolved through its transparency. Glass was able to allow the healing rays of the sun into dark, dank interior spaces. Again, a mix of traditional wisdom and new scientific discoveries in the early twentieth century convinced many people that sunlight had preventative and curative properties. There are kernels of truth in this idea as sunlight indeed will kill some bacteria; however, the perception of natural light as a therapeutic force was probably more important than actual facts.

The prominent British public health reformer Edwin Chadwick, a follower of miasma theory, was one of many who stressed the dangers of low-lying fogs as carriers of disease. In his 1889 book *The Present and General Condition of Sanitary Science*, Chadwick stressed the problem this created in his view for below grade structures.

> I have for a long time collected observations of the height of attacks of epidemics on the population of tall buildings, and have found the attacks to be generally confined to the cellar dwellings or the lower floors, whilst the occupants of the upper floors have been distinctly exempted from them, that is to say, the occupants of dwellings above the range of visible fogs, made-up of the heavier, low-lying, and visible fogs.[2]

Of course, much of this London fog was actually particulate air pollution, not sewer gases, but the notion that basement spaces were disease-ridden was standard fare. The desire to banish these unhealthy fogs with natural light was one of the impetuses of glass vault-lighting, one of the earliest examples of structural glass. Variously called decklights, sidewalk lights, or pavement lights, these elements consisted of rows of translucent glass set into a framework of either iron or concrete, usually as part of a sidewalk; this at a time when many commercial basements extended under the adjoining footway. Additionally, different sorts of prismatic glass were invented in order to enhance the spread of daylight into the deeper recesses of a cellar through light refraction. Aside from their health-promoting function, vault lights also made economical use of daylight at a time before inexpensive electricity and lightbulbs would transform the illumination industry (figure 5.1). Vault lights were a big, competitive business: firms such as Jacobs & Sons in New York City continually advertised their diverse line of products, while also filing dozens of patents for minor improvements to the lenses, frames, etc. Of course, vault light glass is not truly structural, as the surrounding support would not weaken much from the removal of the glass forms; however, the small, sturdy modules were able to resist the pounding forces of sidewalk traffic that would otherwise easily smash through a thin pane. That being said, in the nineteenth century vault lights were sometimes criticized as a pedestrian hazard as they became slippery in wet weather and also were not immune to breakage that resulted in gaping maws on the sidewalk.

Above ground, the earliest commercially successful structural glass element was likely the glass brick system invented by the Swiss engineer Gustave Falconnier on or about 1886, the year he was granted his first patent in his home country (figure 5.2). In an 1889 American patent application for a "Glass Building-Block," he wrote about the expanding possibilities for glass as a building material,

> It is well known that under the improved modes of making glass its production has been greatly cheapened and its toughness improved, whereby it has become better adapted for use in the construction of the ornamental parts of buildings, particularly for window-sills, the covering of façades, and in the construction of the walls of various structures.

Falconnier's system, which he gradually improved upon over two decades, consisted of blown-glass "briques en verre soufflé" plugged

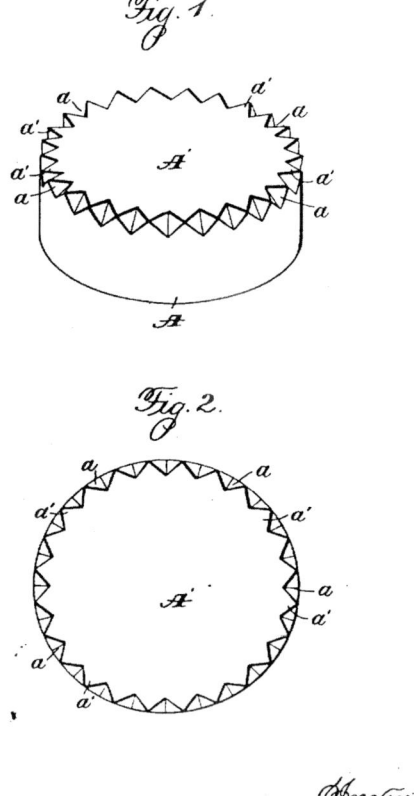

FIGURE 5.1 Jacobs & Sons, Advertisement for Vault Lighting, 1890s, US Patent Office/Public Domain.

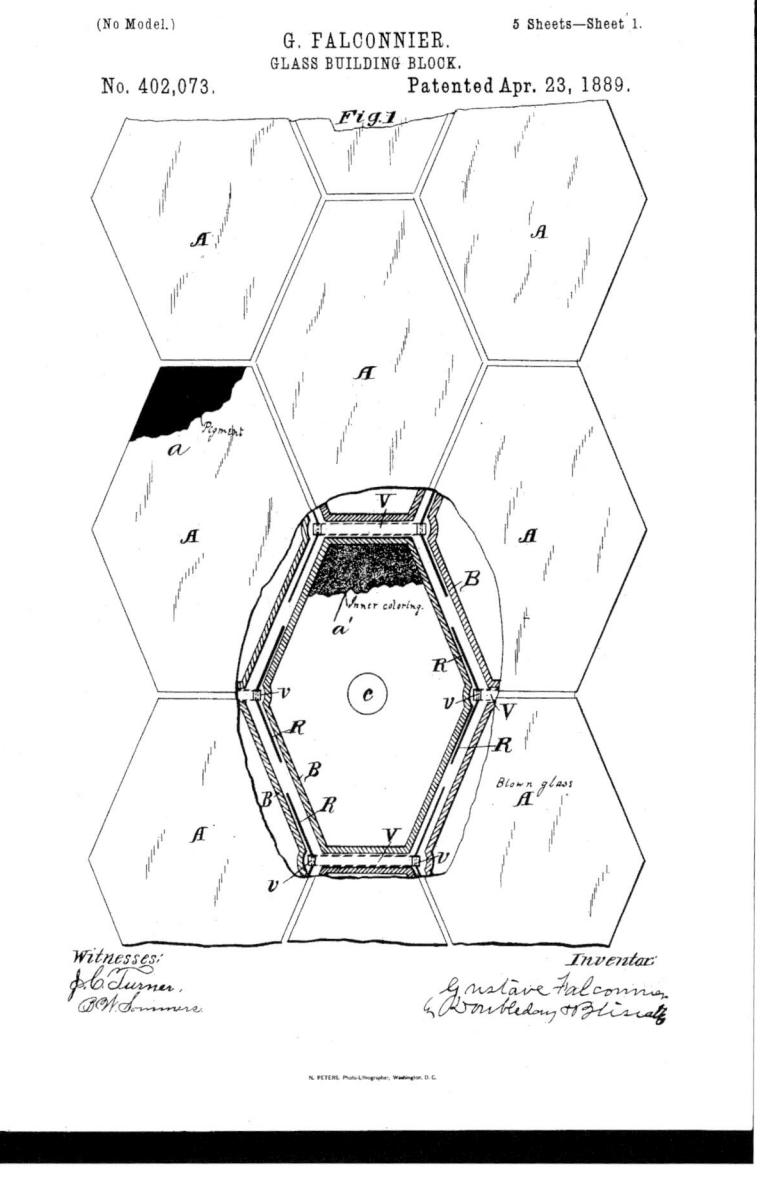

FIGURE 5.2 Gustave Falconnier, Glass Bricks, 1890s, US Patent Office/Public Domain.

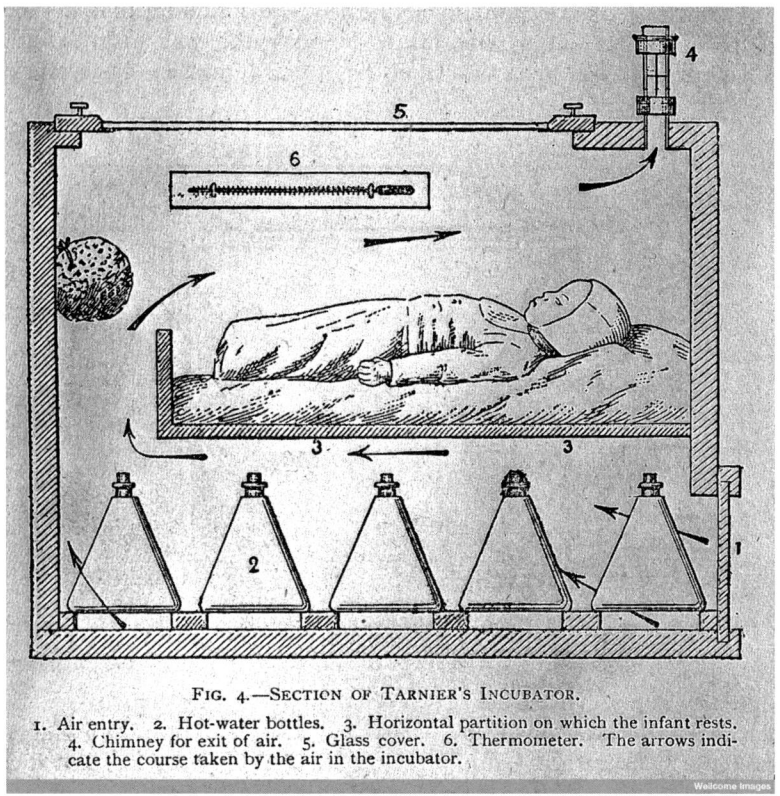

FIGURE 5.3 Stephane Tarnier, Baby Incubator, 1890, credit: Wellcome Library, London, CC by 4.0.

with molten glass during production. The bricks were blown into a mold that produced characteristic forms: convex on the two broad faces with a square or hexagonal shape that tapers at each end. Falconnier marketed the hollow bricks in a variety of refracting capabilities and colors, although a light aqua is most common. Because they were airtight, the bricks functioned like double-paned windows and had a significant insulating advantage over a building made of sheet glass. Falconnier's blocks were slotted so that they could be mortared together, although in some installations small metal glazing bars were utilized between them. It should also be noted that Falconnier and the broader glass block industry benefited from the doubtful presumption that nineteenth-century glass was somehow impermeable to fire; linked to the fact that it had been through the crucible during its manufacture, the belief that glass had already been through a "trial by fire" gave it added technological gravitas.

Suitable for building small glass structures such as garden hothouses, Falconnier licensed his bricks across northern Europe, including to Glashütte Gerresheim of Düsseldorff and the Haywards Company in London.[3] At Chicago's World's Columbian Exposition of 1893, a pair of small greenhouses made of Falconnier's bricks was located next to the grand Horticultural Building. While the engineer received an "Award" at the Exposition, its praise seemed rather dubious, as the citation stated, "Their adaptability for conservatories intended for plant cultivation has not yet been fully demonstrated, but for conservatory vestibules and other rural effects they are well adapted." As Falconnier subsequently tried to market the product outside of the horticultural context, advertising for the bricks often referred to their cleanliness and suitability for surgical and scientific spaces. Falconnier's system was never a huge success: one of the major deficiencies to it that undoubtedly hurt its marketability was the fact that the slotted design made it difficult to replace a broken brick without disassembling a large part of a wall.

It is important to recognize that the Falconnier's system was just one example of a high-profile glass building material; perusing government documents such as the Trade Reports put together by the US Bureau of Manufactures shows that glass brick producers were quietly introducing related products throughout Europe and the United States. In 1904, the US Department of State requested that its European consular officers compile "information in regard to the manufacture of paving bricks from glass, the material used in the manufacture of such bricks, and their value for the purpose named." The resulting report sounded like a glass utopia was on the near horizon, detailing all manner of glass construction products across Europe.[4] A few years later, the German branch of the Luxfer Company—most famous for its refracting tiles—introduced a product called *Glaseisenbeton*, literally "glass-iron-concrete." This scheme, sometimes called the "Keppler-System" after the company's director, Friedrich Keppler, was rather like a vault-light panel that could be mounted vertically as a partition wall without structural responsibilities. Creating a translucent curtain akin to Falconnier's, *Glaseisenbeton* led to the development of the French firm Societe de Saint Gobain's more prominent Nevada tiles after the latter company acquired the rights to Keppler's design.[5]

Perhaps the strongest link between structural glass tiles and health was that made through the design of Pierre Chareau's Maison de Verre (1928–32, figure 5.4), a Paris townhome that served as both living quarters and a doctor's office. Chareau was professionally known more as a furniture designer and decorator than as an architect, and the Maison de Verre represented his most substantial building project. He had received the commission based on his close personal relationship with the owners, Annie and Jean Dalsace, who it is thought had a substantial amount of input into the design of the structure. The most striking part of the Maison de Verre and the source of its nickname is, of course, the two double-story curtain walls made up of Saint-Gobain's solid Nevada tiles grouped in sets of twenty-four and put into prefabricated steel frames. There are in fact two curtain walls, one at the front facade and one on the garden side; both turn a corner of the structure. The Nevada tiles are about 8 inches square, and their thickness combined with a mottled surface keeps them translucent. For this reason, transparent pieces of sheet glass were integrated into the facades to provide a view, giving them the look of an assemblage as opposed to a purist curtain. These sheet glass windows were operable, allowing for fresh air ventilation. In this way the Maison de Verre resonates with the contemporary design of sanitariums for tuberculosis patients and also with the related French investment in

FIGURE 5.4 Pierre Chareau, Maison Verre, 1932, credit: CC BY-SA 3.0.

écoles de plein air, essentially outdoor schools that promoted sunlight and air as curative forces.

Architecturally speaking, the Maison de Verre is something of a *sui generis* example of glass building, and because Chareau was an unknown and the house was somewhat hidden in a courtyard in Paris' Left Bank, it really had very little immediate impact on architectural discourse. While it was, of course, known to Le Corbusier, its quirky design did not emerge into the light until the 1960s, when Richard Rogers and the critic Kenneth Frampton brought it some attention just a few years after Reyner Banham had first salvaged Taut and Scheerbart from a similar oblivion.

The notion that the Maison de Verre represented a "milestone in early modern architectural design," as is often claimed, is quite dubious, because it is really an architectural oddity; truly the building stands out much more for the implicit connection made between glass and sanitation. Never has the glass interior of a medical office called more attention to itself than that of Jean Dalsace. He was a gynecologist, and large swaths of the ground floor and part of the first floor—both areas where the glass facades have their greatest impact on the interior—were built to serve his practice. In addition to the facade glass, the interior of the office also featured a variety of glass partition walls, some transparent with adjustable metal screens, others translucent. Waiting room, reception, exam rooms, surgical suite, study: Dr. Dalsace's medical world was encased in glass. As a practical matter, French journals on hygiene from this era repeatedly advocated the use of glass and other nonporous materials as a defense against microbes in a post-Pasteur world. The so-called heliotherapy represented one of the major treatments for tuberculosis during this era. More emphatically and on a symbolic level, patients at the Masion de Verre in essence entered a huge glass incubator, warmed by the heating pipes that ran under the floor by the glass walls.

Critic Kenneth Frampton, who wrote a long article for *Perspecta* in 1969 that helped to bring the Maison de Verre out of the underground and into the modernist canon, was aware of the effect of the "incubator metaphor," although he articulated it differently. In recognizing the impact that the Maison de Verre had had on the French-American architect Paul Nelson, Frampton noted that "Nelson appears to have been impressed by its creation of a world within a world, the internal realm being all but totally isolated from the outside by a continuous translucent membrane."[6] Importantly, Frampton is referring to Nelson's utilization of translucent panels in a medical setting at the Surgical Pavilion for the

Suez Canal Hospital (Ismalia, 1937). Nelson also utilized the glass wall as an enclosure in several other medical buildings that he planned in the 1930s, including the unbuilt Maison des Docteurs (1933), elevations for which show a translucent screen of glass blocks shielding the patients from the outside world.

Le Corbusier, who lived and worked near the Maison de Verre during its construction, also endeavored to utilize St. Gobain's Nevada brand glass tiles in the hygienic context. While experimenting with them in various ways at the Salvation Army building known as the Cité du Refuge (1929–33, figure 5.5), one of the most successful implementations was in the creation of a clerestory for the wall of that building's infirmary. The City of Refuge had been commissioned by the Salvation Army with financial support from the Princess Edmond de Polignac (nee Winnaretta Singer in the United States), who wanted to provide shelters and services for the urban poor and homeless. In some ways the whole enterprise represented an exercise in bringing hygiene to the outcasts of society; aside from the use of glass bricks, Le Corbusier's implementation of an early glass curtain wall played into the symbolism of cleanliness and modernity. Of course, sheet glass could drive what I term the "incubator metaphor" just as well as glass blocks, and at the City of Refuge Le Corbusier in a sense created a giant, multipurpose incubator for the downtrodden. Importantly, the City of Refuge represented one of the architect's first attempts at designing a sealed building whereby all of the interior air was circulated by a purifying system and no windows were operable for ventilation; in this manner the inhabitants were watched over and cared for like premature infants sealed in a glass box. Of course, there is some irony in the fact that incubators were designed to provide supportive warmth, something that Le Corbusier's south-facing curtain wall did all too well, as the dormitory rooms and nursery at the City of Refuge became unbearably hot during the summer months.

During this era, a combination of increased knowledge about sunlight's germicidal properties combined with residual sun-worshipping mysticism and the experiential joy of bathing in solar energy together spurred the utilization of glass in architecture. As Le Corbusier once wrote, "Glass is the most miraculous means of restoring the law of the sun."[7] This impulse led to the production of one of the oddest health products of the era, Vita glass. Vita glass was promoted on the basis of the healing properties of the sun, an issue that came into

FIGURE 5.5 Le Corbusier, City of Refuge, 1933, VIEW pictures (UK), credit: © F.L.C./ADAGP, Paris/Artists Rights Society (ARS), New York [2018].

sharp focus after 1920 upon recognition of the connection between vitamin D deficiency and the crippling disease rickets. While rickets is primarily caused by malnutrition, lack of adequate sun exposure is also a contributing factor. Glass comes into the picture when a series of experts, notably including the English biologist Leonard Hill, argued that sheet glass was blocking the healthful ultraviolet rays of the sun from entering buildings. Hill wrote that "ordinary window glass filters out the protective rays," and became a champion of Vita glass, a type of sheet, not structural, glass with a chemical formula (basically low iron content) that allowed more ultraviolet light to pass through into the interior.[8] Devised by Francis Lamplough, Vita Glass was licensed to Chance Brothers, who then brought Pilkington Brothers onboard to assist with production. Together the two companies created a joint marketing business and then prepared to soak up the resulting riches. Competing products arose as well, with high-profile endorsements from architects including Frank Lloyd Wright, who intended to use pro-UV glass for his legendary 1930 curtain walled towers in New York at St. Mark's-in-the-Bowery.

Alas, as related by historian John Sadar, the anticipated lucre never really amounted to much for companies that invested in the product. A number of factors worked against it: Vita glass was expensive; a newly published research highlighted the risks that ultraviolet exposure had for skin and eyes, and, most importantly, anyone desiring to bathe in the sun probably will just go outside rather than sit in front of a window in the glare. While interest in sun therapy has never really abated, the Vita glass market did, and the glass was discontinued in the 1930s. Like the case with Wright's proposed towers, the Great Depression also had an impact in canceling the product. In the current era, the specialized glass market produces only what one could call anti-Vita, panes that aggressively block ultraviolet light in order to protect health but also furnishings from the fading of exposure.

Another type of glass marketed to the health market, in this case the pigmented structural material known by a bevy of trade names including Sani-Onyx, Carrara, and Vitrolite, was introduced primarily as a hygienic product. This structural glass was mostly opaque, garnered through a process whereby fluoride was added to the molten material before annealing. Originally offered in only white and black, Sani-Onyx, the first product, was manufactured by the Marietta Manufacturing Company beginning in 1900. The name says it all, as Sani-Onyx was promoted in the sanitation context, as an easily cleanable wall surface for bathrooms, kitchens, and hospitals: at one point Marietta published a catalog titled "The Story of Sani Onyx for Hospitals." In fact, the generic name "sanitary glass" was often specified regardless of brand. Next, Penn-

American Plate Glass proffered its more astutely branded Carrara glass, a name which referenced the famous Italian marble; white structural glass was, of course, much less expensive and more easily worked than stone, as it could be curved, incised, sandblasted, and textured. Pittsburgh Plate Glass eventually bought the rights to Carrara, and in the 1920s advertised both its nonabsorbent qualities—"the ideal material even for urinals"—and cleanliness: "Aseptic walls for the operating room." This fundamental notion about glass—its innate cleanliness—is still in play today. Recent developments in antimicrobial applications including silver, polymers, and photocatalyic coatings have been shown to effectively destroy bacteria on glass.

Pittsburgh Plate Glass (PPG) also asserted that the honed version of Cararra would diffuse bright sunlight and lessen glare when used on walls. The final product to appear was the most commercially visible: Vitrolite, a brand name based on the words "vitreous marble." Its slogan: "The Aristocrat of Sanitary Materials." Between 1916 and 1935 Vitrolite was manufactured by the aptly named Vitrolite Company of Chicago (figure 5.6), which sold the rights to its eponymous product to Libbey-Owens-Ford in 1935. In the United Kingdom, Pilkington Brothers acquired the rights to the European Vitrolite franchise in 1932.

Vitrolite and its brethren underwent a remarkable transformation beginning in the 1920s and accelerating in the 1930s. In an effort to broaden the market away from the mostly utilitarian, sanitary spaces where it all began, producers of structural glass mounted a campaign to redefine it as a fashionable, modern-looking material suitable as an architectural centerpiece on facades, restaurant interiors, and even mausoleums. The Marietta Company published a catalog in the 1920s that demonstrated the shift. "Beautiful Sani-Onyx for Your Walls" advised consumers repeatedly that "Sani-Onyx adapts itself so perfectly to any modern type of architecture, No other wall material is quite so modern—so modernistic, in fact." At some point in this endeavor Marietta recognized that the unappealing vibe of the original, hygienic-sounding name was a liability, and started promoting an alternative one, Rox. Marietta seemed to struggle with its advertising copy at times, as one memorable brochure promised that Sani-Onyx was "'different,' without being freakish."

This new push to refashion the reputation of structural glass relied both on its highly polished sheen and a key new quality: color. Orchid, emerald, walnut, princess blue: as the shift took hold, a huge

FIGURE 5.6 Vitrolite advertisement, 1933, Public Domain.

spectrum of evocative names came on the scene. Soon, over forty different colors were available from the various brands: solids, pastels, and even milky agates were splashed across consumer magazines such as *House & Garden*. Polychrome structural glass came into fashion as part of a broader trend toward overt color in design that was facilitated by technological advances not just in glass but in paint and plastics as well. For example, the invention of nitrocellulose lacquers around 1923 enabled car manufacturers to offer new, colorful models; notably, the iconic, always-black Model T was retired in 1927 by Ford in favor of the new colorful Model A. Likewise, the makers of the thermoplastic known as Bakelite started producing colorful jewelry in the 1920s. An article in the *Saturday Evening Post* of 1928, "The New Age of Color," captured the trend.

> The effects of our chromatic revolution are everywhere apparent. One need not leave his fireside to observe equally striking signs of the new invasion. Hangings, draperies, and floor coverings tell the same new story. The craze for colored glassware for table and parlor use has produced new hues and effects. Even the humble agateware of pantry and kitchen refuses to be denied a part in the general symphony of color.[9]

While in the 1920s structural glass manufacturers first worked to reintroduce their sanitary products so as to ride the polychrome wave, it was not until the 1930s, when the marketing might of Libbey-Owens-Ford (LOF) and Pilkington got behind the product, that Vitrolite et al. really came to the fore in architecture. Those two companies blanketed popular media with advertisements, while also hiring star interior designers—LOF employed both Bruce Goff and Harold Van Doren, while PPG hired Walter Dorwin Teague—in promotional roles. For example, Goff designed a number of model restaurant interiors for LOF filled with striking red Vitrolite counters, tables, and partition walls.

The attempt to get structural glass out of the bathroom, so to speak, was given a huge boost by the US government's efforts to increase commercial investment and consumption during the Great Depression. The attention focused today on the pro-consumption policies modeled on the economic theories of John Maynard Keynes after the Second World War has in many ways overshadowed the astounding increases in the retail economy that had already happened between the wars. New retailing strategies, especially the introduction of widespread consumer credit, combined with the booming economies of the mid-1920s to substantially increase the importance of this sector to national economies. When retail sales plunged as a result of the post-1929 economic crises, the Roosevelt administration eventually stepped in with the so-called New Deal, a package of stimulus programs designed to employ Americans while also fomenting consumption.

One little known part of the National Housing Act of 1934 was called the Modernization Credit Plan, and it provided federally guaranteed loans of up to $50,000 for shops that renovated their premises. Colloquially known by the slogan "Modernize Main Street," the program led LOF to sponsor a juried competition under the same name in 1935. When the winning designs were published in the *Architectural Record* that October, they had positioned Vitrolite as the preferred cladding for modern stores, "what an intelligent public taste will demand."[10] For example, Suren Pilafian and Maurice Lubin's submission for "Problem B Apparel Shop," for which they garnered the first prize, featured a streamlined facade with a typical Art Deco rounded corner, all clad in black Vitrolite. While the jury remarked that "the design would be equally effective in color," the architect's intention was to contrast the polished black exterior with accents provided by chromium ribbons and gas-tube lighting. Continuing inside, both the vestibule floor and all interior partitions were specified to be constructed out of LOF's prized new acquisition.

Pilafian and Lubin's modest shopfront design may have been influenced by Owen Williams's spectacular Daily Express Building that had been constructed on Fleet Street in London in 1932 (figure 5.7). Anticipating the all-glass curtain wall of later skyscrapers like the Lever Brothers building, Williams's Art Deco midrise structure utilized Vitrolite cladding on the spandrels and as an opaque vertical accent. Almost seamlessly united with the plate glass windows—thin chrome-plated ribbons serve as joinery—the black panels resonate with the color of newsprint, a design consonant with the first floor windows that allowed passersby to ogle the printing presses operating therein. The decorative sheath of black Vitrolite functioned somewhat like a billboard for the newspaper, which commissioned two more buildings with near-identical facades, first in Glasgow (1937), and then in Manchester (1939).

The Daily Express building panels represented one of the first examples of what would later be called spandrel glass, a market that developed in the 1950s alongside the curtain wall. Spandrel glass was mainly a plate glass product, and is indicative of an era when the chemical experimentation with glass coatings first came into commercial production. Companies such as LOF, PPG, and Pilkington would spray fine powdered ceramic "frits" on tempered plate glass, which would then be baked into the sheet. LOF marketed their spandrel product with a nod to Vitrolite, calling it Vitrolux, "a color-fused, heat-strengthened polished plate glass."

FIGURE 5.7 Owen Williams, Daily Express Building, London, 1933.

PPG, purveyor of Cararra glass, also seized the stimulus opportunity, marketing Teague-designed facade modernization kits, all centered on the smooth, polished finish of structural glass. These kits anticipated the contemporary facade systems that play such a large role in the market today. In September of 1936, the company kicked off a national tour of twelve model storefronts constructed of actual building materials with an exhibit in midtown Manhattan. Promising a "motorized caravan" that would traverse the East Coast and Midwestern markets served by the company, PPG endeavored to distribute plans to architects and builders.[11] A PPG catalog from that same year, "Producing Bigger Profits with Pittco Store Fronts," promised buyers that a new storefront would "take the fullest and most profitable advantage of the great modern selling magic of 'eye appeal.'" Not since the halcyon days of the surge in glass store fronts of the 1800s had glass so captured the retail imagination, now colonizing not just the display windows but the entire visible surface of the exterior. In pursuit of this retail nirvana, PPG customers could seek a government loan, or simply apply for the company's own Pittsburgh Time Payment Plan.

Glass blocks

While opaque structural glass such as Cararra washed across the buildings of many cities and towns in the 1930s, a newly improved American product, the industrially manufactured glass block, appeared on the market in 1932 and offered yet another way of building a glass paradise. This new type of glass block, a product of the Corning Glass Works, was manufactured out of the material called Pyrex, a brand name that had been introduced in 1915 for a new line of hygienic cookware made out of heat-resistant borosilicate glass. Amidst the glass boom of the 1930s, Corning started producing first cast, and then hollow Pyrex blocks for the building trade. In an article for the trade journal *American Architect* in 1932, Walter Teague announced the new product, promising that "a wall of these blocks sparkles and shimmers softly with an ever-changing radiance."[12] While acknowledging that they were not truly load bearing, Teague promised that the blocks could support 4,700 psi, enough to sustain some light-duty supportive roles (his figure is inaccurate, as hollow glass blocks generally have a compressive strength of less than 800 psi). In 1938 Corning allied with PPG to create a new company that manufactured glass blocks, the Pittsburgh Corning Corporation.

The major competition to Pittsburgh Corning came from the Owens-Illinois Company, which had been formed in 1929 by the merger of the Owens Bottle Company and the Illinois Glass Company. Owens Illinois had long ruled the blown glass bottle market, but sought to increase its share of industrial glass through the introduction of new products such as structural glass. Two years before making its first commercial shipment of "Insulux" brand blocks in 1935, Owens-Illinois had dramatically premiered its product in 1933 when it sponsored the "Owens-Illinois Glass Block Building" at the 1933 Chicago world's fair, an event known by its official title "A Century of Progress International Exposition." At the exposition, the glass block building—which housed a display of Owens-Illinois bottles as well as gardening equipment and flowers from the cosponsor James W. Owen Nurseries—stood 100 feet wide and 60 feet deep, with a 50-foot central tower designed in the popular "frozen fountain" stepped fashion so characteristic of Art Deco styling (figure 5.8). While this building is often cited as a breakthrough in the glass block industry, in fact it represents only another iteration of the glass greenhouse type that had been a part of almost every world's fair for nearly a century. Like Falconnier's structures at Chicago's 1893 fair, glass blocks remained outside the mainstream of architecture. One notable feature about the Owens-Illinois pavilion was its color; the hollow blocks had been painted with bright translucent color in the post-production process, so that the building admitted colored light and also shimmered with color when the interior was lit in the evening. This show of polychrome illumination, resonant with Scheerbart's vision of the future, was not unique, however, to the Owens-Illinois structure, as the Century of Progress made great use of colored light spectacles throughout the grounds. Spurred on by

FIGURE 5.8 Owens-Illinois Glass House at A Century of Progress, 1933.

the producers of electricity and illumination, the so-called architecture of the night—originally the title of a General Electric publication from 1930—found a complementary material in glass blocks. Often combined with structural glass storefronts, milky white opal glass panels and glass blocks created a festive atmosphere at the world's fair or on urban streets. In contrast to the restrained simplicity of Richard Kelly's lighting of the Seagram building, Art Deco architectural illumination reveled in garishness and the carnivalesque.

Reviewers of the Owens-Illinois pavilion recognized the limitations of the glass block building, one recording that the blocks were "not intended as a load-bearing material ... [but are] expected to prove highly useful as a curtain wall material in all kinds of commercial and industrial buildings."[13] This observation nails the obvious limitation of glass blocks versus window glass; the former's load-bearing potential is not enough to really justify them structurally, and, most importantly, glass blocks are not transparent in the least. So except for situations that require light without views, such as in a factory, glass blocks have the effect of limiting, rather than enhancing the openness of a structure, which is of course why Chareau and others were forced to puncture their opaque glass exteriors with sheet glass.

The Manhattan Laundry in Washington, D.C. (1936), provides an excellent example of a glass block curtain wall in a commercial context (figure 5.9). Designed by Alexander M. Pringle & Bedford Brown IV, the structure housed an industrial plant devoted to dry-cleaning and a rug washing operation as well as related offices. The facade features a glass brick curtain wall framed by enameled metal panels, the translucent surface of the overlarge glass bricks—they appear to be Owens-Illinois 12-inch square Insulux blocks—allowing a view of the floor slabs and structural beams of the interior. Like Chareau at the Maison de Verre, Brown, who designed the facade, inserted sheet glass casement windows into the glass block curtain in order to provide views; this is the paradox of glass block buildings: they in fact can be rather claustrophobia-inducing. Another issue that impacts the use of glass blocks is their relative inflexibility: permanently fixed and unshaded, they may insulate well but allow too much solar gain. Pringle and Brown also utilized square glass blocks of a smaller size for the interior partition walls, creating a compelling effect of shadowy figures floating on glass screens.

Glass of all kinds combined again in this era to inspire the notion that humanity had entered a new age of glass. Perhaps the best example of

FIGURE 5.9 Alexander M. Pringle, Manhattan Laundry, 1936, picture by S. Eskilson.

this visionary perspective can be found in the Crystal Chapel designed by Bruce Goff in the 1940s. A nondenominational religious space on the campus of the University of Oklahoma, the Crystal Chapel was to be funded by a private donor. It consisted of a 150-foot-tall pink granite tower matched to panes of translucent pink glass forming a diamond-like, faceted pair of wings. The color and additional strength were to be attained by sandwiching fiberglass within two sheets of tempered plate that were to be framed with a stainless steel structure. Seemingly embracing the Scheerbart/Taut vision of crystalline architecture, Goff's chapel uses sheet glass but in such a way as to create an illusion of a hard, crystalline structure. Perhaps as some sort of cosmic commentary on the fate of crystal architecture, the Crystal Chapel was never built because the patron was found to be mentally incompetent.

Some years earlier, Walter Teague had written in 1932 that "if there is any such thing as human progress it is most certainly out of the shadows and into the light—literally as well as figuratively …Today we have the means to enclose ourselves in walls that are only as much walls as we please."[14] In this paean to glazed surfaces, Teague invoked Wright's famous 1928 essay on what the latter considered a "super-material." While Teague and Wright rhapsodized poetically about artistic and human potential, other authors offered a more materialistic viewpoint, with a 1938 *Architectural Forum* article announcing that "The Glass Age Arrives" in a piece sponsored by glass block manufacturer Pittsburgh Corning. Likewise, *Popular Mechanics* promised in 1940 that "You can now live in a glass house and if your pocketbook is fat, furnish it with everything from glass book ends to bedroom suites." In an associated advertisement, LOF promised that "Modern use of glass makes houses roomier, living more convenient, homes more attractive … rentable … salable."[15] Scheerbart had written in 1914, "Colored happiness/Only comes in a glass culture," and, like so many commercially reified utopias, his dream had finally come true.

It is perhaps too easy to overstate the aesthetic impact of structural glass by focusing on some of the handful of structures that truly attained the dreamy, floating effect which it was possible to provide. For example, the circular sheath of glass blocks that surrounds the grand staircase of George Fred Keck's Herbert Bruning house in Wilmette, Illinois, positively dazzles in either day or night, providing light but also privacy and insulation. Likewise, Wright's dramatic installation of Pyrex glass tube fenestration—he had experimented with various types of production glass blocks before settling on his customary unique approach—at the SC Johnson Administration Building (1939) and Research Tower (Racine, Wisconsin 1950) is a wonder to behold (although the Administration Building leaked horribly because of the lack of silicone caulks in the 1930s). The Museum of Modern Art even featured glass blocks in the offices of their new building by Goodwin & Stone, where a curved interior wall shimmered behind the exterior curtain. However, truth be told, the general employment of glass brick during its boom years is more often undistinguished, if not regrettable. *Architectural Forum* recounted in 1940 that "never has a new building product caught on so quickly," with over twenty million having been sold in the preceding five years. However, it had already become apparent that a great deal of those blocks had been sold based on what the magazine termed the blocks' "novelty value." While defending the material's popularity, *Architectural Forum* also admitted that "Glass blocks have been used for book-ends, barfronts, and bathtubs—and, in all too many cases, misused."[16] Clearly, countless builders had gravitated to the material as a novel, trendy infill for voids and partitions in all manner of vernacular architecture. Glass blocks were truly everywhere, but dazzling they were not.

The rapid decline of glass block as a prestigious material was in a large part a function of its popularity and consequent overuse. Versus plate glass sheets, which required specialized skills and materials to install, glass blocks were cheap and had been designed to be mortared together like common brick, and so could be implemented in the most modest, even DIY, project. This situation was lamented in 1947 by Mary Roche, who was writing for a lifestyle section of the *New York Times*. "One of the first building materials to become associated with the general conception of modern architecture was glass block. Unhappily, it soon acquired the less pleasing tag of 'modernistic,' thanks to the antics of designers who slapped it up everywhere with more enthusiasm than common sense."[17] As this quote makes clear, the fact that glass block was conceived of as a part of Art Deco was by this time also working against it. Roche argued that since "this fad has petered out," homeowners could now make use of glass block for certain pragmatic improvements. In barely a dozen plus years glass block had fallen from the height of extravagant glamour—harbinger of the age of glass—to a minor embellishment suitable for modest industrial structures, below-grade windows, garages, and perhaps screening bathroom fixtures, as Roche had recommended, and Le Corbusier implemented in his own apartment at the Immeuble Molitor.

Despite this cultural setback, Pittsburgh Corning and Owens-Illinois continued to produce standard 6 × 6 feet translucent blocks while also marketing new products in the 1950s through to the 1970s. At that time, so-called sculpted glass modules, essentially large 12 × 12 inch hollow glass blocks with incised decorative patterns, entered the market. Available either clear or colored, these were often used as accent pieces in vernacular architecture; they have a funky vibe that is redolent of the era.

Another new "artistic" product was the intaglio block, whereby frits were used to cover part of the face of the block, leaving a stylized glass shape such as an hourglass. While PPG remained committed to the product—the company seemed to be behind a 1977 *New York Times* article titled "Glamorous Glass Bricks Are Booming"—the reality was that "they have been in the fashion doghouse and were badly used for a long time."[18] In many ways the die was cast and just two modest markets—mundane infill and decorative novelty—defined the material and largely still do.

The fate of Vitrolite et al. tracks roughly the same as that of glass blocks. Its popularity and ubiquity in the 1930s fade in the postwar years, where it is grouped with other newly unfashionable Art Deco staples, all of which must have seemed rather kitschy and overstylized when compared to the emerging aesthetic of restraint associated with the Miesian variant of the International Style. A sense of the decline of Carrara glass, for example, can be garnered through a perusal of *Sweet's Catalogue of Building Construction* over the decades. Sweet's eponymous Catalogue, founded in New York in 1906 by Clinton Sweet, soon became one of the most important annual advertising venues for construction material producers. Throughout the interwar years, Carrara glass and its brethren had been prominently featured in advertisements in *Sweet's*. PPG actually continued to promote Carrara as a spandrel material into the 1950s, even as plastic and ceramic materials cut further into the market for structural glass; but by the early 1960s it had disappeared from the catalog and from the profession.

The resilience of the glass block

Anyone surveying the architectural glass field in the late 1970s would walk away convinced that the float glass plate curtain wall reigned supreme while the formerly ubiquitous glass blocks, bricks, and structural panels were consigned to novelty status if not complete oblivion. This analysis would prove partly correct—Vitrolite et al. were never to return—but in fact the glass block was on the verge of reclaiming a piece of the evanescent world dominated by plate glass. Two of the first artistic redeployments of glass blocks came from an architect known widely for his expertise with concrete: Tadao Ando. Working in Osaka, in the late 1970s Ando designed two courtyard houses that make effective use of screening glass walls. One factor that probably enabled Ando to embrace the glass brick was that in Japan the material was not freighted with baggage; there, it had not been overexposed in casual structures, fashionable and then unfashionable, etc. Rather, for Ando the blocks had a distinguished pedigree in "serious" architecture, especially the work of Chareau and Le Corbusier that Ando had informally studied as an autodidact.

Glass block proved to be an effective medium for Ando's developing style that borrowed from both Japanese and Western traditions. Translucent glass block walls were an ideal fit for Ando's Japanese modernism, an architecture that concerns itself with the deep interplay of light and shadow while also reveling in fluid spaces that feature perceptually blurred boundaries. Of course, there is also an obvious analogy with the translucent Shoji screens that decades earlier had had such an immense impact in the West. Furthermore, the lantern-like glow of an illuminated glass block wall fits comfortably into the Shinto spiritualist element of Ando's spaces. In his first deployment of glass blocks in the three-story Ishihara House (1978), Ando used them as the facing of a stepped curtain wall that covers three sides of a narrow interior courtyard that is open to the sky. On either side of the courtyard at the upper level are two evenly spaced bedrooms, and ghostly shadow figures could be seen moving from across the empty space.

The next year, 1979, Ando saw completed his Horiuchi House in Osaka, where he made use of a freestanding wall of glass blocks that clearly resonates with the tradition of the Shoji screen, but here brought outside the space of the building proper. The Horiuchi House is composed according to Ando's familiar tripartite rectangular plan with a courtyard in the center space. While in structures like the Azuma House Ando forcefully blocked out the street with an unfriendly concrete wall, for the Horiuchi House he engages with the urban space by using the glass blocks as a mediating element, their translucence suggestive of a leaky boundary, as sunlight and shadow can traverse the public and private realms. While outside the medical context of an incubator, one gets the same sense of a pristine membrane that separates the spare interior from the dirt and chaos of the urban environment. Inside the home, plate glass has been used on the three courtyard facades in place of the glass blocks of the Ishihara interior, the transparent sheets opening up the space in comparison.

In the contemporary era, the fact that Ando's name could be added to the canonical lineage of the glass block along with Le Corbusier and Chareau has helped to establish a parallel artistic thread for the material, one that seems to be insulated from the otherwise sullied reputation of this staple of basement windows. For this reason a number of notable architects have experimented with glass blocks, albeit often in a bespoke form, as the standard commercial blocks still suffer from the association with their vernacular use. For example, 2013 saw the debut of Hiroshi Nakamura's Optical Glass House (Hiroshima), which employs a screen of 6,000 cast glass bricks to separate a garden courtyard from the bustling city streets. Like Ando, Nakamura made use of the translucency and sound insulating qualities of the blocks to create a sensually blurred boundary between private and public spaces.

In Japan, the Shoji symbolism employed by Ando has been joined by a second traditional metaphor, that of the lantern. Japanese lanterns, or *tōrō*, have a long history as an architectural embellishment, especially for temples. In addition, the emotional power of lanterns can be witnessed through the floating paper *tōrō* released as part of the Buddhist Festival of Obon, a celebration of ancestral ties. The Japanese lantern is a perfect archetype for night architecture that uses illuminated glass blocks or some other type of structural glass. For example, Shin Takamatsu's Kirin Plaza (Osaka, 1987) featured neon illumination hidden behind a grid of opalescent glass (figure 5.10). The four rectangular towers of glass are naturally a milky white, although the illumination system allowed for a colored light show to be programmed on demand. Glowing like *tōrō*, these light towers also call to mind the stylized geometry and glowing glass elements of Art Deco buildings from the 1930s. (To cite one example, see Harry Sternfeld's WCAU tower in Philadelphia from 1930.) The Kirin towers also responded to the glittering spectacle of Osaka's Shinsaibashi-suji street, home to walls of glittering digital billboards. Takamatsu has written about the frenetic nature of this central commercial location and his attempt to engage with it: "the characteristics of the locale as well as an indifferent detachment from that context must be exploited and overwhelmingly intensified in the architecture." Along these lines he produced a powerful hybrid of lanterns, Art Deco, and billboards that all came together to form a remarkable glass monument: Kirin Plaza was demolished in 2009.

Renzo Piano's 2001 Maison Hermès represents an even more conspicuous example of glass block luminous architecture that invokes the symbolism of the lantern (figure 5.11). Situated in Tokyo's fashionable Ginza shopping district, the twelve-story Maison Hermès' curtain walls are faced in over 13,000 oversized (42.8 cm × 42.8 cm × 12 cm) hollow

FIGURE 5.10 Shin Takamatsu, Kirin Plaza, 1987, credit: CC BY-SA 3.0.

glass blocks that were custom made by the Italian specialty firm Seves. While the actual steel glazing bars are hidden behind the edges of these translucent blocks, a painted metallic edge invokes the internal structure in an effect something like that of Mies's famous mullions. What makes the glass block wall of the Maison Hermès unique is really its sheer size: substantial technological advances in the steel framing system allowed these "structural" blocks to reach a height of 50 meters and also meet

FIGURE 5.11 Renzo Piano, Maison Hermès, 2001.

earthquake codes: of course, no glass block can actually sustain the dead load of such a height. In a compelling twist, Piano sublimated the work of the shop window into his glass block facade, as a small number of the blocks act as vitrines, displaying shoes, scarfs, and the like to passersby.

Miles away from Ginza in both distance as well as sentiment—yet invoking the Japanese memorial language of the floating lantern—stands another glittering glass block tower, Madrid's 11 March Memorial (2007, figure 5.12). There, the 15,000 glass blocks are curved outward on one short end and inward on the other so that they can be nestled one into another and form a haunting glass cylinder: a "shimmer of hope" reaching 11 meters above the ground. Designed by a collaborative group led by Esaú Acosta, the memorial tower—dedicated to the almost 200 people killed by terrorist bombs in March 2004—is designed to funnel light down into an underground room. As was the case with the Maison Hermès, new structural technologies have quietly allowed for the building of tall glass structures that denizens of an earlier era could only visit in their dreams. In the case of the 11 March Memorial the technical advance in play is the cyano-acrylate adhesives that were perfected in the 1990s. Cured under ultraviolet light, this liquid mortar is so thin (3 mm) and transparent that it is invisible; with only the most minimal steel fittings, the memorial at the Atocha railroad station embodies the potential of glass as a symbol of a hopeful spirit.

FIGURE 5.12 FAM, Atocha Station Memorial, 2007.

Structural glass facades

Keeping in mind the slippery nature of the term "structural" when it comes to architectural glass, the last few decades of the twentieth century witnessed the rise of a new iteration of the term, this time referring to ever-larger curtain wall enclosures. The architectural narrative here shifts from designers to engineers, as a number of new glazing strategies are devised to meet the goal of the all-glass building. The structural strength of glass itself changes only incrementally up until the twenty-first century. In terms of size, tempered float glass becomes widely available in standard thicknesses—for commercial use generally 6–12 millimeters but for certain projects reaching as high as 32 millimeters—and sheet sizes. The ribbon width of most float glass lines increased gradually from 8 to about 10 feet today, while the length of the sheet is determined mainly by the availability of handling equipment. It is important in this regard to remember that glass is heavy—a 12 millimeters thick large sheet weighs around 1,000 pounds—and unwieldy as a construction material. Another limit with respect to plate glass size is the tempering ovens, which generally handle smaller sizes than the float line; also, laminates, coatings, and insulated glazing units all place restrictions on the maximum size pane. Today, tempered, laminated glass is widely available in sheets that measure 120 × 180 inches, while specialty firms have produced dramatically larger sizes.

A number of ancillary technological developments have also facilitated the structural glass industry. As noted above, new adhesives that allow for effective glass-to-glass bonds played a key role. Glasbau Hahn was one of the pioneering companies in this regard, working with experimental cements as early as the 1930s, and later proffering silicon and cyanoacrylate. Hahn was also a major contributor starting in the 1950s to the most truly structural utilization of glass, the glass fin. Glass fins consist of a bonded sandwich of two or three sheets of float glass that are placed perpendicular to a glass curtain wall along the vertical joints. Acting somewhat like mullions, glass fins provide lateral stability that resists bending from the wind load without introducing intrusive, opaque structural materials such as steel. Starting in the 1960s, Hahn also devised what was the final piece in the puzzle of frameless glass walls: suspended glazing. A literal implementation of the curtain analogy, suspended glazing refers to structures wherein the glass sheets are hung from fixtures at the top of the facade. Because this system prevented the glass sheets from collapsing under their own weight, it allowed for dramatic new facades that appeared dematerialized in comparison to the evident structure in a conventional curtain wall.

One of the earliest suspended glass walls can be found in Ipswich, England, where Norman Foster oversaw the Willis Faber & Dumas Building that was completed in 1975 (figure 5.13). This curved structure features a suspended wall of almost 40 feet, consisting of six sheets hanging vertically with interstitial glass fins to provide stability. Foster had grown up in Manchester, and that city's gleaming Daily Express Building (1939) with its facade of glass and black Vitrolite had an evident impact on the Willis Building's design. While basically frameless, the Willis Building also featured "patch plates," rectangles of stainless steel that bolted the glass sheets one to another. In subsequent years, these fixtures have been superseded by less visible attachments, mainly point-fixed glass spider fittings.

The question arises, what does this new iteration of the glass wall mean; how does it signify? Decades and decades after Scheerbart, it would be hard to imagine that a structural glass facade was dallying in expressionist poetics. Similarly, this era seemed separated from the canards of classic functionalism: clarity, honesty, and principled purity. For Foster and his early partner Richard Rogers, the answer is usually sought in the

FIGURE 5.13 Norman Foster, Willis Faber & Dumas 1975.

architectural trend known as British high-tech. Not really a movement per se, high-tech suggested a devotion to and faith in technological progress as a unifying human accomplishment. The term "high-tech" was quite fashionable both in and outside of architectural circles in the era, signifying the cutting edge of culture. Of course, one can see something paradoxical in employing this architectural language for a firm as bland as Willis, an insurance (and reinsurance) company with roots in the nineteenth century: conceptually it seems something of a reach.

In a parallel to the situation in the 1930s, when glass companies marketed ready-made Vitrolite storefronts, starting in the 1970s the major glass manufacturers quickly devised new systematized products that allowed for the ubiquitous deployment of structural glass facades. Corporate atria, hospitals, museums, schools, malls, airports: nowadays, structural glass facades may be literally transparent but they are also largely invisible in the public's imagination; it required a glass enclosure that is exceedingly captivating to grab the attention of the average urban viewer. Toyo Ito's Sendai Mediatheque (2000, figure 5.14) is one of the few structures that has effectively met this high bar. The emerging digital age provided a cultural context for the Mediatheque—a combination library, digital media access point, gallery, and theater—that Ito understood and was able to express through architecture. The south facade features a structural glass wall that is double glazed with a substantial three-foot air gap in between the two panes. The building's fluid interior spaces and dramatic woven vertical tubes are completely exposed at night through this facade; Ryue Nishizawa has dramatically described his reaction to the resulting transparency: "It was almost as if an x-ray photo was

FIGURE 5.14 Toyo Ito, Sendai Mediatheque, 2000.

instantaneously exposing every part of a darkened interior to view—the transparency was that shocking... This was the elevation of a substantial, powerful, and intense building." While embodying the digital age, Ito's Mediatheque also rests on elements of Japanese tradition. The sense of blurred boundaries and the way that at night it lights up like a lantern both recall deeply ingrained threads from his homeland.

Because of the Mediatheque's double walled glass facade and the way the outer pane is not nestled neatly into the frame of the roof, the building gives off a sense of how dynamic flows of information are percolating inside and through the walls and tubular steels webbed structures. While transparent, the double wall, which is supported by glass fins, creates visual complexity as ghostly shimmering reflections and refractions dance before the viewer's eyes. At least since 1984, when the Canadian author William Gibson published the visionary science-fiction text called *Neuromancer*, there have been attempts to envision cyberspace, or, as Gibson famously annointed it, the matrix. Ito's Mediatheque for the first time created an astonishing space that lets the visitor feel on a visceral level an almost spiritual flow of information crisscrossing the universe. As Roland Barthes wrote in another context but still capturing the essence of the digital stream, "writing ceaselessly posits meaning but always in order to evaporate it." In Ito's phantasmagoria, the building is slippery and discursive; one can grasp it for a moment but then the view evaporates and is renewed. Historically, such a strong conceptual match between a building's design and its purpose is a rare treat indeed.

The same year that the Mediatheque opened in Sendai, the digital behemoth Apple started opening retail stores across the globe that also represent a powerful contemporary utilization of the "high-tech" aesthetic: although, of course, no one would apply such an obsolete term today. Working with architects Bohlin Cywinski Jackson, glass engineers Eckersley O'Callaghan, and specialty glass producer sedak GmbH & Co, Apple sought to create high-performing retail outlets that would further enhance the brand's reputation for top shelf design. Of course, the focus on architectural glass forms a natural match with the company's familiar touchscreens and love of smooth, polished surfaces, and as Ito had shown, glass has perhaps found its greatest architectural role as a harbinger of advanced digital culture. Of the 300-plus stores Apple has opened since 2001, the branch located on Fifth Avenue in New York City (2006, figure 5.15) has garnered the most praise and set the stage for many subsequent emporia.

FIGURE 5.15 Bohlin Cywinski Jackson, Apple Cube, 2006.

The Fifth Avenue store itself is below grade: all that is visible at street level is a glass cube vestibule that leads to an interior stairwell. Measuring 10 meters in each dimension, the cube consisted of 106 panels stitched together with over 250 steel fittings. Many of these attachments were laminated into the glass so that they were nearly invisible. In an extension of glass fin technology, the cube also featured laminated glass beams and columns: Truly structural, in the cube glass actually carried both live and dead loads.

The Fifth Avenue store cube also featured an example of what has become one of the hallmarks of the retailer's stores, the structural glass staircase. Eckersley O'Callaghan had overseen the first glass stair at the Soho store that opened in 2002. A conventional design in that the glass sides stretched down to the floor in a way that defeats the desired effect of weightlessness, it was replaced in 2011. The redesigned structural glass stringers float in the air; they were made of a single piece of laminated glass each 13 meters long and weighing over two tons. Eckersley O'Callaghan also created the first spiral version of the staircase for the Apple store in Osaka (2005), utilizing a solid structural glass balustrade and stainless steel handrail and hardware. Another advanced technology behind these designs is chemical tempering, which allows for the toughening of glass that will not fit into a conventional oven. Over the years, the engineers have worked assiduously to decrease the amount of steel hardware as they work toward the goal of a pristine glass structure.

Accolades aside, within just a handful of years the structural glass cube at the Fifth Avenue store had become technologically obsolete and Jobs insisted that it be redone. The same team of engineers and architects reunited, and, with the addition of the facade company seele (sedak's parent company), endeavored to create the cube Mark II (2011). The new cube, although bigger than the first, saw a tremendous decrease in the amount of glass panels and hardware: from 106 to 15 sheets of glass and from 250 to only 40 fittings. A major change was the size of the glass panels; sedak was able to supply tempered, laminated sheets that measured an astonishing 18 × 3.6 meters. Of the hardware that remained, even more of it was embedded out of sight into the glass structural pieces. Today, even the Mark II has been visually superseded by a new, even more minimalist design, in this case the so-called Zorlu Lantern in Istanbul. Designed by Foster + Partners (a later iteration of the firm that started it all with Willis Faber & Dumas in 1975), the Zorlu Apple store features a clerestory roof that is made up of just four huge glass panels (each 10 × 3 meters) bonded together with silicone adhesive minus the steel fittings. These four walls are mounted by a carbon fiber reinforced plastic roof that imitates the brushed metal sheen of an iPhone.

Another challenge that has faced glass producers in the last two decades has been the rise of curvilinear exterior forms in building. Beginning in the late 1990s, the digital turn in architectural design catalyzed a taste for unique flowing shapes. Whether inspired by the Deleuzian-based fold theory promoted by Peter Eisenman, or simply a matter of exploring the stylistic potential of new parametric modeling software, this trend has resulted in an increased demand for structural panes that are curved or bent in a way that defies the planar history of glass. The 2006 renovation of the Gare de Strasbourg featured one such dramatic facade treatment, as over 6,000 square meters of laminated safety glass were cold bent in order to create a wave of glass that appears to rush outward from the original nineteenth-century edifice (figure 5.16). The Strasbourg station represents a striking architectural fusion of old and new structures, while also renewing the long-held dream of a functionalist winter garden, a hub of transportation that echoes with Joseph Paxton's Great Victorian Way.

The sea of glass that has been built up since the 1970s on the exteriors of buildings has at times been matched inside by glazed walls. No firm has used interior glass walls more eloquently than SANAA, the partnership

FIGURE 5.16 Jean-Marie Duthilleul, The Gare de Strasbourg, 2006

formed in 1995 by two former employees of Toyo Ito, Kazuyo Sejima and Ryue Nishizawa. Perhaps their most stunning, if understated interior—a quiet, contemplative space that contrasts with the frenetic energy of the Mediatheque or an Apple Store—was the one SANAA designed for the Toledo Museum of Art that opened in 2006 (figure 5.17). A pavilion that is separated from the main museum, the building houses its extensive collection of glass objects. (It should be noted that the city of Toledo, which calls itself "the glass capital of the world," has a strong history in the manufacture of industrial glass having served as the headquarters of Libbey-Owens-Ford from 1930 until it was absorbed by Pilkington in 1986. In 2006, the year that the glass annex opened, Pilkington was itself purchased by Nippon Sheet Glass of Japan.) SANAA's glass pavilion is a one-story structure wherein the galleries are formed by sinuously curving glass walls. The walls are nestled into grooves in the floors and ceilings so as to create a sense of stability and permanence. Because glass can transmit sound and the different areas of the annex have varying climate control needs, SANAA created interstitial spaces between the galleries that insulate while also adding a sense of mystery for the viewer contemplating these inaccessible backstage spaces. Because of the floor to ceiling glass walls, the galleries at the glass pavilion feel like a giant glass vitrine, the visitor wrapped in a cocoon of glass like an infant in an incubator.

FIGURE 5.17 SANAA Kazuyo Sejima and Ryue Nishizawa, The Toledo Museum of Art Glass Pavilion, Toledo Ohio, 2006. Photo credit Iwan Baan.

The walls of the Toledo glass annex consist of a specialty type of float glass that Pilkington sells under the trade name Optiwhite. First produced in 1984, Pilkington's Optiwhite is one of a class of low-iron sheet glasses that have exceptional light transmittance and remain almost completely colorless in most conditions. The product was an obvious choice to give the sense of unadulterated visual purity that SANAA sought for the Toledo glass pavilion. On another note, as a corollary to its admirable transparency, Optiwhite according to Pilkington also has "high solar heat transmittance," a feature of glass in architecture that has been bedeviling its practitioners since Victorian times. The next chapter takes up the ongoing issue of glass, sunlight, and sustainability.

6 SHADE

As early as 1851, when the Crystal Palace established glass as an industrial building material, architects recognized that sunlight could be a curse as well as a blessing. Starkly put, glass skins are an environmentalist's nightmare. The gradual awareness during the modern era of the thermal inefficiency of glass has led to multivalent attempts to counter its high emissivity and poor insulating characteristics. A multitude of shading strategies have been employed to reduce or completely block sunlight, ranging from conventional curtains to the total elimination of windows in some structures. Le Corbusier, of course, worked throughout his career to partially block daylight, and his endeavors to develop the brise-soleil have led in recent decades to stunning new screens such as the sheath on Jean Nouvel's Doha Tower (2011), which has played a highly visible role in redefining the brise-soleil as a signifier of glamour and sizzle.

Simultaneously, in South Asia, Geoffrey Bawa and others have synthesized modernist and regional traditions in response to the climate and abundant sunshine, initiating the trend known as "tropical modernism." Beginning in the 1960s yet another technological revolution began in the glass industry, initiating the era of composite multi-skins, nano-coatings, and smart glazing. Culturally, the rise of the sustainability movement in architecture has changed the way many architects view glass. At the same time that glass has reached an apotheosis of sorts as a symbol of glittering wealth and technological prowess via shimmering skyscrapers and worldwide Apple stores, critics have lashed out at it as a shallow, even unethical, celebration of conspicuous consumption.

In hindsight, there should have been a greater sense of foreboding regarding the climactic complications of glass architecture. Despite the fact that they were built in mild, temperate regions, nineteenth-century glass structures were known colloquially as "hot houses." As related in Chapter 1, this was the whole point of the endeavor, to create an artificial hot and humid climate in which to raise tropical plants. Joseph Paxton's Great Conservatory at Chatsworth (1840), for example, was nicknamed the Great Stove for a reason. This was the glory of these glass structures: their transparency welcomed both visible light and infrared solar heat, and then trapped that heat inside the glass sheath. Additionally, glass is a poor insulator, and glass conducts hot and cold temperatures with ease to the interior where they are often not desirable. Warm in winter, yes, but also very, very hot in a summer heat wave.

Paxton's Crystal Palace of 1851 represented the first large-scale attempt to transition this greenhouse-derived architecture into something that was habitable for people as well as plants. Recall, the Crystal Palace was glazed with over 300,000 panes each measuring 49 × 10 inches: the roofs required over seventeen acres of glass. The panes were only one-thirteenth inch thick, a measurement that prevented the glass from blocking more than about 10 percent of the infrared heat. At the same time, a single glass skin provides almost no insulation from outdoor ambient air temperatures that will quickly impact the interior.

With decades of experience at Chatsworth, Paxton was aware of this issue and, as the Great Exhibition was a summer event, he planned multiple strategies to keep the interior temperature at a comfortable level. The first line of defense initiated by Paxton was, paradoxically, to remove glass from the glass building. Many of the ground story walls and some of the vertical elevations had wooden infill panels that created wall space for displays while also blocking the sun. Furthermore, Paxton saw fit to cover almost the entire horizontal sections of the roof with calico fabric, a translucent cotton textile that diffused the visible light while blocking a portion of the solar heat. Importantly, Paxton put these shades on the outside of the Crystal Palace, where the absorbed heat could be washed away by the wind. In contrast, internal curtains would have blocked the visible light but let the heat into the building, and once it is in, it is in. Paxton also engineered a ventilation system that made some use of evaporative cooling. Despite these efforts, a series of heat waves in London during the summer of 1851 led to a number of instances of extreme interior temperatures. The *Times* reported in June,

> On Saturday the oppressive heat proved too great even for the attraction of the Crystal Palace, and since it was opened we have hardly seen so small an attendance there. In vain did ladies appear in the thinnest muslin dresses, and gentlemen walk about with their

hats in their hands. The wind would not blow in such a direction as to secure a thorough draft, and in the desperate effort to find relief from their suffering some clustered around the fountains.[1]

It is clear that the interior temperature of the Crystal Palace repeatedly soared into the 90s Fahrenheit, and in July Paxton ordered the removal of thousands of panes of glass on the east and west elevations in order to allow for cross-ventilation that could clear out some of the overheated air. While these panes were later restored, continual spells of warmer weather through August made the Crystal Palace often uncomfortable for visitors. As the ventilation system proved at best marginally effectual, the only successful strategy for cooling the Crystal Palace involved covering and removing the glass that was its veritable raison d'être: cooling the glass house by making it not a glass house.

At the same time that the Crystal Palace established glass as an architectural material, it also underscored an environmental flaw that was not to be easily overcome. In subsequent decades in the nineteenth century there is a great deal of writing about glass architecture but really very little building; it is arguable that the underlying thermal inefficiency of glass, which might be easy to account for and dismiss in a speculative essay, was continuing to confound practicing architects. For example, a November 1898 article in Lyon's *Revue des Deux Mondes* argued blithely that internal ventilation could overcome any climate issues. Advocating a strategy that anticipated Le Corbusier's famous *mur neutralisant*, the author opined that "Double glass walls in a house would admit of the circulation between them of cold or warm air, thus regulating the temperature." After the turn of the century, Paul Scheerbart also speculated about double glazing and effective ventilation systems, but the essential thermal problem created by building with glass in an era before industrial air-conditioning was simply unsolvable with the thin, transparent panes available at the time. Jump ahead as far as Walter Gropius's Dessau Bauhaus building of 1926 and the story is largely the same as it was in 1851. As Sheldon Cheney recounted,

> Now I have heard it whispered that this Glass Box, though grown out of a philosophy of use, though held up as the type example of a new architecture developed from a strict logic of structure, fails a little of its practical purpose. It is said that an all-glass building traps an intolerable amount of heat in the summer.[2]

Windowless stores

Cheney was writing in 1930, on the cusp of a decade that saw new opportunities in glass architecture while also witnessing instances where architects rejected glass altogether for practical reasons other than solar gain, as was the case with Chicago's 1933–34 world's fair, the Century of Progress Exhibition. After two successful seasons, Chicago's Century of Progress International Exposition closed in October 1934. Within one year no major exposition structure was left standing; however, one aspect of the fair's exhibition buildings—their elimination of all windows— would become a central tenet of the subsequent design of retail spaces that led to a fundamental reorganizing of one of the most visible architectural spaces of the twentieth century, the department store.

Three weeks after the fair ended, leading mass-market retailer Sears, Roebuck and Company opened a new store in Chicago, known as the Englewood store, establishing the fair's place in the history of commercial architecture. The *Chicago Daily News* opined that the Englewood store proved that the Century of Progress exposition was as architecturally significant as the vaunted Columbian Exposition of 1893: "The new plans [for Sears] show plainly the influence of A Century of Progress and indicate that the big exposition may exert an effect comparable to that of the Columbian Exposition of 1893, which set styles in American architecture for a generation." While somewhat under the radar, the revolutionary windowless design of Sears' stores of the 1930s was first conceived at the Century of Progress.[3]

Early in the exposition's planning, the exhibition's architectural commission had decided to eliminate natural light from the interiors of the buildings. Toward this end, almost all the major fair buildings— the Hall of Science, Travel and Transport, the Electrical Group, and the General Exhibits Group—were built with few or no windows. Director of Works Daniel Burnham (son of the organizer of the 1893 exhibition) explained this decision in 1932: "Practical considerations dictated this windowless feature. Everyone familiar with exhibition buildings knows that sunlight for day-time illumination is a variable quantity." Burnham argued that plentiful artificial light was more easily controlled, and that the windowless design opened up more flexible wall space for exhibits. While in 1851 Paxton had out of necessity relied on natural light at the Crystal Palace, he had also recognized that glass can conflict with good display practices and so had placed wooden walls on much of the ground floor. At the Century of Progress, the expense of glass was also taken into account, as the frugal years of the Great Depression mandated inexpensive skins made of Masonite and asbestos board.

The major buildings at the Century of Progress were designed by the commissioners and featured a range of general exhibits, but many large corporations also sponsored branded structures and hired their own architects to build them. The Sears building was designed by George C. Nimmons, who created a windowless design highlighted by a moderne rectilinear tower, a variation on both the fair's style and Sears's trademark architecture (figure 6.1). A source of astonishment to visitors, the Sears store highlighted the company's vast distribution network through a huge diorama. As discussed in Chapter 1, the history of department store glass architecture had begun in France in the nineteenth century. Between 1867 and 1876, a group of architects, including Louis August Boileau and his son Louis Charles Boileau had built and enlarged the opulent Bon Marche store in Paris, the first department store building. The architects of Bon Marche had solved the problem of illuminating the store's interior mainly by utilizing natural light. While employing gas and electrical illumination, the store relied heavily on its large windows complemented by a series of glazed courtyards to light the merchandise.

FIGURE 6.1 George Nimmons, Sears Pavilion, A Century of Progress, 1933.

When Nimmons finished work on his first post-fair store in Chicago in 1934, the editors of *The Architect and Engineer* immediately recognized the influence of the Century of Progress exposition.

> Sears had already had some experience with a windowless building, for its building at the Century of Progress exposition in Chicago had no windows. The Sears display department, in working in this World's Fair structure, had soon found that the absence of windows greatly simplified the task of injecting power and drama into the displays ... [Les] Janes and his display department felt that they had learned something of great importance from their work at the World's Fair.

Nimmons had been planning the Sears store in the Englewood neighborhood of Chicago, Sears's headquarters city, for several years. The store was originally intended to be built with many windows; however, under the orders of Sears's National Director of Design and Store Arrangement Les Janes, Nimmons abruptly revised the construction plans and eliminated all of the windows in the building (figure 6.2).

FIGURE 6.2 George Nimmons, Sears Englewood Store, 1934, credit: Chicago Architectural Photographing Company, Chicago—Photographic Images of Change, University of Illinois at Chicago. Library. Special collections department.

Newspapers reporting on the store's opening ceremonies in November 1934 announced that "the new store is built in the modernistic windowless architectural style introduced at the World's Fair." While the editors of *Architectural Forum* added, "Sears' executives and Architects Nimmons, Carr, and Wright may well have started a train of development that will eventually lead to the complete elimination of the window in certain types of commercial buildings." The key issue for Nimmons was not so much the problem of solar heating, as the Englewood store was one of the first to see fully implemented air-conditioning. However, Nimmons argued that outside air could "interfere" with the ventilation systems and, in fact, the machinery may have struggled against the radiant heat of an abundantly glazed structure. Nimmon's main goal was to strictly control the interior retail environment. Other than light shafts that provided daylight in order for customers to evaluate fabrics, window openings and sunlight produced glare and simply got in the way of Sears' display experts. The store gained about 15 percent more display space from the elimination of windows, prevented damage to merchandise from ultraviolet light, and also prevented the influx of both urban grime and street noise.

The Englewood store was not a lone experiment at Sears in the 1930s as the company built five more windowless stores over the next few years. This series of stores, along with several more completed in the early 1940s, popularized the windowless designs across major urban areas. During the 1940s, prominent industrial designer Raymond Loewy won a commission from industry giant Federated Stores to build a new department store. This store, Foley's (Houston), featured the familiar blank facade pioneered by Nimmons. In 1947, Hecht Company opened a large windowless store in Silver Spring, Maryland, while 1948 saw May Company's windowless expansion in Los Angeles by Albert C. Martin and Associates. Other windowless stores included Millron's in Westchester, California (1949, Gruen and Krummeck), and the Burdine's department store in Fort Lauderdale, Florida (1947, Abbott, Merkt, and Company).

Since 1950, the windowless style established at Sears has become the norm in retail architecture. Take even an extreme example of exterior glazing such as the 2004 Dior store on Ometesando Avenue in Tokyo and you will find an interior isolated from the glass (figure 6.3). Designed by Kazuyo Sejima and Ryue Nishizawa who together form SANAA (an acronym for Sejima and Nishizawa and Associates), Dior

FIGURE 6.3 SANAA, Dior Omotesando, 2004.

Omoteando is a 30-meter-tall five-story boutique that glows like a crystal palace. The double wall skin consists of an outer glass curtain that is given sculptural depth by an inner layer of white acrylic panels. These panels flow and billow like frozen drapery, altering the materiality of the skin in the viewer's eyes. However, inside the store this remarkable glass exterior is virtually ignored, as the display artists sought to create rather conventional staged set pieces featuring the different lines of Dior merchandise. In the eyes of the store's interior designers it would seem that the store's facade may as well be as windowless as a Sears. Sejima herself has noted the paradox.

> I'm not 100 percent happy with the building, but I feel that originally we are so different—Mr. [Bernard] Arnault is a very rich man, and he wants to sell as much Dior as possible. And we are not so interested in that. We divide exterior and interior. The exterior is very beautiful and behind the wall is their intention.[4]

Likewise, contemporary Apple stores that are legendary because of their dramatic glass enclosures such as the 5th Avenue glass box in New York (Bohlin Cywinski Jackson) or Foster + Partners' newest Istanbul iteration, in fact, separate the glazing from the customer's sight lines. Both these stores are essentially below grade, and the dramatic glass enclosures—as is also the case at Dior Omotesando—function more as a billboard than as an integrated source of natural light and views. Ironically, the Dior Omotesando store is as windowless as a Sears in spite of all that glass.

Air-conditioning

Another aspect of the new retail environment that Nimmons designed in 1934 for Sears was the implementation of effective air-conditioning. This technology, without which the widespread adoption of glazed curtain walls never could have occurred, ironically saw its first widespread use in windowless buildings. At the same time that Sears was essentially sidestepping the issue of thermal gain, Le Corbusier was in the middle of his vaunted struggle against it that was complicated as he was working in regions where the magic bullet of modern air-conditioning was not available.

Notably, in 1935 Le Corbusier made his famous first trip to the United States. Organized by the Museum of Modern Art, Le Corbusier's sojourn was an apparent failure insomuch as he received no new commissions, although it undoubtedly helped to burnish his American reputation in the long run. Upon his return to France, Le Corbusier published a memoir of the trip called *Quand les cathédrales é´taient blanches: voyage au pays des timides* ("When the Cathedrals Were White: Journey to the Country of Timid People," published in French in 1937), in which he expressed his general disappointment with American architecture mixed with a few moments of wonder. One major disappointment was his feeling that Americans had failed to embrace the new designs made possible by glass. In a rather poetic passage regarding skyscrapers he opined,

> Americans have established a type of window and they use it remorselessly throughout the USA. I should like to bring remorse to the souls of the architects and say to them: "In your offices, however high they may be, these cottage windows are annoying. They lead you up a blind alley: the space that you have gained by height—a treasure—is not being used, you do not seize it. You have missed out! In your eyries you seem to be in cellars!"

While Le Corbusier did not visit Chicago and Nimmons' new Sears store in 1935, Le Corbusier's admiration for Radio City at Rockefeller Center was prompted by the complex's similar interior environment. "No windows anywhere ... Silent walls. 'Conditioned' air throughout, pure, clean, at a constant temperature." In his travel memoir, Le Corbusier took pains to find a place for a chapter about his own reputed invention of air-conditioning, one which he portrayed as an "idea of genius" that had been subverted by lesser bureaucratic souls. Le Corbusier's system had two parts, *la respiration exacte* and *le mur neutralisant*. *Respiration exacte* was based on the work of Gustave Lyon, and it was essentially a ventilation system that could move filtered air throughout a building. *Le mur neutralisant*, which Le Corbusier claimed to have invented himself—although the idea had appeared in print decades previously—referred to a double-glazed system whereby heated or cooled air would circulate in the gap in such a way that the architect believed could maintain a year-round temperature of 18°C throughout the structure.

As he recounted in *When the Cathedrals Were White*, Le Corbusier had first proposed the dual system for the Centrosoyus Palace in Moscow, where it was rejected, after which he had planned to install it in the Salvation Army's City of Refuge (Paris, 1933). At the City of Refuge, Le Corbusier oversaw the first installation of a fully glazed curtain wall in Paris, which he intended to be fully sealed and double-glazed so as to allow for the functioning of the *mur neutralisant*. The curtain wall fronted a dormitory and faced south, so that the reduction of solar gain was paramount (figure 6.4). Unfortunately, budget limitations led to the elimination of both the *mur neutralisant* and the double glazing, so that the City of Refuge residents inhabited un-air-conditioned rooms facing the sun with only an un-tinted pane of drawn sheet glass as a barrier: a barrier that could not be opened for ventilation. Despite the fact that temperatures inside the building leapt into the 30s Celsius, Le Corbusier considered the building's "conditioned air" a success. With notable understatement he recorded, "Difficulties did not develop except at the height of the summer, during heat waves." Despite Le Corbusier's persistent campaign to leave the building as it was, the city of Paris ordered that the hermetic seal of the south facade be broken, and forty operable windows—Le Corbusier called it "the disemboweling of our building"—were installed in 1935. In his memoir, Le Corbusier related this experience back to his trip to the United States, where he noted that most new air-conditioned buildings had signs instructing the

FIGURE 6.4 Le Corbusier, City of refuge, South Façade, 1933, VIEW pictures (UK), credit: © F.L.C./ADAGP, Paris/Artists Rights Society (ARS), New York [2018].

occupants to keep the windows closed so as not to interfere with the air-conditioning, as if this somehow explained why he had enclosed the City of Refuge residents in a hothouse.

While Le Corbusier would eventually abandon the *mur neutralisant* for other measures, his interest in creating a gap between the glass layers in a curtain wall and integrating it with the ventilation system proved prescient. In recent decades, dual layer glass facades have been utilized to solve a range of practical problems. The simplest version of this technology is the buffer facade, in which an air gap of 1–4 feet is left between two glass layers, somewhat shielding the interior air of the building from the radiant heat or cold of the outer skin. Buffer facades also serve effectively as sound insulation. The Hooker Building, completed in 1980 by Cannon Design and later known as the Occidental Chemical building, features a meter-wide gap between an outer tinted and insulated sheath and an inner wall of clear glass. An independent ventilation system draws in outside air at the base of the facade and then exhausts warmer air out of the top of the building to aid in cooling. Another variation on the ventilated dual facade integrates the air-handling of the interstitial space with the internal air-conditioning. In these so-called extract-air systems, the facade gap becomes a major exhaust channel for the interior ventilation.

Both of these buffer strategies result in sealed buildings without any operable windows, a situation which has been widely derided in recent years as the cause of "sick building syndrome," an engineering problem that became something of a cultural meme in the 1980s as people became concerned about the largely recirculated air in many office towers. Combined with alarmist stories about the invisible emissions from fire-retardant chemicals, paint, plastic, and the like, sealed buildings came to be viewed as the culprit for a whole host of nonspecific chronic complaints from office workers. Reminiscent of the fresh-air "cure" for tuberculosis of the nineteenth century, critics argued that sealed buildings were a threat to public health. In response to this criticism, in the late 1980s architects devised the twin-face facade, which essentially reverses the roles of the two glass curtains. Now the inner skin is tinted and insulated, while a single-layer outer skin completes the facade. The advantage to a twin-face facade for a skyscraper is that outside air can be drawn into the gap and the inner skin has operable windows that allow the inhabitants to naturally ventilate the interior. Because of the high winds at skyscraper elevations, a single-facade system with operable windows could at times introduce a gale into the interior. There is an environmental trade-off here as allowing people to open up windows at will in a large building inevitably leads to higher heating and cooling costs versus a sealed structure.

While Le Corbusier offered up exotic air-handling systems, it was two unprepossessing glass technologies that were developing in the 1930s—double glazing and tinting—that would enable architects to better handle thermal gain for decades to come. The otherwise unknown American engineer C. D. Haven is commonly cited as the "inventor" of double-glazed windows, although of course the basic idea of layering sheets of glass in order to enhance a window's insulating qualities had been informally employed for centuries. Libbey-Owens-Ford first adopted Haven's idea of creating a window with one frame but two panes separated by a sealed air space: the company christened the new product Thermopane. Thermopane windows—LOF's trade name eventually came to be used generically to refer to any brand of "insulated glazing units" (IGUs) as they are called today—entered the market in the late 1940s. The underlying idea is the same as for dual facade systems in that double-glazed windows create an air gap, generally of about a half inch, that helps prevent the two layers of glass from radiating heat and cold at a time when the interior and exterior temperatures diverge or the outer skin is heated up by sunlight. Newer versions of IGUs substitute argon or krypton gas for air in the sealed chamber, as these heavier gases have lower thermal conductivities because their molecules move more slowly.

The other technology that made the glass curtain wall a reasonable cladding solution in the postwar era was tinting. Again, glass makers had experimented with adding alloying materials to glass in order to change its light transmissibility for many years, but the process was not successfully industrialized and marketed until the 1940s. Tinting can consist of a general darkening of the glass or a selective blocking of parts of the spectrum so as to give the glass a particular color. When LOF introduced tinted glass in the 1940s their product was initially blue-green, a color choice that allows for high rates of visible light transmission. Tinted windows reduce glare and are heat-absorbing while also blocking a large amount of visible light. However, there are also a number of drawbacks to conventional tinted glass. First, in order to make the glass darker it needs to be thicker, and this added weight meets additional cost and more difficult handing of large sheets. Second, because it is heat-absorbing, tinted glass heats up in the sun and then radiates that heat into the interior of the building. Finally, less solar gain means less visible light, and this impacts the view as not everyone wants to see the world through dark glass. In this regard tinting can also be deceptive, as tints that block a lot of the visible spectrum do not in practice block much more of the infrared light that heats up an interior. Lastly, the invention of tinting added a new dimension to the calculation of thermal movement and has resulted in a great deal of breakage and water infiltration.

Just as the first large clear glass curtain wall on Willis Polk's Hallidie Building (1918) was introduced by a relatively unknown architect in a smaller city, the first integrated employment of double-glazed tinted windows was advanced by the successful, if rather uncelebrated, architect Pietro Belluschi of Portland, Oregon (figure 6.5). In 1948 Belluschi, working outside of his traditional style, oversaw the completion of the twelve-story Equitable Building, a sealed and air-conditioned concoction featuring a facade of blue-green tinted Thermopane windows. Belluschi, who later served as the Dean of the School of Architecture at MIT, is recognized for this achievement in more specialized literature, but his rather modest bank building was quickly overshadowed by the United Nations Secretariat (1952) and Lever House (1952), both of which made use of the same glass products but in taller structures in a high-profile city.

The slow penetration of double-glazed tinted glass is evident in the construction of Mies van der Rohe's two sets of apartment buildings in Chicago from the 1950s as well as his Seagram building. The first pair of residential towers, 860–880 Lake Shore Drive (1951), was constructed with single-pane clear glass windows. In order to grapple with the resulting solar gain and create a modicum of uniformity, Mies employed a system of interior silver curtains to block the light. While successful at reducing glare, once the infrared light has entered the building, the battle against the sun's radiant heat has been lost. The second set of towers, known as the Esplanade Apartments, were completed five years later with double-glazed, gray-tinted windows. Mies also came up against the dearth of color choices in tinting when he designed the Seagram Building (1958), as LOF was unable to provide bronze tinted glass from their line without disrupting production at great cost. Seagram's general contractor eventually located a small foundry that could produce the glass using older technology.

Skidmore, Owing, and Merrill's Lever House exemplifies the problem of thermal contraction and expansion that has plagued many of the first-

FIGURE 6.5 Peter Belluschi, Portland Bank, 1948, Public Domain.

generation tinted-glass skyscrapers. By the 1990s, it was estimated that the entire original glazing, both windows and spandrel panels, had been broken by the sun. In 2001, SOM replaced the entire facade with new glass that made use of subsequent technological breakthroughs. As had been the case for Le Corbusier at the City of Refuge, remediation of early glass facades has been one constant over the past several decades.

Shading strategies

In so much as there is a continuum developing in modern architecture during the mid-century that spans from the total elimination of glass at the Sears' stores to the tinted curtain wall that is fully exposed to the sun, then the partial blocking of the sun through passive shading fits somewhere in the middle. Since humans first populated the earth, relief from the sun has been a matter of comfort and survival. Especially in the arid desert climes of North Africa and Arabia, multiple shading strategies had developed over the centuries. Perhaps the most successful shading element developed in the Arab East was the vertical wooden screen known as a *mashrabiya*. Originally devised in order to cool containers of drinking water with both shade and a constant stream of air, in the fourteenth century Egyptian artisans began a tradition of elaborately carved wood latticework that swept through Cairo and across North Africa. Now used to cool people as well as water, skilled artistry was combined with structural solutions—thermal expansion and contraction could destroy joinery—to create a form of passive cooling that spread from India to Spain. Often used to shade an oriel window and provide privacy as well as cooling, Europe's colonial empires brought knowledge of the *mashrabiya*—called a *moucharbieh* in French—to Europe.

In the more temperate climes of central and northern Europe there was really no need for elaborate shading devices in the built fabric dominated by insulating masonry walls: that is, until the onset of the modern age of glass. Perhaps receiving more credit than is his due for transmitting rather than originating a new architectural form, Le Corbusier is inextricably linked to the development of shading devices in Europe. At the same time that he was experimenting disastrously with air-conditioning, Le Corbusier also mused about another strategy to reduce thermal gain, the deeply set windows, louvers, and baffling collectively called brise-soleil. Le Corbusier admired the flexibility of the *mashrabiya*, and he speculated about both fixed systems and movable irises that could provide greater flexibility. In one of his more artful passages, Reyner Banham noted the irony of the return of shade just as glass walls were first asserting themselves on the skyline.

> As has been said, the invention of the sun shade or *brise-soleil* is an example of the process by which the advantages of the traditional massive wall were argued back one at a time. The transparent glass

membrane, admitting the ineffable joys of sunlight, sufficient to stop rain blowing in and people falling out, could not exclude overdoses of the ineffable.[5]

The most iconic type of fixed brise-soleil devised by Le Corbusier consists of concrete shutters extending from the plane of the facade on both the vertical and horizontal axes. While Le Corbusier outlined the form in 1933 in a speculative plan for an Algerian office building and in his influential book *The Radiant City*, he found his first suitable commission in the Ministry of Education building constructed in Rio de Janeiro between 1936 and 1943 (figure 6.6). The Swiss architect traveled to Brazil in both 1929 and 1936, and the latter sojourn had a major impact on a group of Brazilian architects including Lúcio Costa, Oscar Niemeyer, and Alfonso Reidy. The tropical climate in Rio demanded a solution to solar gain if modern glass office buildings were to be built in such a torrid climate; at the Ministry of Education, the northern sun-facing facade combined deep-set windows with three movable louvers set on the horizontal within each bay. The brise-soleil was only utilized

FIGURE 6.6 Oscar Niemeyer et al., Ministry of Education, 1943, Public Domain.

on the one side as the east and west walls are windowless and the shaded southern facade features a glass curtain wall.

In the 1940s, Brazil experienced a building boom that represents one of the greatest moments in the history of tropical modernism. The synergy created by experimenting with forms from both Brazilian vernacular and colonial era architecture together with the impetus provided by Le Corbusier and his appropriation of the *mashrabiya* led to a number of exciting new buildings. For example, Costa's Guinle Park housing blocks known as Nova Cintro and Bristol both feature a mélange of screens made of both concrete and ceramic materials (figure 6.7). The screens have a sculptural depth in order to provide greater protection from the sun. Costa also made use of organic screens, as the brise-soleil was also intended to serve as the support for a garden of Brazilian Trumpet creepers and the like that would provide further shade. Costa's employment of alternating patterns—some with curving decorative flourishes and some made up of modernist grids—on these facades

FIGURE 6.7 Lucio Costa, Parque Guinle, 1954, Public Domain.

created a syncopated energy that contrasts with the relative monotony of many of Le Corbusier's own exterior elevations.

As the International Style spread across the tropics in the 1940s and 1950s, regional architects learned to make climactically sound choices that at times contradicted the authoritarian principles of high modernism. Because he faced the challenge of the sun on a day-to-day working basis, Sri Lankan architect Geoffrey Bawa, for example, learned how to practice sustainable architecture long before the term came into fashion in the West. In his 1959 A.S.H. de Silva House, Bawa rejected the flat roof line of Le Corbusier in favor of a pitched roof that provided better sun protection and drainage. Unfortunately, as the International Style proliferated in the tropics, not enough architects and builders made these types of allowances for the climate. Instead, quite the opposite occurred as thousands of office towers and apartment blocks rose up that featured unshaded glass curtain walls in sealed buildings matched with massive air-conditioning systems. Many of these glass towers did not even make simple allowances for the transit of the sun. Part of the problem arose from the increasing prominence of large global corporations and hotel chains that were headquartered in more temperate regions and brought with them expectations about architecture and artificial climate—remember Le Corbusier's 18°C dictum—that were not responsive to the thermal reality.

The age of glass also resulted in thermal disasters in more temperate climates. Aside from Le Corbusier's City of Refuge, another pair of the most notorious structures was created by legendary architects Frank Lloyd Wright and Louis Khan. Wright's SC Johnson Administration Building (1936) in Racine, Wisconsin, made use of Pyrex tubes as a clerestory; inoperable and unshaded, they led to an environmentally unpleasant interior that is perhaps unsurprising given Wright's sometimes whimsical approach. But the windows at Kahn's Alfred Newton Richards Medical Research Laboratory at the University of Pennsylvania (1957–61) were even more thermally calamitous, and the fact that Kahn intended to introduce a new type of functional architecture at the building added an ironic twist. While Kahn did implement some of the earliest insulated glazing units at the Richards Laboratory, the basic lights are made of unshaded quarter-inch polished plate glass. As some of the individual panes measure over 70 square feet, the solar gain and glare was such a major problem that the occupants resorted to covering the windows with sheets of cardboard out of sheer desperation. A 2015 renovation has finally remediated this situation, as the glass was replaced with Viracon's VLE-70 (70 referring to the percent of visible light transmittance), a laminated low-e glass that allowed the architects to retain the building's original appearance while vastly improving its thermal performance.

In Le Corbusier's own postwar work, the brise-soleil was to become such a standard element that his name has become inextricably attached to it. Typical sentiment was expressed by the British architect Clive Entwhistle in a letter written to Le Corbusier in 1946: "I take this opportunity on behalf of young people here to thanks you for your latest gift to architecture: the brise-soleil, a splendid element." Le Corbusier also employed the screens in his second remediation of the City of Refuge's southern facade after it had been destroyed in the Second World War. There, colorful sun baffles were added in 1952 to finally give the inhabitants some relief from "overdoses of the ineffable."

Le Corbusier was of course not the only European modern architect working to deploy shading devices in the 1930s. Paul Nelson and Oscar Nitzchke, for example, worked together in 1934 to design a surgery pavilion in Ismailia to serve the Westerners working on the Suez Canal project. Basing his work on the Egyptian practice of hanging textiles outside of buildings, Nelson devised a scheme he called the "para-soleil envelope," essentially a layered buffer zone of adjustable metal louvers set on the horizontal. The space above the louvers is shaded by a projecting concrete roof that maximizes the amount of air kept out of direct sunlight. In acknowledging and acting upon the need to conceive of the facade as a deeply layered transitional space, Nelson should be credited as an innovative forerunner of the climactic interstitial zones created by contemporary twin-face facades.

By the 1960s, as a repetitive series of glass box skyscrapers sprouted up in cities around the world, the technology seemed settled: single-face facades with tinted, double-glazed windows enclosing a sealed structure. In 1963, Victor Olgyay published the first edition of his ungainly titled if prescient text *Design with Climate Bioclimactic Approach to Architectural Regionalism*. Olgyay was one of the first authors to attempt to comprehensively understand the impact of regional climates on all aspects of building practice while also drawing attention to the fact that too many architects gave little more than passing attention to issues of energy costs and consumption. Before Olgyay's book, few architects were well versed in terms such as "long-wave radiation," "sun path diagrams," or "mean-radiant temperature impact." In the section on solar control it is clear that the technology was lagging at the time; Olgyay made note of the advantages of heat-absorbing glass, but he focused the chapter almost entirely on passive solar control strategies using sun screens.

Olgyay was something of an outlier in the 1960s, but the prevailing lackadaisical attitude toward the expense of artificial climate in buildings with glass skins was something that would be widely reevaluated after the events of 1973. In October of that year the major Arab oil exporting states instituted a series of dramatic price hikes combined with embargoes on deliveries to a number of their major customers including the United States, the United Kingdom, and Japan. The oil embargo was a geopolitical move that was designed to disrupt the global economic system in response to the support that Israel had received during the Yom Kippur War. Led by Saudi Arabia, the embargo lasted six months but its long-term effects resonate through to this day in many sectors of the industrialized economies of Asia and the West.

In terms of the age of glass, the complacency that had characterized the design of the mid-century skyscraper was forever transformed as architects quickly adapted to the new economic and political realities. For example, in January 1974 the Houston-based architectural firm Caudill Rowlett Scott (CRS) published a manifesto of sorts titled *A Bucket of Oil*. Headquartered in a city with a desert climate that was also dominated by the petroleum industry, CRS used the book to taut their "humanistic approach" to energy conservation. "The main thrust of this book is to return to fundamentals as we retreat from affluence and the spendthrift days of energy unlimited." Regarding glass in architecture, the book is filled with oversized drop quotes with ominous messages: "1/4 plate glass allows 80 percent of the solar energy to penetrate" and "there is no single solution to use or stop solar radiation."

What most comes through from the book is a sense of urgency bordering on panic, as the authors imagine a coming age of car-free urban areas devoid of "megastructures" and the need to adjust to simple domestic pleasures in small homes that are collectively heated and cooled. While in hindsight some of these predictions for the future seem unduly influenced by the prevailing sense of crisis, one rubricated concluding statement absolutely stands the test of time "We must innovate to save those buckets of oil." Within a few short years, experimental structures like the aforementioned Hooker Building started to appear. Combining tinted double-glazing with a buffer facade and movable louvers in the interstitial space, the Hooker Building was partly motivated by a public relations nightmare besetting the Occidental Chemical Company that had purchased Hooker Chemical. In a notorious environmental disaster, Hooker's earlier disposal of toxic waste products had led to appallingly dangerous conditions for the residents of a neighborhood called Love Canal that had to be evacuated and shuttered in 1978.

Perhaps the best-known example of evolving solar control devices was the brise-soleil designed in 1981 by Jean Nouvel for the Institut du Monde Arabe in Paris (1987, figure 6.8). A cultural as well as an aesthetic triumph, the IMA's southwest curtain wall features 240 photosensitive screens that adjust automatically to daylight conditions. Acknowledging the roots of the brise-soleil in the *mashrabiya*, Nouvel's design added a frisson of exoticism to the field of thermal control. In reality, the brise-soleil at the IMA was architecturally important more for symbolic reasons than for technical ones. The climate of Paris is quite temperate, and for this reason the metal apertures are placed in the protected space inside of the curtain wall. In a more challenging thermal environment, this design would allow too much heat to radiate through the glass and also be conducted through the heated metal screens.

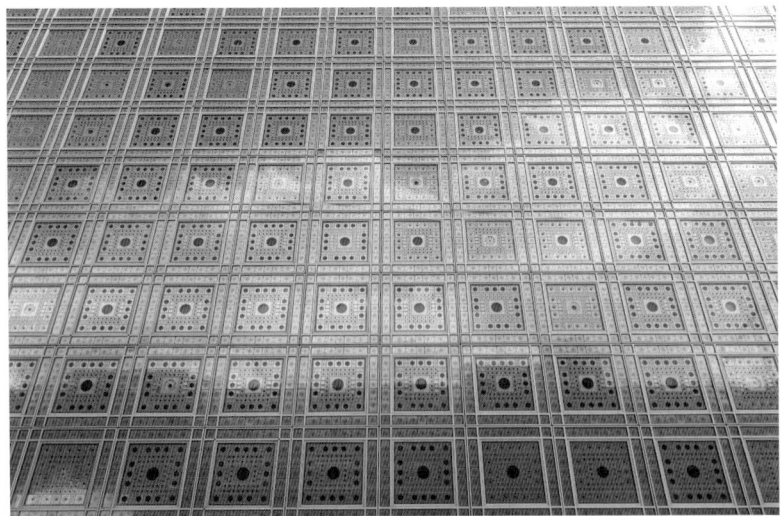

FIGURE 6.8 Jean Nouvel, Institut de le Monde Arabe, 1981.

FIGURE 6.9 Jean Nouvel, Doha Tower, 2012.

Nouvel was offered the opportunity to employ the *mashrabiya* form in a desert environment in 2005, when he won the commission to design the Doha Tower in Qatar (2012, figure 6.9). The reflective glass skin is surmounted by an aluminum *mashrabiya* in traditional geometric patterns. This outer sheath was designed with concern for the solar orientation, as the pattern is adjusted to block 25 percent of the light from the north, but almost 60 percent of the daylight from the more troublesome eastern and western elevations. As opposed to the brise-soleil in Paris, which had more of a cultural than a thermal significance, that of the Doha Tower provides a fine example of how the Gulf States have recently made inroads in terms of greening their commercial architecture.

The brise-soleil has become something of a marker of status in recent architecture, as witnessed by the career of Santiago Calatrava, whose elaborate moving sun screen for the Milwaukee Art Museum (2001) launched the architect into the cosmos of starchitecture. Similarly, in September 2016 the David Adjaye–designed National Museum of African American History opened on the Mall in Washington, D.C., giving renewed visibility to the beauty of the brise-soleil. Adjaye's iron screen recalls the folk art of the American south while also using variable densities in order to properly deflect the daylight from different areas of the building based on its solar orientation.

Green glass buildings

In concert with the development of more sophisticated sun screens and buffer zones, glass itself has gone through continual technical development that vastly improved its thermal performance over first-generation tinted glass. The new science of large area coatings on glass led to a series of new products including Vari-Tran, a reflective layer offered by LOF after 1968. Vari-Tran, short for "variable light transmission," was a metal and silica coating applied to glass through a vacuum process. Its gold or silver reflective sheen is familiar to connoisseurs of 1970s commercial architecture, and was often applied to tinted glass in order to soften glare while reducing solar heating by about 80 percent. Beginning with Vari-Tran, it is in the last decades of the twentieth century that the technology of glass starts to defy simple explanation, as chemical strategies comprised of first pyrolytic and then diode sputtered processes come to the fore, while new equipment includes electron beam evaporators, planar and rotatable cylindrical magnetron cathodes, and large aperture bent glass coaters.

Tinting and reflective coatings both proved effective at reducing solar gain, but they also greatly reduced visible light transmittance, leaving buildings potentially dark and gloomy. The next generation of coatings made use of so-called heat mirror technology, which serves to reflect infrared light while having minimal effect on visible light transmittance. Heat mirror glass is more commonly known as low-emissivity, or low-e glass, a reference to how the coating reflects rather than radiates heat energy. Since low-e does not absorb heat energy like tinted glass, the panes themselves do not heat up and transmit high temperatures. Low-e coatings are able to keep heat either inside or outside of a building depending on the application. While low-e coatings were originally produced in the 1980s as a series of metallic layers applied to a plastic laminate, newer systems have allowed for the coating to be applied to the glass itself. Currently, advances in coatings are continuing to approach the visible light/solar heat ideal, whereby spectrally selective glass can be completely transparent but able to block as much solar heat as was desirable for the regional climate.

Oil price shocks in the 1970s combined with mounting awareness of the massive energy costs of the urban landscape and a greater worldwide attention to environmental issues led in the 1990s to a critical mass of architects engaged with the trend known as sustainable architecture. Probably the most high-profile organization dedicated to the cause of green building is the US Green Building Council, a nongovernmental, nonprofit organization founded in 1993. The USGBC is best known for establishing the LEED ("Leadership in Energy and Environmental Design") rating system that awards different levels of certification to buildings that meet certain sustainability criteria. While LEED standards have been attacked as arbitrary at times, there is no doubt that they created a system, however imperfect, that gave a framework for evaluating and publicizing green architecture. LEED standards in 2016 were updated to their fourth iteration, and glass manufacturers now commonly taut the ability of their products to earn points in the rating system. While high-efficiency glass can have an impact on a variety of LEED criteria and the process is highly technical, the greatest upside is found in the ability to optimize energy performance. Since the establishment of the USGBC, a multitude of sustainable architecture organizations have arisen worldwide, including the UK Green Building Council, the World Green Building Council, and Architecture 2030.

The green building movement has led to a sea change in the priorities of architects and builders, and the last two decades have witnessed a wealth of new buildings that use all of the available technology to defeat solar gain and heat loss through glass walls. While the United States saw the establishment of LEED standards, European nations have led the way in green building. Germany, with its long-standing commitment to *Grünkultur* as a societal ideal, was a natural location for two of the first sustainable towers, Foster + Partners' 1997 Commerzbank and Renzo Piano's Debis Tower (1998). The fifty-three-story Commerzbank was designed to be naturally ventilated as much as possible in Frankfurt's temperate climate, with the central atrium operating like a low-pressure chimney that draws air from the operable windows of the three office wings (figure 6.10). The building was also designed with attention to its solar orientation, and its twin-faced facade has an outer IGU with ventilation slots and an inner single pane with the gap acting partly as a *mur neutralisant*, with warm or cool air flowing through the interstitial space depending on the season. The heating and ventilation system is integrated with both the windows—it will not function if they are opened—and the louvers situated between the glass skins. Furthermore, the winter gardens are surrounded by

FIGURE 6.10 Foster + Partners, Commerzbank, Frankfurt, 1997.

canted glass walls that reduce the veiling reflectance and also serve as passive solar collectors in winter.

The Debis Tower in Berlin also demonstrated the full range of modern sustainable glazing strategies (figure 6.11). On the south, east, and west elevations the high solar gain is mitigated by a twin-faced facade enclosing a 27 inch interstitial gap. The inner skin has occupant-operable windows, while the outer skin consists of automated glass louvers that

FIGURE 6.11 Renzo Piano, Debis Tower, Berlin, 1998.

are opened and closed by the building's control systems depending on the thermal environment. In addition, external brise-soleil panels can be adjusted in order to reduce glare. These aluminum louvers are paired with a ceramic sun screen at lower elevations. The base of the building features a covered street—reminiscent of the nineteenth-century arcades—that is glazed with ceramic fritted lights and structural fins. And the list goes on: together, Piano Workshop reports that hot weather energy consumption should be only half that of a conventionally sealed building.

Importantly, Piano Workshop also noted that Debis "is clad in a very elaborate, maintenance-intensive curtain wall." Notably, Piano tauts that the maintenance catwalks inside the facade also serve as another layer of fixed sun screen. This type of plural layers of sun-defeating instruments brought both expensive initial design challenges and continuing upkeep costs and retrofitting, not to mention that the layered high-tech aesthetic of the building may not be for everyone. The point from a sustainability perspective is simple: glass remains an energy extravagance. The need for architects and engineers to devise performative multilayered systems could be diminished if only people would give up on the dream of glass. The fact is if you build a relatively short twenty-two-story tower like the Debis—not to mention a startlingly high 20-meter atrium curtain wall like that at Kisho Kurakawa's gorgeous National Art Center (Tokyo, 2007)—and cover it in glass, you are choosing to utilize a lot of energy. Like the environmentally conscious private jet traveling globetrotter who rationalizes their lifestyle through the absolution of carbon offsets, the patrons and architects of "sustainable" glass structures seek absolution where there is none. Instead, perhaps just do not use all that glass.

While tall buildings have been known to cast deep shadows in urban areas, the inverse situation, heat and glare, has caught the attention of the public recently. The impact on street life of some glass towers was made manifest through two notorious buildings, London's 20 Fenchurch Street (2014) and Dallas's Museum Tower (2013), which together have undermined the unreflective celebration of glass cladding. In London, Rafael Vinoly's so-called Walkie Talkie building's concave facade concentrated light so intensely that it melted parts of a car parked on the street below the south facade. While an awning has remediated the immediate problem, the building earned the derisive nickname Walkie Scorchie as a result while also being "awarded" the Carbuncle Cup that is named in recollection of Prince Charles's famous remark. Conversely, the architectural firm NBBJ in 2015 proposed their "No Shadow Tower," actually two buildings which would use glass to reflect diffuse daylight into the darkened areas at the base of the buildings.

In Dallas, the forty-two-story Museum Tower has since its completion concentrated an intense amount of sunlight on to the adjacent Nasher Sculpture Center. In an ironic twist, the Nasher had been designed by solar-aware architect Renzo Piano so as to take maximum advantage of natural light. In order to deflect negative publicity, the owners of the luxury condominium tower, the Dallas Police and Fire Pension System, at first made plans for remediation with reflective film, but in 2015 decided to drop these efforts and "express the thanks of the Board to the Nasher Sculpture Center for their efforts."

Glass architecture has often been driven by technology, and several recent strategies have emerged that solve problems associated with glazing. One of the most problematic aspects of glass walls from the ornithologist's perspective has been that they kill birds. It has been estimated that bird strikes on buildings end the lives of hundreds of millions of creatures each year. Almost all glass cladding kills birds, either because it is opaque and reflects the sky or transparent, and birds are unable to see the barrier. Additionally, nighttime illumination, especially up lighting, often draws birds into deadly collisions. Research has shown that outfitting buildings with low reflectance (under 15 percent) glass is effective, as are ceramic frits that abide by the "two by four rule," creating the impression that there is no space more than 2 inches vertical and 4 inches horizontal; birds will shy away from such a pattern. A bird-deterrent pattern can also be applied to the glass using ultraviolet coatings that are invisible to the human eye, while most sun screens will naturally serve as a visual indicator of the buildings presence. While these strategies partially ameliorate the problem, once again the glass is an indulgence: more glass, more dead birds.

The future of glass

Unsurprisingly, a number of new glass technologies are concerned with options for making glass that harnesses, rather than just blocks, solar radiation. Why can a window not also serve as a solar panel? The issue comes down to the opacity of photovoltaic cells. Current solar panel/window combinations either utilize opaque strips amidst the clear glass or greatly diminish the visible light. Because there is a trade-off between power efficiency and transparency when trying to absorb infrared light while allowing visible light inside, the goal of today's emerging photovoltaic technology is to create solar cells that do not block visible transmittance at all. One promising new technology, transparent luminescent solar concentrator, seems well on the way to creating transparent solar cells, although the work is still experimental at this point.

As has so often been the case in the past, speculative glass technology has at times been given a futuristic tint, as aspirational projects are often celebrated even though many are always just around the next corner, and have yet to arrive. As long ago as 1990, Bernard Tschumi created his Glass Video Gallery (now known as the Tschumi Pavillion) as a structurally glazed space for viewing the then novel medium of music videos for the Groninger Museum in the Netherlands. Tschumi asserted that "The appearance of permanence (buildings are solid; they are made of steel, concrete, bricks, etc.) is increasingly challenged by the immaterial representation of abstract systems (television and electronic images)." While this analogy is still valid—Toyo Ito repurposed it a decade later for digital technology at the Sendai Mediatheque—the promise of cladding as screen remains more the province of science fiction movies than a meaningful part of architectural practice. Tschumi's Glass Video Gallery itself has become something of a relic and an homage to the architect, with the Groninger often commissioning designers to situate new works there. For example, in 2015 the Rotterdam firm Shift layered it with translucent cyan, magenta, and yellow film to create a polychrome confection.

Past is present at times: David Benjamin and Soo-in Yang, founders of the design practice The Living, have also espoused a techno-utopian vision of the future of glass that resonates with some of the same themes of progress that Joseph Paxton claimed for his Great Victorian Way in the 1860s. Yang and Benjamin proffer a future where a network of interconnected smart buildings imbedded with sensors are able to adapt to changes in weather and air quality in real time. One of their most compelling glazing projects is called The Living Glass, a type of silicone membrane that is slit in such a way that its contraction causes fishlike gills to open and close in response to the climate. In 2015, The Living offered a new take on the facade, showcasing the Amphibious Envelope at the Chicago Architectural Biennial. Reinterpreting the insulated glazing unit as a terrarium-like ecosystem, the Amphibious Envelope "can self-regulate indoor oxygen levels, self-clean, and provide dynamic shading." And also frogs live in it. The underlying premise of these projects—that the built environment will be able to cooperate and communicate with their inhabitants in a symbiotic fashion—bodes well for a new age of glass.

While so much has changed with glass technology, Singapore's Gardens by the Bay twin conservatories show also how much has stayed the same. The two structures, known as the Flower Dome and the Cloud Forest, are devoted to the tropical horticulture of this region, albeit at different elevations with varying humidities, and for parts of the year receive an immense amount of solar radiation. The Cooled Conservatory Complex features two of the largest air-conditioned colonial era greenhouses in the world, and rather ironically are predicated on sustainable practices. They were constructed with all of the latest glass technologies—spectrally selective insulated glazing units utilizing low-e glass with high visible light transmittance—and yet, like Paxton before them, the British architectural firm Wilkinson Eyre also installed a series of woven cloth exterior shades to cover up all that glass.

7 THE POLITICS OF GLASS

As a major part of the modern built environment, glass has continually been inveigled one way or another in the realm of politics, broadly speaking. Since at least the Elizabethan era, glass has often quietly functioned as a marker of social class—something it still does today—while also at times taking a more visible role on the geopolitical stage. Albeit indirectly, even the Crystal Palace came to serve as an allegorical invocation of British trade policies under the Empire. However, as touched upon in Chapter 4, during the halcyon years of the avant-garde, political readings of steel and glass architecture truly came to the fore. Expressionism, functionalism, *sachlichkeit*: pick your rubric—none of them have fixed meanings anyway—and there will be political ramifications for glass architecture in the years following the First World War. Modern glass cycled through moments of politicization, depoliticization, and repoliticization in changing historical contexts: glass has at times been defined as Socialist, Communist, Capitalist, Bolshevik, and none of the above. While the discourse was fluid, the overarching sense was that glass, insomuch as it was a striking component of modern aesthetics, was a material favored by political progressives who rejected the old order and sought a future of utopian, universal harmony of some sort.

It was in Germany that the political readings of glass have been most evident in the past century. While some 1920s architects such as Walter Gropius and Ludwig Mies van der Rohe sought to downplay the political implications of modern architecture, others such as Laszlo Moholy-Nagy or Hannes Meyer pretty unequivocally linked modern architecture with Marxist themes of social justice and a rejection of nationalist commitment. Meyer had the most staunchly political reading of modern architecture during his tenure at the Bauhaus (1927–30), which of course led to his abrupt dismissal. Confirming his political enemies' view of him, Meyer then emigrated out of Germany in to the Soviet Union, where he became one of the most high-profile European architects who worked to implement Stalin's first Five-Year Plan of industrialization. While many modern architects hedged on the political implications of what the founders of CIAM (including Meyer) called "Architecture and Its Relation to the State," Meyer told a Soviet magazine soon after his arrival in 1930, "I am going to work in the USSR where a truly proletarian culture is being hammered out, where socialism originates and where the society exists for which we have fought here under capitalism."[1] As a key member of the Pan-Russian Society of Proletarian Architects, the most doctrinaire society of Soviet architects, Meyer's strident orthodoxy cast a pall over modern architecture for those uncomfortable with his politics. *Kulturbolschewismus*, indeed.

While Meyer broadcasted his allegiance to left-wing politics, both Moholy-Nagy and Mies, as well as other key figures in modern design such as Jan Tschichold, learned to downplay the linkage between Communism and the new architecture. Mies attempted to navigate the treacherous political situation in Germany of the early 1930s, famously pleading his case to Nazi officials including Alfred Rosenberg and anyone in the Gestapo who would listen. Despite his desperate advocacy, in the end Mies opted to close the final iteration of the Bauhaus in 1933 after Nazi officials demanded that he fire Ludwig Hilberseimer and Wassily Kandinsky in order to remain open. At this point the story becomes fraught for the architect of glass,[2] as while others fled the country he would spend the next four years trying to find an accommodation with Germany's new overlords and convince them to adopt modernism as the Nazi house style. In 1933 he entered the competition for the Berlin Reichsbank, in 1934 he signed on to affiliated organizations of the regime including the *Volkswohlfahrt* and Joseph Goebbels's *Reichskulturkammer*, and in 1935 Mies submitted plans for the German Pavilion at the Brussels World's Fair. The ending of this doomed campaign is well known: Hitler anoints Albert Speer as his principal architect, and the infamous Speerian structures of the National Socialist regime, defined by their retrograde emphasis on mass and monumentality, are planned so as to ignore the virtues of glass.

The establishment of the Hitler–Speer architectural partnership and its promulgation of kitschy, classical theatrics still today defines the regime as an avowed enemy of progressive modernist aesthetics. There would be no glass walls. The question remains, was this an act of destiny, representative of the flawed souls of the National Socialists, or a more fortuitous event that could have turned out differently? The alternate history of Nazi modernism hangs on only a few threads, and paramount is a passing remark Hitler made in a 1933 speech to an event billed as a Culture Congress, where he spoke in favor of "a functionalism of crystalline clarity." The suggestion is that Hitler may have been open to the aesthetics of glass, and the fact that Mies had his fair share of Nazi-affiliated students, patrons, and other supporters such as Hans Weidemann bears this out. There is a parallel here to the history of communication design, where the National Socialists are most associated with blackletter type and idealized representational images; again this was not fully the case as another Bauhaus luminary, Herbert Bayer, produced a number of works for the Nazi government after the Bauhaus was closed. The key point here is that there is nothing innately progressive about glass or steel or sans serif type, and the writing of history has cemented ideological trends that were not writ in stone.

Philip Johnson

The American architect Philip Johnson—known for both his promotion of Mies and his adulation of Hitler during this era—provides another interesting prism through which to view the politics of glass. Independently wealthy and well traveled in Europe, Johnson had been inspired to study the new architecture after his chance meeting in 1929 of Alfred H. Barr, Jr., the founding director of the Museum of Modern Art. In 1931, upon writing a review of the Berlin Building Exhibition organized by Mies, Johnson seemed committed to the depoliticized view of the new architecture. He noted that Mies rejected functionalist austerity in favor of luxury, and for this reason he is "disliked by any architects and critics, especially the Communists." Johnson exulted over Mies' use of plate glass walls that contributed to "the feeling of openness that, perhaps more than anything else, is the prime characteristic of modern architecture."[3] At this point Johnson was formulating the notion of the International Style along with Henry-Russell Hitchcock, and it would appear that the transition from politicized 1920s experimental modernism to postwar corporate neutrality was proceeding apace. Except, upon attending a Nazi rally in a suburb of Berlin in 1932, Johnson experienced an epiphany and soon would become a staunch promoter of National Socialist doctrine.

For the most part it would appear that Johnson's architecture and his politics remained separate, especially because in 1934 Johnson resigned as the Director of Architecture at MoMA in order to devote himself exclusively to radical activism on behalf of populist demagogue Huey Long and the notorious anti-Semite Rev. Charles Coughlin. However, there was a transitional year, 1933, when Johnson had not yet relinquished his curatorial position and published an article, "Architecture in the Third Reich," in the Harvard University literary magazine *Hound & Horn*. Pointedly, Johnson in this article tried to remove Mies from any connection to the Bauhaus. Of the latter he noted, "Nor is it possible they will adopt the Bauhaus style. It is not monumental enough and it has irretrievably the stamp of Communism and Marxism, Internationalism, all the 'isms' not in vogue in Germany today." Johnson briefly surveyed the different factions in German architecture, including "the young men in the party, the students and revolutionaries who are ready to fight for modern art." Johnson offered up the depoliticized Mies as the future of German building and someone supported by Nazi modernists. "In architecture there is only one man whom even the young men can defend and this is Mies van der Rohe." Again, Speer and Hitler would derail this vision for Mies.

As is well known, in the late summer of 1938 Mies left Germany for Chicago—three months before the terror that the Nazis snidely referred to as Kristallnacht, "Kristall" being a term for plate glass shop windows—and in 1940 Johnson began the process of shedding his activism and reengaging with architecture, this time as a student-practitioner at Harvard. In the later 1940s and 1950s Mies and Johnson become linked through numerous projects at MoMA, Seagram, etc. But one iconic yet modest structure of 1949, Johnson's Glass House pavilion on the grounds of his estate in New Canaan, CT, brings together the architects and their shared experience of Nazi Germany (figure 7.1). Mies is a secondary figure at this point, as he stands mainly as the inspiration for Johnson's Glass House, a building that the American architect readily admitted began with Mies (whose own Farnsworth House would not be completed until 1951). The year after the Glass House was completed, Johnson published an explanation of the structure's ancestry in *Architectural Review*. Most of this explanation was predictable, yet the caption of one photo of the house stood out starkly.

FIGURE 7.1 Philip Johnson, Glass House, 1949.

> The cylinder, made from the same brick as the platform from which it springs, forming the main motif of the house, was not derived from Mies, but rather from a burnt wooden village I saw once where nothing was left but foundations and chimneys of brick. Over the chimney I slipped a steel cage with a glass skin. The chimney forms the anchor.

Presumably, this anecdote refers to Johnson's infamous propaganda trip on the heels of the Wehrmacht invasion of Poland in 1939, an experience he described as a "stirring spectacle." Peter Eisenman would later interpret this caption as exemplary of Johnson's "personal atonement and rebirth" after his detour into fascism.[4] Under this reading, the glass skin of the house serves as a metaphor of postwar transparency, with Johnson exposing and acknowledging the "horrors of war."

But a different reading is also possible: not of atonement but of reflection on an exciting part of Johnson's life. One could argue that Johnson was in fact taking up one of the most recognized themes of Speer's monumental architecture, its ruin value. As Johnson never really said much about Nazi architecture at the time when he became fully engaged with the movement, his opinion of Speer has often been imputed as negative although it is in the end unknowable. Speer's promotion of what he called *Die Ruinenwerttheorie* (the theory of ruin value), a Romantic sentiment with a long history in Western culture, was a key part of his grandiose plans for the remaking of Berlin. Under this interpretation, the glass skin of Johnson's house is not a transparent membrane of atonement, but a crystal vitrine encapsulating the spectacular destruction of an empire that had so invigorated him.

The transparency metaphor

Whatever the meaning of the Glass House in particular, more broadly speaking, there is more than a little irony in how the new, depoliticized International Style made one of its first appearances at the United Nations. Harken back first to 1927, when the forerunner of the United Nations, the League of Nations that had been founded in 1920 amidst the ashes of the First World War, held an architectural competition to build a new headquarters in Geneva, Switzerland. The League of Nations was intended to foster world peace, and its founding also marked some of the earliest employments of the "transparency" metaphor in European politics whereby international disputes would be solved in a logical fashion in an open forum. Over 300 architects submitted proposals for the Palace of the League of Nations, a group that included Hannes Meyer, Le Corbusier, and Erich Mendelsohn among other notables. While many of these examples of the new building may seem in hindsight to have been well matched to the League's idealist quest for a new age of world peace and transparency, in a notorious rejection of modern styles the jury selected a staid Beaux-arts design by Henri Nénot that was never built. How much the political tone of many modern architects played into this decision—a result often depicted as only a stylistic defeat—is unclear. Of course, this snub of Le Corbusier et al. directly led to the formation of modern architecture think tank and advocacy group Congrès internationaux d'architecture moderne (CIAM) in subsequent months. While the political situation of its membership was complex, in CIAM's initial La Sarraz Declaration of 1928, the focus was on the issue of academicism and the desire to remove political concerns from architecture insomuch as they supported conservative styles. "Within the same order of ideas, all the prescriptions of the State which, in one form or another, tend to influence architecture by giving it a purely aesthetic direction are an obstacle to its development and must be vigorously combated." In line with the thinking of Johnson and Mies, CIAM helped to steer the new architecture out of a direct linkage to ideology. Not that the politics of the new building had by any measure disappeared after

1928, as the whole fraught episode would in some ways be repeated—with many of the same protagonists and a similar outcome—just a few years later with the disputed competition for the Palace of the Soviets in Moscow.

Leap ahead twenty years to 1947–51 with the design for the United Nations headquarters in New York City by Wallace Harrison, Oscar Niemeyer, and Le Corbusier, and it would appear that the dream of international transparency had finally been made manifest through the UN Secretariat Building, a thirty-nine-story tower that shimmers with twin tinted green glass curtain walls. Whatever its architectural faults, as a symbolic statement of the imagined new age of world peace the Secretariat stood as a striking rejoinder to the monumental classical styles that had been promulgated by the totalitarian regimes of the 1930s and 1940s. Glass had truly come into its own as an anti-ideological symbol of human progress and rational resolutions: depoliticized glass had won a stirring, if illusory, victory at last.

Once it became firmly established as a fundamental tenet of modernism, the transparency metaphor soon faced attempts to problematize or even dismantle it. Notably, an article by Colin Rowe and Robert Slutzky, "Transparency: Literal and Phenomenal," opened up several new directions of inquiry for architectural theorists of the 1960s. However, the most serious contestation came through a book published in 1975 by the French theorist Michel Foucault. In Foucault's groundbreaking book *Discipline & Punish: The Birth of the Prison*, he recounted the late-eighteenth-century crusade of London's Jeremy Bentham, an eccentric polymath who had spent decades trying to convince the British government to accept his idea of a new type of prison building. Bentham's panopticon, devised along with his brother Samuel, consisted of an annular building with a guard tower at its core. Windows in the tower would be shaded by blinds and facing outward toward the ring of individual cells that were themselves backlit by windows on the exterior. In this manner, a small number of guards could surveil a large group of prisoners who would be unable to know when and by whom they were being watched. While the panopticon prison had never been built in Bentham's lifetime, its basic principles were eventually utilized in a handful of prisons. For Foucault, the panopticon was not a building type but instead served as a metaphor of how power functioned in modern, "free" societies: the glass windows of the panopticon are complicit in a dark purpose, helping to facilitate a new type of internalized social control that induces "a state of conscious and permanent visibility that assures the automatic functioning of power." This dystopic vision of architectural transparency as a facilitator of the disciplinary mechanism stands in stark contrast to the uplifting reading preferred by most modern architects.

Outside of the academy and its theoretical concerns, the original transparency metaphor has continued to thrive in architectural practice; Germany was to witness one of the most overt invocations of the metaphor in the last decade of the twentieth century. After the crumbling of the Iron Curtain in 1989 and the subsequent official reunification of East and West Germany, a great deal of attention was focused on the political and symbolic reconstitution of Germany, with the architecture of a restored Berlin foremost on people's minds. And at the very center of it all stood the half-ruined hulk of the Reichstag building that had been originally constructed in 1894 to house the Imperial Parliament. A typical nineteenth-century ornamental neo-baroque splendor of an official edifice, the original Reichstag building designed by Paul Wallot featured a glass and steel cupola that had been derided at the time as an affront to conventional taste. Later, the structure had become synonymous with Nazi totalitarianism because of a fire that damaged the building in 1933 and was utilized as a pretext for mass arrests and the suspension of civil rights in Germany. New layers of meaning accumulated upon the Russian conquest of Berlin and the destruction of the city. After the war, while the Reichstag building sat in West Berlin right on the border with the East, it stood for decades freighted with a sense of hopelessness and conflict. Thus, when Germany was reunified in 1990, the idea of reestablishing a national parliament in Berlin and repurposing the building back to its original function represented an immense symbolic opportunity for architecture.

The Reichstag building was renovated between 1995 and 1999 with Foster + Partners serving as lead architects (figure 7.2). Norman Foster had won an initial international competition in 1993, but his original winning design—which did not include the dome but rather a vast transparent canopy—was substantially modified over the next two years. While the building's original dome had been removed in the 1950s because of its disrepair and Foster was against including a new one, in the end the British architect was pressured to erect a new cupola to crown the structure. Ah, the Reichstag building dome, probably no other architectural feature has so robustly laid claim to the notion that democratic politics represents a triumph of transparency. The allegory is heavy-handed yet effective:

FIGURE 7.2 Norman Foster, Reichstag Dome, 1999.

the dark years of the middle twentieth century were characterized by the ponderous monuments of Speer and Hitler, and now this bright, shining dome of liberty has ushered in a reborn era of freedom and civility.

It has been called a beacon, a lighthouse, a fishbowl, or simply "light and space"; the dome of the Reichstag building established a new paradigm for government architecture even though the basic allegory of transparency had been around almost as long as industrial plate glass. Hannes Meyer, for example, had referred to that symbolic element in describing his 1927 proposal for the League of Nations. After the war, the West German government in Bonn had repeatedly invoked the message through glass curtain walls on a new crop of rather understated modern government buildings. What made the cupola at the Reichstag building special was how loud and strong the message became when it was beamed from the top of such an iconic structure.

Of course, the fundamental notion that glass equals democracy is strictly a subjective one. And as the age of glass accelerated in the 1930s, all sorts of governing institutions had laid claim to its declarative properties. The Reichstag building context seems straightforward: Stalin and Hitler favored imperial classicism wrought of stone and democracy values the lucid clarity of glass. But what about the dictator's compatriot Mussolini? In 1932, fascist house architect Giuseppe Terragni had opined in regard to his House of Fascism, "Here is the Mussolinian concept that fascism is a glass house into which everyone can peer, giving rise to the architecture that is the complement of this idea: no encumbrance, no barrier, no obstacle between the political hierarchy and the people."[5] Decades later, the East German government had built the stunning Palace of the Republic, a glittering, if fashionably reflective (it was the 1970s), glass box that heralded the modern, progressive nature of life behind the Iron Curtain. Clearly, the populist interpretation of glass is a flexible one. This same ambiguity existed in regard to the Reichstag cupolas, both Wallot's and Foster's, did they signify democracy or nationalism or something new (?): a century apart both architects faced the arduous task of trying to please an entire Bundestag full of clients of various political stripes.

Reengaging with the medical analogy introduced in Chapter 5, it is notable that some architectural critics saw the Foster renovation as an attempt to resuscitate a hospice-ready patient with modern technology. Like a baby in an incubator—although at the other end of life's spectrum—the Reichstag building was to be treated with a glass membrane that would pull it out of its enervated state of being. All too often the experience of glass structures is interpreted strictly from the street viewing the exterior. The case could be made that the sense of transparency combined with the feeling of impregnability that one feels inside the building looking out is the more important one; there is something comforting without being suffocating while swaddled inside a glass wall.

Annette Fierro has argued that in France during the presidency of François Mitterrand (1981–95) that nation likewise employed the political metaphor that links the transparency of glass with democratic accessibility. In elucidating how Mitterrand sought to suggest that he had "open[ed] previously closed cultural institutions to the general public," Fierro cites widespread use of glass in the Grands Projets of the early 1990s; she finds nuggets of meaning in the smallest details of the construction of buildings such as I. M. Pei's Grande Pyramide at the Louvre (1989, figure 7.3), where the architect specified crystalline low-iron plate glass. In my view, however, Fierro's most trenchant observation is one that in a sense contradicts her own thesis: she points out in the preface to her book that the glass buildings of the Grands Projets are "Laden with subject matter questionably beyond their capacity to convey." In this writer's view at least that is the crux of the study of glass: can the material really sustain a discourse? Does glass really have the capacity to consistently stay on message? Outside of the broadest invocation of

FIGURE 7.3 I. M. Pei, Grande Pyramide Louvre, 1989.

transparency, it is arguable that the Reichstag or the Louvre exists today outside of academic discourse as spectacles on the tourist pilgrimage, delightful buildings that shimmer on a summer afternoon.

As the term "transparency metaphor" became a buzzword of contemporary governments—and for this Foster's Reichstag building dome should be given the most credit for popularizing the notion—there has been a trickle-down effect of the symbolism on buildings across the globe. Foster repeated himself, for example, in the design of London's City Hall (2002), which the firm notes "advances themes explored in the Reichstag, expressing the transparency and accessibility of the democratic process." Yet can this political glass metaphor truly stick to the building in the way that classically styled stone edifices continue to exude gravitas? Take London's City Hall: in 2015 it served as the stunning location shot for several scenes in Sam Mendes's latest iteration of the James Bond franchise *Spectre*. Far from being a signifier of transparent government, the building served in the movie as the anti-democratic headquarters for a global surveillance operation financed by the arch villain under the cover of a public–private partnership (figure 7.4). It was easy to flip the building from one meaning to the next as Foster's high-tech style with its hint of Toyo Ito's framing of digital media is ideologically flexible in a way that belies its stated message.

FIGURE 7.4 Norman Foster, London City Hall, 2002.

FIGURE 7.5 Legat Partners, Waukegan City Hall, 2004, credit: Legat Architects, Inc.

To cite one last and more modest structure, take the City Hall designed by Legat Architects for the faded industrial town of Waukegan, Illinois (figure 7.5). Completed in 2004, this striking building makes use of the transparency analogy in that the City Council chambers are clad in glass in order to provide "public visibility of the government in action," according to the architects. Of course, cynics have made the case that these buildings are pernicious insomuch as they shill for an idealized vision of government transparency that rarely exists in practice. Whether in Berlin, London, or Waukegan, clarity in glass does not necessarily make for clarity in process.

Postmodern glass

There is another pivotal historical moment when political theory crashed into glass architecture in the late twentieth century, albeit in a less direct, populist manner. This episode rested upon the 1984 publication of Fredric Jameson's article "Postmodernism, or The Cultural Logic of Late Capitalism," in the *New Left Review*.[6] Jameson, one of the preeminent theoreticians of Postmodernism, presented a heterogeneous selection of "readings" of various aspects of Western culture in the article, including an analysis of John Portman's Westin Bonaventure Hotel in Los Angeles (figure 7.6). The Westin Bonaventure had been completed in 1976, and represented the first example on the Pacific coast of Portman's pioneering style that combined the architect's signature soaring atria with other spectacular touches such as glass elevators and elaborate water elements. The thirty-five-story cylindrical hotel, which would serve as an anchor to the gradual redevelopment of downtown Los Angeles, is sheathed in bronze-tinted, opaque reflective glass that is typical of the era.

Jameson's argument focused largely on the interior atrium and multilevel retail zone, which he argued signified a "mutation in built space itself" that he termed "hyperspace." He noted the bewildering layout of the lobby, and suggested that it was emblematic of a new type of postmodern hyperspace that could not be cognitively mapped by individuals, a shallow series of surfaces that stood as an allegory of our inability to "map the great global multinational and decentered communicational network in which we find ourselves caught as individual subjects." Jameson, or James Bond? The latter is told by a wizened old criminal in *Spectre*, "You're a kite dancing in a hurricane, Mr. Bond."

FIGURE 7.6 John Portman, Westin Bonaventure, 1976.

For Jameson, the glass sheath of the Westin Bonaventure also played a role in its postmodern messaging. His words are worth quoting at length.

> Now one would want rather to stress the way in which the glass skin repels the city outside, a repulsion for which we have analogies in those

reflector sunglasses which make it impossible for your interlocutor to see your own eyes and thereby achieve a certain aggressivity toward and power over the Other. In a similar way, the glass skin achieves a peculiar and placeless dissociation of the Bonaventure from its neighborhood: it is not even an exterior, inasmuch as when you seek to look at the hotel's outer walls you cannot see the hotel itself but only the distorted images of everything that surrounds it.

Jameson views this repulsion as featuring a sleight of hand versus the earlier modernist separation of building and street; for him the older phenomenon was transparent and honest in its forcefulness, while the Westin Bonaventure repels through reflection that does not clearly announce its intention. For Jameson, the Westin Bonaventure thereby repels the disordered street, and substitutes its own totalizing environment, one that demands collective behavior in line with a corporatized capitalist culture. This political critique captured the imagination of a generation of academics who in the 1980s were just starting to wade into the turbulent waters of postmodern theory en masse. There is a strange coda to this scholarly milestone: the Westin Bonaventure became perhaps the most unlikely site of theory-minded pilgrimage one could imagine. While lacking the exoticism of a Walter Benjamin–inspired sojourn to the Paris Arcades, nonetheless generations of aspiring semioticians have no doubt gazed upon the now-quite-unassuming reflective skin of the Westin Bonaventure while feeling a frisson of anticipation that they might just get lost in Portman's convoluted lobby.

There is of course an underlying theme of social class in Jameson's Marxist-inflected thinking. While in his writings the intersection of glass and class was partially obscured through the obtuseness of theory, in other contexts the role of glass as a marker of wealth—which has been in play from the material's early Elizabethan use at Hardwick Hall—is supremely evident. In early office towers, for example, proximity to natural light through windows formed part of a clear hierarchy as the lower the stature of the employee, the farther they worked from the light. Le Corbusier recognized the combination of symbolic light and height in his tour of New York City in 1935. "The great masters of economic destiny are up there, like eagles, in the silence of their eminences. Seated in their chairs, framed by two plate glass windows which fuse their rooms with the surrounding space, they appear to us made out of the substance of this event which is as strong and violent as a cosmic mutation." Likewise, finance critic Michael Lewis wrote in 2011 of an anecdote regarding the pinnacle of Frankfurt's Commerzbank headquarters.

> The Commerzbank Tower is fifty-three stories high and unusually shaped: it resembles a giant throne. The top of the building, the arms of the throne, are more decorative than useful. The interesting thing, said the German financier, who visited often, is the glass room at the top, from which one looks down over Frankfurt. It is a men's toilet. Commerzbank executives had taken him there to show him how, in full view of the world below, he could shit on Deutsche Bank.

Today, Steve Hermann–designed Beverly Hills glass homes and glittering residential spires like Christian de Potzamparc's One57 are symbolic arbiters of social class. While some have asserted that glass can blur public and private spaces in a way that promotes collective life, others see a continuing role for glass as a fortress material, its crystalline sharpness demarcating economic inequality with precision and certainty.

NOTES

Preface

1 Henry Chance "On the Manufacture of Crown and Sheet Glass," *Journal of the Society of Arts*, February 15, 1856, pp. 222–231.

2 Pittsburgh Plate Glass Company, *Glass History Manufacture and Its Universal Application*, 1923, p. 1.

Chapter 1

1 Cecil D. Elliott, *Technics and Architecture: The Development of Materials and Systems for Building* (MIT Press, 1992). Elliott provides a more detailed description of all three types of glass manufacture.

2 *Sir Robert Peel's New Tariff*. London, James Gilbert, 1845.

3 Henry Chance, op cit.

4 "Manufacture of Glass for the Crystal Palace," *Illustrated London News*, December 21, 1850, p. 470.

5 John Loudon, *Remarks on the Construction of Hothouses* (J. Taylor, 1817) p. 2.

6 John Dix, *The Glasshouse*, (Phaidon, 1996).

7 Paul Hollister, "The Glazing of the Crystal Palace," *Journal of Glass Studies* Vol. 16 (1974), pp. 95–110.

8 Siegfried Giedion, *Space, Time, and Architecture the Growth of a New Tradition* (Harvard UP, 1941).

9 Thomas A. P. van Leeuwen, *The Skyward Trend of Thought* (MIT Press, 1988). Van Leeuwen dissects the suppression of the poetic, imaginative thread that fomented the construction of tall commercial structures in the United States.

10 John Ruskin, *The Opening of the Crystal Palace* (Smith, Elder and Co., 1854).

11 Karl Marx first floated the idea of commodity fetishism in *Capital*, published in German in 1867 and English in 1887.

12 Thomas Richards, *The Commodity Culture of Victorian England, Advertising and Spectacle 1851–1914* (Stanford UP, 1990), p. 3.

13 Daniel Defoe, *The Complete English Tradesman* (Charles Rivington, 1726), iii.

14 Defoe, pp. 312–13.

15 Claire Walsh, "Shop Design and the Display of Goods in Eighteenth-Century London," *Journal of Design History*, Vol. 8, No. 3 (1995), pp. 157–176.

16 *The Tradesman; or Commercial Magazine*, Vol. 3, No. 1, July 1809, pp. 26–31.

17 Frank Lloyd Wright, *Architectural Record* July 1928 "VI The Meaning of Materials—Glass" from Frank Lloyd Wright, "In the Cause of Architecture: VI. The Meaning of Materials – Glass" pp. 11–16.

18 Julia Scalzo, "All a Matter of Taste: The Problem of Victorian and Edwardian Shop Fronts," *Journal of the Society of Architectural Historians* Vol. 68, No. 1, pp. 52–73.

19 Quoted in Johann Friedrich Geist, *Arcades: The History of a Building Type* (MIT Press, 1983), p. 528.

20 Jonathan Beecher, *The Utopian Vision of Charles Fourier* (Beacon Press, 1971), pp. 242–243.

21 Geist, op. cit., p. 55.

22 Meredith Clausen, "Frank Lloyd Wright, Vertical Space, and the Chicago School's Quest for Light," *Journal of the Society of Architectural Historians* Vol. 44, No. 1 (March 1985), pp. 66–74.

Chapter 2

1 Alastair Duncan, *Modernism: Modernist Design 1880–1940 The Norwest Collection* (Antique Collectors Club, 1998).

2 Robert Ellis et al., *Official catalogue of the Great exhibition of the works of industry of all nations,* 1851, p. 125.

3 Jasmine Allen, "Stained Glass and the Culture of Spectacle, 1780–1862," in *Visual Culture in Britain* Vol. 13, No. 1 (2012), pp. 151–156.

4 Quoted in Richard Altick, *The Shows of London*, (Belknap Press, 1978).

5 Caryl Coleman "Sea of Glass" *Architectural Record*, vol. 2 #8 March 1898, pp. 265–285.

6 George Hotchkiss, *Industrial Chicago* (Goodspeed Publishing Company, 1891–1896), p. 794.

7   Ibid., p. 796.

8   Otto Antonia Graf, "Enspacement: The Main Sequence from 4 to 6 Analysis of Wright's Steel Cathedral Project," in Robert McCarter, Ed., *On and By Frank Lloyd Wright A Primer of Architectural Principles* (Phaidon, 2005), pp. 144–169.

9   Several years later at the University Club, Martin Roche tried a more conventional solution, using clear glass for the bottom sections of each of his stained glass windows in order to preserve the lake views to the east of the building.

10 Frank Lloyd Wright, op. cit., p. 15.

11 Carel Blotkamp, et al., "Theo van Doesburg," in *De Stijl: The Formative Years 1917–1922* (MIT Press, 1982), esp. pp. 11–18.

Chapter 3

1   P.B. Wight, "Recent Fireproofing in Chicago," *Inland Architect* (April 1885), pp. 52–53.

2   Theodore Turak, "Remembrances of the Home Insurance Building," *Journal of the Society of Architectural Historians* Vol. 44, No. 1 (March 1985), pp. 60–65 and Gerald R. Larson & Roula Mouroudellis Geraniotis, "Toward a Better Understanding of the Evolution of the Iron Skeleton Frame in Chicago," *Journal of the Society of Architectural Historians* Vol. 46, No. 1 (March 1987), pp. 39–48.

3   William Lebaron Jenney, "The Steel Skeleton, or the Modern Skyscrapers,–The Engineering Problems," *Inland Architect* (January 1900), Vol. 34, pp. 2–8.

4   "W.L.B. Jenney, Architect," *The American Architect* Vol. XCII, No. 1645 (July 6, 1907), pp. 5–6.

5   Montgomery Schuyler "Architecture in Chicago Adler & Sullivan," *Architectural Record*, February 1896, pp. 3–48.

6   Charles Waldheim, Charles Waldheim and Katerina Ruedi Ray, Eds. *Chicago Architecture: Histories, Revisions, Alternative* (University of Chicago Press, 2005), p. 366, note 17.

7   *Guardian*, April 2, 2015, http://www.theguardian.com/cities/2015/apr/02/worlds-first-skyscraper-chicago-home-insurance-building-history.

8   For more on the economics of electrical power see Thomas Leslie, "Glass and Light The Influence of Interior Illumination on the Chicago School," *Journal of Architectural Education* Vol. 58, No. 1 (September 2004), pp. 13–23.

9 Thomas Leslie, "'As Large as the Situation of the Columns Would Allow': Building Cladding and Plate Glass in the Chicago Skyscraper, 1885–1905," *Technology and Culture* Vol. 49, No. 2 (April 2008), pp. 399–419.

10 Jenney, op. cit.

11 Barr Ferree, "The High Building and Its Art," *Scribners* (March 1894), pp. 297–318.

12 John W. Root, "A Great Architectural Problem," *Inland Architect* (June 1890), pp. 67–71.

13 George Hill, "Some Practical Limiting Conditions in the Design of the Modern Office Building," *Architectural Record* Vol. 2, No. 4 (April–June 1893).

14 Carol Willis has written an in-depth accounting of how the availability of daylight determined the overall plan and interior layouts of commercial architecture in this era "Light, Height and Site: The Skyscraper in Chicago," in John Zukowsky, ed., Chicago Architecture and Design, 1923–1993(Munich: Prestel, 2000), 119–140.

15 A. T. Andreas, *History of Chicago from the Earliest Period to the Present Time* (Chicago: A. T. Andreas Publisher, 1886).

16 Hotchkiss, op. cit., Volume II, p. 793.

17 Ibid., p. 21.

18 J. W. Yost, "Influence of Steel Construction and of Plate Glass upon the Development of Modern Style," *Inland Architect* Vol. 28, No. 4 (November 1896).

19 First published in *Chicago Economist* then *Architecture and Building*, September 10, 1892, pp. 128–129.

20 Peter Wight, "Modern Architecture in Chicago," *The Pall Mall Magazine* Vol. 18 (May–August 1899), pp. 293–308.

21 Schuyler, "The 'Sky-Scraper' Up to Date," *Architectural Record* Vol. 8, No. 3 (January–March 1899), pp. 231–257.

22 Louis Sullivan in *Lippincott's* Vol. 57 (March 1896), pp. 403–409.

23 The panel papers were reprinted in *Inland Architect* Vol. 28, No. 4 (November 1896), pp. 33ff. The partnership founded in 1880 by Adler and Sullivan had frayed under economic pressure and after 1894 their only new, joint commission was for the Schlesinger & Mayer Department store (1898).

24 A lively writer, one wonders what could have been if Adler had only been able to edit more of Sullivan's essays for clarity.

25 Siegfried Giedion, *Space, Time and Architecture the Growth of a New Tradition* (Harvard University Press, 1941).

26 Edward A. Renwick, *Recollections*, 1932, p. 189, Unpublished Manuscript.

27 Elevation drawing of the Gage Building. *Inland Architect* Vol. 33, No. 2 (March 1899), p. 20.

28 Bruno Taut, *Modern Architecture* (The Studio Ltd., 1929), p. 66.

29 Meredith Clausen "Frank Lloyd Wright, Vertical Space, and the Chicago School's Quest for Light," *Journal of the Society of Architectural Historians* Vol. 44, No. 1 (March 1985), pp. 66–74.

30 K.C. Clark, *Inland Architect* April 1898, p. 29.

31 Any discussion of the Luxfer Prism Company begins with Dietrich Neumann, "'The Century's Triumph in Lighting': The Luxfer Prism Companies and Their Contribution to Early Modern Architecture," *Journal of the Society of Architectural Historians* Vol. 54, No. 1 (March 1995), pp. 24–53.

32 "The Century's Triumph in Lighting," *The Inland Architect and News Record* 34 (January 1900), The Technical Review of the Building Arts: 39–40.

33 Tim Benton, *The Villas of Le Corbusier and Pierre Jeanneret 1920–1930* (Birkhäuser, 2007), pp. 47–78.

34 Le Corbusier, *Toward an Architecture* (Getty Publications, 2007), p. 120.

35 Ibid., p. 98.

36 Quoted in Bruno Reichlin, "The Pros and Cons of the Horizontal Window The Perret—Le Corbusier Controversy," *Daidalos* (13 September 1984), Reichlin details the dispute and elucidates how Perret and Le Corbusier's conception of the window demonstrated differing conceptions of public and private space.

Chapter 4

1 Walter Gropius, "Architectural Details: Walter Gropius," *Architectural Record* Vol. 137 (February 1965), p. 133.

2 Reyner Baham, "The Glass Paradise," *Architectural Review* (February 1959), pp. 87–89.

3 Illinois State Association of Architects, *The Inland Architect and News Record*, Vol. 9, No. 9 (June 1887), pp. 88–90.

4 Rosemarie Haag Bletter has gone into the history of the expressionist glass and crystal allegory in her article, "The Interpretation of the Glass Dream-Expressionist Architecture and the History of the Crystal Metaphor," *Journal of the Society of Architectural Historians* Vol. 40, No. 1 (March 1981), pp. 20–43.

5 Neumann, op cit., p. 43.

6   David Nielsen, *Bruno Taut's Design Inspiration for the Glashaus* (Routledge, 2016).

7   Arthur Korn, *Glass in Modern Architecture*, Dennis Sharp, Ed. (Design Yearbook Limited, 1967).

8   Keith Dills, "The Hallidie Building," *Journal of the Society of Architectural Historians* Vol. 30, No. 4 (December 1971), pp. 323–329.

9   William Polk quoted in "The World's First Glass Front Building," *The Architect and Engineer of California* Vol. LIII (1918), pp. 71–73.

10 Arthur Korn, *Glass in Modern Architecture* (Barrie & Rockliff 1967, 1929).

11 Quoted in Julia Bekman Chadaga, *Optical Play Glass, Vision, and Spectacle in Russian Culture* (Northwestern University Press, 2014), p. 126.

12 Quoted in Eve Blau and Nancy J. Troy, *Architecture and Cubism* (MIT Press 1997), p. 232.

13 Bruno Taut, op. cit., p. 93.

14 Walter Gropius, "Program of the Staatliche Bauhaus in Weimar," 1919.

15 Sheldon Cheney, *The New World Architecture* (Longmans, Green and Co., 1930), pp. 306–308.

16 Lewis Mumford, "The Skyline: House of Glass" *The New Yorker* (8 August 1952), p. 49.

17 Aline Louchheim, "Newest Building in the New Style," *The New York Times* (April 27, 1952), p. X9.

18 "The Monotonous Curtain Wall," *Architectural Forum* Vol. 111 (October 1959), pp. 143–147.

19 Thomas Ennis, "Building is Designer's Testament," *The New York Times* (November 10, 1957), p. 1.

20 "New Silhouette on City's Skyline," *The New York Times* (April 27, 1952), pp. 113 and 235.

21 Aline Louchheim, op. cit., "Newest Building in the New Style," *The New York Times* (April 27, 1952), p. X9.

22 Lewis Mumford, "The Skyline: Magic with Mirrors II," *The New Yorker* (22 September 1951), pp. 99–106.

Chapter 5

1 Paul Scheerbart, *Glasarchitektur*, quoted in Dennis Sharp, ed., p. 46.

2 Edwin Chadwick, *The Present and General Condition of Sanitary Science, an Address* (London: Printed for the author by James Meldrum, 1889), p. 8.

3 Kristel de Vis, et al., "The Use of Glass Bricks in Architecture in the 19th and 20th Centuries: A Case Study," Interim Meeting of the ICOM-CC Working Group October 3–6, 2010.

4 "Glass Paving and Building Bricks," *Scientific American Supplement* No. 1538 (June 24, 1905), pp. 24642–24643.

5 Neumann, op cit., p. 46.

6 Kenneth Frampton, "Maison de Verre," *Perspecta* Vol. 12 (1969), pp. 77–109; 111–128.

7 Le Corbusier Translated by Paul Stirton annotated by Tim Benton, "Glass, the Fundamental Material of Modern Architecture," *West 86th: A Journal of Decorative Arts, Design History, and Material Culture*, vol. 19, no. 2 (Fall-Winter 2012), pp. 282–308.

8 Quoted in John Stanislav Sadar, "'Vita' Glass and the Discourse of Modern Culture," in Grace Lees-Maffei, Ed., *Writing Design Words and Objects* (Berg, 2012), pp. 103–117 . Sadar has performed admirable research into this formerly obscure subject.

9 Quoted in Stephen Eskilson, "Color and Consumption," *Design Issues* Vol. 18, No. 2 (Spring 2002), pp. 17–29.

10 "Modernize Main Street Competition Awards," *Architectural Record* Vol. 78 (October 1935), pp. 208–265.

11 "Model Store Fronts Exhibited," *New York Times* (September 9, 1936), p. 38.

12 Walter Dorwin Teague, "Structural and Decorative Trends in Glass," *American Architect* Vol. 141, pp. 40–43, 110–112.

13 "Glass-Block New Building Material," *Scientific American* Vol. 149, No. 3 (September 1933), p. 128.

14 Walter Dorwin Teague, op. cit., "Structural and Decorative Trends in Glass," *The American Architect* Vol. 141 (May 1932), pp. 40–43, 110–112.

15 James McQueeney, "The Glass Age," *Popular Mechanics*, vol. 73 no. 3 (March 1940), pp. 337–344.

16 "Glass Block," *Architectural Forum* Vol. 72, (May 1940), pp. 327–330.

17 Mary Roche, "New Ideas and Inventions" Home Section, *The New York Times* (May 4, 1947), no pagination.

18 Warren Platner quoted in Carter Horsley, "Glamorous Glass Bricks Are Booming," *The New York Times* (November 17, 1977).

Chapter 6

1 *Times*, June 30, 1851, p. 5. Quoted in Henrik Schoenefeldt "The Crystal Palace, Environmentally Reconsidered," *Architectural Research Quarterly* Vol. 12, No. 3/4 (2008), pp. 283–294.

2   Cheney, op. cit., p. 306.

3   Parts of this section originally appeared in Stephen Eskilson, "Sears Beautiful," *Chicago History* Vol. 39 No. 2 (Fall 2000), pp. 26–43.

4   Quoted in Arthur Lubow, "Disappearing Act," *The New York Times*, October 10, 2005.

5   Reyner Banham, *The Architecture of the Well-Tempered Environment* (Architectural Press, 1969), p. 158.

Chapter 7

1   Quoted in Claude Schnaidt, *Hannes Meyer: Bauten, Projekte und Schriften*, (Teufen, 1965). Schnaidt noted Meyer's propensity toward the political: "If Meyer had spoken a little more often about art and a little less about politics, if he had merely indulged in reassuring generalities instead of impugning an economic system, if he had built luxury villas instead of co-operative housing estates, he would probably have been entitled to more honors than he has received."

2   Rosemarie Haag Bletter has written cogently, "Mies' architecture is synonymous with modernism and modernism is synonymous with glass."

3   Philip Johnson, "In Berlin Comment on Building Exposition," *The New York Times*, August 9, 1931, p. 97.

4   Peter Eisenman, "Introduction," *Philip Johnson Writings* (Oxford, 1979).

5   Quoted in Michael Z. Wise, *Capital Dilemma Germany's Search for a New Architecture of Democracy* (Princeton Architectural, 1998), p. 16.

6   Fredric Jameson, "Postmodernism, or the Cultural Logic of Late Capitalism," *New Left Review* Vol. I, No. 146, July–August 1984, pp. 52–92. The article's impact was enhanced when it was later included as the title essay in a collection of Jameson's essays on Postmodernism (Duke University Press, 1991).

INDEX

Note: titles of books are given in italics; page numbers in italics refer to illustrations.

Abbott, Merkt, and Company 167
Acosta, Esaú 150
adhesives 150, 152, 157
Adjaye, David 58, *58*, 183
Adler, Dankmar 73
Adler & Sullivan 33, 69, 79
Aesthetic movement 41
AFIMALL, Moscow 57
air conditioning 112, 132, 167, 169–75, 179
airtightness. *See* sealed buildings
Albers, Josef 51–2, 52–3, *53*
Albert C. Martin and Associates 167
Allen, Jasmine 30
Alton Towers 29
American Institute of Architects 73
Amphibious Envelope 190
Ando, Tadao 146–7
Apple store, Fifth Avenue, New York 155–6, *156*, 157, 168
   Mark II 157
Apple store, Osaka, Japan 156
Apple store, SoHo, New York 156
Apple store, Zorlu, Istanbul 157
Apple stores 115, 155, 168
Aquitania (ship) 86–7
Aragon, Louis 20
Arbeitsrat für Kunst 108
arcades 18–22
Arcades Project (Benjamin) 21
Architecture 2030 185
Art Deco
   architectural illumination 114, 142, 148

"frozen fountain" 141
ornamental surface glass 122
at Paris expositions, 1925 and 1937 54
skyscrapers 79
use of glass blocks 138, 145, 146
Art Nouveau 39, 41
Art Sacré group 54–5
Arts and Crafts 41–2
Ateliers d'art Sacré 54–5
Atocha Station Memorial 150, *151*
Atwood, Charles 67, *76*, 77
Au Printemps, Paris 25
Aubel, Marjan van 57
Avery Coonley Playhouse, Riverside, Illinois 46–7, *47*

Bailey, W. and D. 6
Banham, Reyner 90, 114, 176–7
Barr, Alfred 78, 111, 112, 195
Barthes, Roland 155
Bartlett, Frederick 40–1
Baudelaire, Charles 21
Bauen en Frankreich (Giedion) 89
Bauhaus 51–3, 90, 193, 194, 195
Bauhaus Dessau workshop 105–7, *106*, 108–9, 111, 121, 163
Bawa, Geoffrey 161, 179
Bayer, Herbert 195
Beaux-arts 71, 198
Behne, Adolph 108
Belluschi, Pietro 174, *175*
Benjamin, David 190
Benjamin, Walter 21–2, 22, 25

Benson, J. W.. *See* J. W. Benson store, London
Bentham, Jeremy and Samuel 199
Benton, Tim 85
Berlin Building Exhibition, 1931 195
Berlin-Dahlem Botanical Garden 94
Besant, Annie 95
Bicton Gardens Palm House, Devon 6–7
Bing, Siegfried 38–9, 55
bird deterrents 189
Der Blaue Reiter 95
Blavatsky, Helena 94–5
Bletter, Rosemarie Haag 91
Blotkamp, Carel 49
blown glass 1, 100. *See also* crown glass; cylinder glass
Bogert house, Evanston, Illinois 71
Bohlin Cywinski Jackson 155, *156*, 168
Boileau, Louis Auguste 25, *26*, 165
Boileau, Louis Charles 25, 165
Boley Building, Kansas 107
Bon Marché, Paris 25, *26*, 165
Bontemps, Georg 7
borosilicate glass 140
Boston Store, Chicago 69
Boucicaut, Aristide 25
Boullée, Étienne-Louis 22
Bourcicaut, Arthur 12
Bragdon, Claude 96, 109
Braithwaite, Martha 14
Breton, Andre 20
brise-soleil 161, 176–8, 180, 182–3, 187, 188
broad glass. *See* cylinder glass
Brown, Bedford IV 142
Brown, Edith 38
Brown, Ethel 38
Die Brücke 97
Bruning, Herbert. *See* Herbert Bruning house, Wilmette, Illinois
A Bucket of Oil (CRS) 181

buffer facade 172. *See also* double walled glass facades
"bulls eye" panes 6
Burdine's department store, Fort Lauderdale, Florida 167
Burne-Jones, Edward 41–2
Burnham, Daniel H. 91–2, 93, 164. *See also* D. H. Burnham and Co.
Burnham & Root 64, 79, *80*

"cabinet window" 14
Calatrava, Santiago 183
Cannon Design 172
Carrara glass 122, 135, 139, 146
cast plate glass 2–3
cathedral glass 32
Caudill Rowlett Scott (CRS) 181
Cavendish, William, Duke of Devonshire 7
Centrosoyus Palace, Moscow 170
A Century of Progress International Exposition, Chicago,1933–34. *See* Chicago World's Fair, 1933–34
ceramic frits 57, 138, 146, 188, 189
Chadwick, Edwin 124
Champlain Building 67–8, *68*, 69, 69–71
Chance Bros. 7, 30, 32, 134
Chapelle du Rosaire de Vence 55
Chapelle Notre Dame du Haut, Ronchamp 55–6, *56*, 58
Chareau, Pierre 130–1, *130*, 142
Chartres, Duc de 19
Chatsworth, Great Stove Conservatory 7, 162
chemical tempering 156
Cheney, Sheldon 109, 163–4
Chicago Architectural Biennial 190
Chicago Stock Exchange 69, 72
Chicago Window 59, 66–72, 72–4, 76, 77, 79, 85–6
Chicago World's Fair, 1933–34 164–5, 166

Owens-Illinois Glass Block Building 141–2, *141*
Sears Pavilion 165, *165*
Chrysler Building, New York 79
CIAM (Congrès internationaux d'architecture moderne) 89, 194, 198
Cité du Refuge, Paris 132, *133*, 170, *171*, 180
Clark, K. C. 80
Clausen, Meredith 26, 79
claviluxes 95–6
Cluysenaar, Jean-Pierre 23
Coatings. *See also* low-e glass
  antimicrobial 135
  ceramic frits 57, 138, 146, 188, 189
  spectrally selective 184, 191
  technology 184
  variable light transmission 184
Cochin, Charles-Nicolas 5–6
Colburn, Irving 100
Coleman, Caryl 31
color music 95–6
color organs 95–6
colored glass 94, 95. *See also* polychrome structural glass; tinted glass
colored light 94, 95, 96, 97, 141
colored light projections 95–6
Commerzbank, Frankfurt 185–6, *186*, 208
The Complete English Tradesman (Defoe) 13
condensation 20, 107
Congregation Anshi Chesed, New York 33
Congrès internationaux d'architecture moderne (CIAM) 89, 194, 198
Conservatories. *See* greenhouses
Constructivism 47–54, *54*
cookware 140
Cooled Conservatory Complex, Singapore 191
Coonley Playhouse 46–7, *47*

Corning Glass Works 140
Costa, Lúcio 177, 178, *178*
courtyards 79–83
Couture, Thomas 34
Couturier, Pierre 54–5
Crosby Hall, London 40
crown glass 1–2, 6
Crystal Chain (Die Gläserne Kette) 107
crystal metaphor 12, 94, 108, 114, 121–2, 123, 144, 168, 196
Crystal Palace 8–12
  legacy 11–12, 17, 91, 99
  political reading of 193
  Pugin as primary detractor 29
  shading and ventilation 162–3
  sheet and pane size 2, 8
  statistics 8
curtain walls 99–109. *See also* facades
curvilinear exterior forms 157–8
cyano-acrylate adhesives 150, 152
cylinder glass 2, 7, 100. *See also* drawn glass

D. H. Burnham and Co. 70, 77
Daily Express Building, Glasgow 138
Daily Express Building, London 138, *139*
Daily Express Building, Manchester 138, 152
d'Alembert, Jean le Rond 5–6
dalle de verre 55
Dalsace, Jean 130, 131
Dana House 44–5
daylighting 64–5, 69, 165
  control 182
  Luxfer Prism tiles 74–5, 80–2
  refection of 188–9
  vault lights 125
De Lange House, Alkmaar, Holland 49, *50*
De Silva House, Galle 179
De Stijl 48, 49, 52, 53
Debis Tower, Berlin 186–8, *187*

INDEX 219

Debret, Francois 19
decklights 125
Defoe, Daniel 12–13
Denis Maurice 54
department stores 12, 25–6, 79, 164, 165
Design with Climate Bioclimactic Approach to Architectural Regionalism (Olgyay) 180
Deutscher Werkbund exhibition, Cologne, 1914 101
  Glashaus 96–7, *97*, *98*
Deutsches Luxfer Prismen Syndikat 97, 129
Diderot, Denis 5–6
Dior Omotesando, Tokyo 167–8, *168*, 169
Dip-Tech 57
display windows. *See* shop windows
Dix, John 6
Doesburg, Theo van 48–54
Doha Tower, Qatar 161, 183, *183*
double glazing 93, 173, 174, 180, 181–2. *See also* insulated glazing units (IGUs)
double walled glass facades 154–5, 163, 168–9, 170, 172, 180, 181–2, 185–8
drainage 19–20
drawn glass 1, 100
dual layer glass facades. *See* double walled glass facades

Early Modern Architecture Chicago: 1870–1910 exhibition, 1933 78
Ecclesiological Society 31
Eckersley O'Callaghan 155, 156
Eesteren, Cornelius van 49
Eggeling, Viking 53
Eiffel, Gustave 25
860–880 Lake Shore Drive, Chicago 110, 114–15, *115*, 174
Eisenman, Peter 157, 197
electric lighting 63, 112, 148, 164

Ellis, Peter 102, *103*
Emerson, Ralph Waldo 72
Encyclopédie (d'Alembert) 5–6
Encyclopédie (Diderot) 5–6
energy conservation 181
energy performance 185, 188. *See also* thermal performance
Entwhistle, Clive 180
environmental issues 189–90
Equitable Building, Portland, Oregon 174, *175*
Esplanade Apartments, Chicago 174
L'Esprit Nouveau (journal) 83, 84
excise tax 4
Exposition des Arts Décoratifs at Industriels Moderne, Paris, 1925 54
Exposition Internationale des Arts et Techniques dans la Vie Moderne, Paris, 1937 54
expressionism 51, 95, 97, 107–9, 113–14
  and functionalism 9, 11–12, 89–90, 92, 105
exterior shades 162, 191
extract-air systems 172

facades 151–9. *See also* double walled glass facades
Faguswerke, Alfeld 101, *101*, 102
Falconnier, Gustave 98, 125, *127*, 128–9, 141
FAM Arquitectura y Urbanismo 150, *151*
Farnsworth House, Plano, Illinois 196
Feininger, Lionel 51
Ferree, Barr 64
Fierro, Annette 202
fire permeability 128–9
Fisher Building 70
Flachat, Christophe-Eugène 24
float glass 118–19, 151, 159
fluoride additive 134
Foley's department store, Houston 167

Foote, Samuel 30
Ford & Brooks 38
Foster, Norman 152, *153*, 200–1, *201*, 202, 203, *204*
Foster + Partners 157, 168–9, 185–6, *186*, 200
Foster-Munger Company 32, *33*
Foucault, Michel 199
Fourcault, Emile 100
Fourcault glass 100
Fourier, Charles 22–3, 91
Frampton, Kenneth 131
Friedrichstrasse skyscraper, Berlin (unbuilt) 114
frit printing 57, 146, 188, 189
Froebel, Friedrich 42
Fuller, George A.. *See* George A. Fuller Company
functionalism, and expressionism 9, 11–12, 89–90, 92, 105
Furness Abbey 28

Gage Group 74–5, 77
Galeries Lafayette, Berlin 26
Galeries Lafayette, Paris 25
Galleria Vittorio Emanuele II, Milan 19
Gardens by the Bay, Singapore 191
Gare de Strasbourg 157, *158*
Garnier, Charles 26
Geist, Johann 23
General Electric 142
George A. Fuller Company 77
Gesamtkunstwerke 41, 46, 48, 51
Gibson, William 155
Giedion, Siegfried 11, 73–4, 89–90, 93, 107
glare control 173, 184, 186, 187
Glas im Bau und als Gebrauchsgegenstа (Korn) 99, 101, 105
Glasarchitektur (Scheerbart) 91, 92, 93–4, 95, 96, 107, 121
Glasbau Hahn 152
Glaseisenbeton 129

Die Gläserne Kette (Crystal Chain) 107
Glashaus pavilion 96–7, *97*, *98*, 122
Glashütte Gerresheim 129
glass blocks 140–6. *See also* Luxfer Prism tiles; Nevada tiles
  Falconnier's glass bricks 125, *127*, 128–9
  Glashaus pavilion 97–8
  load-bearing potential 142
  revival of 146–50
  thermal performance 142
  Wright's compositions for the Luxfer Prism Co. 42–4, *43*
glass bricks. *See* glass blocks
Glass Farm, Schijndel, Netherlands 57
glass fins 152
Glass House, New Canaan, CT 196–8, *197*
Glass in Modern Architecture (Korn) 99, 101, 105
glass screens 142, 148, 157–8
glass staircases 156
glass tax 3, 4
glass tiles. *See* glass blocks
Glass Video Gallery (Tschumi Pavillion) 190
glazing ratio 63–4, 69–70
Goff, Bruce 137, 143–4
Goodwin, Philip 111–12, *111*, 144
Gothic style 28–9, 30, 31, 39, 41, 93–4, 96
Graf, Otto Antonia 42
Grande Pyramide, Louvre, Paris 202
Grands Projets 202
Great Depression 134, 137, 165
Great Exhibition, London, 1851 8, 9–11, 29, 30
Great Stove Conservatory, Chatsworth 7, 162
Great Victorian Way (unbuilt) 24
Green Building Council 185
green building movement 185
greenhouses 5–12, 94, 129, 161–2, 191

Grey Cloth and Ten Percent White (Scheerbart) 93
Groninger Museum, Netherlands 190
Gropius, Walter
    Arbeitsrat für Kunst 108
    and Bauhaus 51
    Bauhaus Dessau workshop 105–7, *106*, 108–9, 112, 121, 163
    and the curtain wall 101, *101*, 102, 105–7
    and expressionism 90, 107, 108
    and functionalism 89, 90, 96–7
    and Paul Scheerbart 121
    political readings of architecture 193
    and stained glass 51, 52, 53
    Tribune Tower competition 73
Gruen and Krummeck 167
Guinle Park, Rio da Janeiro 178, *178*

Hallidie Building, San Francisco 102–5, *104*, 107
Hardman, John Jr. 29
Hardwick Hall 4–5, 17, 207
Harris Manchester College Chapel, Oxford 41
Harrison, Wallace 199
Haven, C. D. 173
Haywards Company 129
heat mirror technology 184
Hecht's Building, Silver Spring, Maryland 167
Herbert Bruning house, Wilmette, Illinois 144
Hermann, Steve 208
high-tech 153, 155
Hilberseimer, Ludwig 194
Hill, George 64
Hill, Leonard 134
Hirst, Damien 57
Hitchcock, Henry-Russell 108–9, 195
Hoff, Robert van 't 48
Holabird, William 69, 71
Holabird & Roche 67–70, *68*, 71, 74–5

Holmes & Son, Norwich 16–17, *17*
Home Insurance Building, Chicago 60, *61*, 62, 64
Hooker Building, Niagara Falls, New York 172, 181–2
Horeau, Hector 24
Horiuchi House, Osaka 147
horizontal orientation 67, 70, 71, 77–9
horticultural applications. *See* greenhouses
hothouses. *See* greenhouses
House of Fascism 202
hygiene and glass 123–40
hyperspace. 205

Illinois Glass Company 140
Illinois Institute of Technology (ITT), McCormick Tribune Campus Center 57
Illinois State Association of Architects 91
incubator, glass 124, *128*
incubator metaphor 131, 132, 147, 158, 202
indoor air quality 172
infirmaries 131–2
ink jet printing 57
Institut du Monde Arabe (IMA), Paris 182, *182*
insulated glazing units (IGUs) 173, 185
Insulux 141, 142
intaglio block 146
interior glass walls 142, 157–8
International Style 77–8, 79, 109, 111, 179, 195, 198
iron and glass conservatories 5–12, *9*
Ishihara House, Osaka 147
Ismailia surgery pavilion, Suez Canal 180
Ito, Toyo 154–5, *154*, 158, 190
Itten, Johannes 51, 52, 90

J. W. Benson store, London 15, *16*
Jacobs & Sons 125, *126*

Jameson, Fredric 205–6
Japanese modernism 147–8, 155
Jardin d'Hiver, Paris 24
Jardin du Roi, Paris 6
Jeanneret, Charles-Édouard. *See* Le Corbusier
Jeanneret, Pierre 84
Jenney, William Le Baron 60, *61*, 62, 63–4, 65
Jewish iconography 33
Johnson, Philip 78, 79, 110, 111–12, 112, 195–8
jours de souffrance 85

Kandinsky, Wassily 95, 194
Keck, George Fred 144
Kehilath Anshe Ma'ariv, Chicago 33
Kelly, Richard 114–16, 117, 142
Keppler, Friedrich 97, 98
Keppler-System 129
Khan, Louis 179
Kimball, George 65
Kirchner, Ernst Ludwig 97
Kirin Plaza, Osaka 148, *149*
Klee, Paul 52
Kokomo Opalescent Glassworks 36
Koolhaas, Rem 57
Korn, Arthur 90, 99, 101, 105, 107
Kraus, Ernst 51
Küpper, Christian Marie Emil. *See* van Doesburg, Theo
Kurakawa, Kisho 188

La Farge, John 34–5, *35*, 36
La Roche, Raoul 84
La Samaritaine, Paris 25
laminated glass 143, 151–2, 180
Lamplough, Francis 134
lantern symbolism 147, 148, 150
Laplanche, Jean-Alexandre 25
Le Corbusier
 and air conditioning 170
 on American Architecture 169, 207

 architectural references to 112
 brise-soleil 161, 176–7, 180
 Chapelle Notre Dame du Haut, Ronchamp 55–6, *56*
 Cité du Refuge 132, *133*, 170, *171*, 180
 Five Points Towards a New Architecture 86, 88
 Immeuble Molitor 145
 Ministry of Education building, Rio de Janeiro 177
 mur neutralisant 170, 172, 185
 The Radiant City 177
 ribbon window 59, 79, 83–8
 and stained glass 27, 57
 United Nations Secretariat building *118*, 199
 use of glass blocks 145
 use of Nevada tiles 132
 Vers une Architecture 84, 87
 When the Cathedrals Were White 169, 170
Leadbeater, C. W. 95
League of Nations, Geneva building competition 198, 201
Ledoux, Claude-Nicolas 22
LEED 185
Leeuwen, Thomas van 11
Legat Partners *204*, 205
Leger, Fernand 55
Leiter II Building, Chicago 65
Leslie, Thomas 63
Lever House, New York 90, *113*, 117, 174–5
Lewis, Michael 208
Libbey glass company 100
Libbey-Owens-Ford (LOF) 100, 111, 135, 137, 138, 144, 158, 173
light courts 79–80
light projection 95–6
"light screens" 44
lighthouse lenses 30
Living Glass 190
Loewy, Raymond 167

London City Hall 203, *204*
long window. *See* ribbon window
Louchheim, Aline 113–14, 117
Loudon, John 6
Louvre, Paris
   grand gallery 23
   Grande Pyramide 202
low reflectance glass 189
low-e glass 180, 184, 191
Lubin, Maurice 138
Luxfer Prism Company 42–4, *43*, 80–2, 97, 129
Luxfer Prism tiles 74–6, 80–3, *81*
Lyon, Gustave 170

Mahler, Alma 90
maintenance catwalks 188
Maison de Verre 130–1, *130*, 142
Maison des Docteurs (unbuilt) 132
Maison Hermès, Tokyo 148–50, *150*
Malevich, Kasimir 108
Manhattan Laundry, Washington, D.C. 142, *143*
Marietta Manufacturing Company 134, *135*
St. Mark's-in-the-Bowery, New York 134
Marshall, Benjamin 103–4
Martin, Albert C.. *See* Albert C. Martin and Associates
mashrabiya 176, 182, 183
Matisse, Henri 55
May Company department store, Los Angeles 167
McCormick Buildings, Chicago 74
McCormick Tribune Campus Center, Illinois Institute of Technology (ITT) 57
medical buildings 130–2
Mendes, Sam 203
Meyer, Hannes 193–4, 201
Meyer Building 79
Mies van der Rohe
   architectural references to 112, 149

Berlin Building Exhibition 195
860–880 Lake Shore Drive, Chicago 110, 114–15, *115*, 174
Esplanade Apartments 174
glass-walled proposals of 108
and Paul Scheerbart 121
and political readings of architecture 193, 194
projects cited by Korn 105
promoted to Nazis by Johnson 196
screen-printed photograph of 57
Seagram Building 115–17, *116*, 174
and thermal movement 110
Millron's department store, Westchester, California 167
Milwaukee Art Museum 183
Ministry of Education building, Rio de Janeiro 177–8, *177*
Mitterrand, François 202
Modern Architecture: International Exhibition, 1932 78, 110
Modern Architecture (Taut) 78
Moholy-Nagy, Laszlo 52, 108, 193, 194
MoMA. *See* Museum of Modern Art (MoMA)
Monadnock building 69
Morris, William 30, 41, 42
Mumford, Lewis 112, 117
mur neutralisant 170, 172, 185
Museum of Modern Art (MoMA) 73, 78, 110, 144, 169, 195, 196
MoMA Building, New York 111, *111*
Museum Tower, Dallas 188, 189
MVRDV 57

Nabis 39
Nabi/Tiffany windows 39, *40*
Nakamura, Hiroshi 148
Nasher Sculpture Center, Dallas, Texas 189
National Art Center, Tokyo 188
National Housing Act, 1934 138

National Museum of African American History, Washington, D.C. 183
National Ornamental Glass Manufacturers Association 32
National Socialism 194–6
natural light. *See* daylighting
natural ventilation 130, 172–3, 185
Nazi Germany 51, 194–6, 197, 200
NBBJ 188
Nelson, Paul 131–2, 180
Nénot, Henri 198
Neumann, Dietrich 83
Nevada tiles 122, 129, 130
The New Architecture and the Bauhaus (Gropius) 108
New Deal 137
Niemeyer, Oscar 177, *177*, 199
nighttime illumination 114–17, 141–2, 148, 189
Nimmons, George C. 165, *165*, 166, *166*, 167, 169
Nippon Sheet Glass of Japan 158
Nishizawa, Ryue 154, 158–9, *159*, 167
Nitzchke, Oscar 180
"No Shadow Tower" 188
Nord-Draht 105–6
Normandy glass 1. *See also* crown glass
Norwest Collection 27
Notre Dame du Haut, Ronchamp 55–6, *56*, 58
Notre-Dame de Toute Grâce du Plateau, Assy 55
Nouvel, Jean 26, 161, 182–3, *182*, *183*
Novarina, Maurice 55

Occidental Chemical Company 172, 182
Ofili, Chris 58
Olgyay, Victor 180–1
opalescent glass 34–6, *35*
Optical Glass House, Hiroshima 148
Optiwhite 159

orangeries 6
organic screens 178
Organic Window 72–7
Oriel Chambers, Liverpool 102, *103*
orientation of building 117, 183, 185
Orléans, Duc d' (later King Louis Phillippe) 19
Osler, Abraham Follett 9–11, *10*
Osler fountain 9–11
Otte House, Berlin 52
Oud, J. J. P. 48
outdoor schools 131
overheating 132, 162–3
Owens Bottle Company 140
Owens-Illinois Company 140–1, 145
Owens-Illinois Glass Block Building 141–2, *141*
Ozenfant, Amédée 83–4

Palace of the Republic, East Germany 202
Palais Royal, Paris
  Galerie de Bois 19
  Galerie d'Orléans 19–20, *20*
Palladian window 71
palm houses. *See* greenhouses
Palmolive Building, Chicago 79
panopticon prison 199
Pan-Russian Society of Proletarian Architects 194
para-soleil envelope 180
Parque Guinle, Rio da Janeiro 178, *178*
Parson, Elizabeth 38
partition walls 142, 157–8
Passage d'Opéra, Paris 19, 20
Passagen-Werk (Benjamin) 21
patch plates 152
patents
  glass blocks/bricks 125, *127*
  long window 85
  Luxfer Prism tile 42–4, *43*
  opalescent glass 34–6
  tempered glass 110

pattern books 32
Patton, Normand 91
pavement lights 125
Paxton, Joseph
   Crystal Palace 8, 162–3
   Great Stove Conservatory, Chatsworth 7, 162
   Great Victorian Way (unbuilt) 24–5
   legacy 99
Peel, Sir Robert 4
Pei, I. M. 202
Pelli, Cesar 99
Penn-American Plate Glass 134–5
Perret, Auguste 83, 87
phalansteries 22, 23
Phoenix Pavilion 44
photovoltaic (PV) panels 189–90
Piano, Renzo 148–50, *150*, 186–8, *187*, 189
Piano Workshop 188
Pilafian, Suren 138
Pilkington Brothers 118, 134, 135, 137, 158, 159
Pittsburgh Corning Corporation 140, 144, 145
Pittsburgh Plate Glass (PPG) 100, 135, 139–40, 146
Pittsburgh process. 100
plate glass production 65, 100
pointfixed glass spider fittings 152
Polignac, Edmond de, Princesse 132
Polk, William 103–5, *104*, 107
polychrome structural glass 135–7, 190
Portman, John 205–6, *206*
postmodern glass 205
Powell, John Hardman 29
Prairie houses 44–7
Pre-Raphaelites 41
The Present and General Condition of Sanitary Science (Chadwick) 124
Pringle, Alexander M. 142, *143*
prismatic glass 125. *See also* Luxfer Prism tiles

privacy laws 85
programmed lighting 148
Pugin, Augustus W. N. 17, 28–30
Purism 83, 85
PV (photovoltaic) panels 189–90
Pyrex 140, 144, 179

quarry stained glass windows 32–3

Radio City, Rockefeller Center 170
Randolph, S. M. 91
reflective glass 184, 205, 206–7
Reich, Lilly 112
Reichstag, Berlin 200–1, *201*, 202, 203
Reidy, Alfonso 177
Reliance Building, Chicago *67*, *76*, 77, 79
Renwick, E. A. 69, 74–5
ribbon window 59, 83–8
Richards, Thomas 12
Richards Medical Research Laboratories, University of Pennsylvania 179–80
Richter, Hans 53
Rietveld, Gerrit 49
Robie House window *45*
Roche, Martin 39–40, 41, *41*, 69, 71
Roche, Mary 145
Rogers, Richard 131, 152
Romanticism 28
Rookery building, Chicago 64, 79, *80*, 82
room depth 64, 87
Root, John Wellborn 64, 79
Rouault, George 55
Roussel, Ker-Xavier 39, *40*
Rowe, Colin 199
Rox glass 135
Ruskin, John 11–12, 17, 94
Russel-Hitchcock, Henry 78

Sacré-Coeur, Audincourt 55
Sadar, John 134
Saint-Simon, Henri de 23–4, 91, 92, 93

Salon d'Automne 87
Salvation Army, Cité du Refuge 132
SANAA 157–8, 167–8, *168*
Sani-Onyx glass 134
sanitariums 130
sanitary glass 134
sanitation 123, 134–5
La Sarraz Declaration 198
SC Johnson Administration Building, Racine, Wisconsin 144, 179
Scalzo, Julia 18
Scheerbart, Paul 90–1, 92–4, 95–6, 107, 121–2, 123, 144
Schlesinger & Meyer Store 73, 79
Schroeder House, Utrecht 49
Schuyler, Montgomery 62, 65, 71
screen printing 57, 58
sculpted glass modules 145
Seagram Building 115–17, *116*, 142, 174
sealants 110. *See also* adhesives
sealed buildings 110, 112, 132, 167, 172, 179
Sears, Roebuck and Company 164
Sears Englewood store, Chicago 164, 166–7, *166*, 169
Second Leiter Building, Chicago 65
The Secret Doctrine, the Synthesis of Science, Religion and Philosophy (Blavatsky) 94–5
sedak GmbH & Co 155, 157
seele 157
Seiden, Rudolph 110
Sejima, Kazuyo 158–9, *159*, 167, 168
Sendai Mediatheque 154–5, *154*, 190
Seves 149
shading 176–83, 190. *See also* brise-soleil
Sharp, Dennis 91
sheet glass. *See* cylinder glass
Shift 190
ship saloons 86–7
shoji screens 44, 147
shop windows 12–18, 138, 139–40
show cases 12

sick building syndrome 172
sidewalk lights 125
silicone adhesives 152, 157
silicone membranes 190
Singer, Winnaretta 132
Skidmore, Owings, and Merrill (SOM) 90, 112–13, *113*, 174–5
skylights 12
skyscrapers 59–65
Slutzky, Robert 199
smart buildings 190
Smythson, Robert 4–5
social aspects
　glass as marker of social class 193, 207–8
　glass as symbol of personal wealth 4–5, 207
　rise of consumer culture 21
　social status of glass 17–18
Societe de Saint Gobain 129
solar control 162–3, 181, 184. *See also* brise-soleil; shading
solar gain 162–3. *See also* thermal performance
solar panels 189–90
SOM (Skidmore, Owings, and Merrill) 90, 112–13, *113*, 174–5
Sommerfeld House, Berlin 52
Space, Time and Architecture: The Growth of a New Tradition (Giedion) 89–90
spandrel glass 138, 146
spectrally selective insulated glazing units 191
Speer, Albert 194, 196, 197
spread glass. *See* cylinder glass
stained glass 27–58
　and constructivism 47–54
　Frank Lloyd Wright 42–7
　at Great Exhibition, 1851 8
　imaging technologies 57
　as an industrial product 31–4
　Le Corbusier 27, 55–7
　Pierre Couturier 54–5

Scheerbart's espousal of 96
    screen and frit printing 57, 58
    Tiffany and La Farge 34–42
    Vicorian revival 27–31
staircases 156
steel framed construction 60–2
Stephen Lawrence Center 58, *58*
Sternfeld, Harry 148
Stone, Edward Durrell 111–12, *111*, 144
storefronts. *See* shop windows
structural glass 121–59
    facades 151–9
    glass and hygiene 123–40
    glass blocks 140–50
    staircases 156
Suez Canal Hospital, Surgical Pavilion 131–2
Suger, Abbot 94
Sullivan, Louis 42, 59, 72–7, 77, 78, 82
sun screen. *See* brise-soleil
sunlight and health 132–4. *See also* daylighting
Suprematism 108
suspended glazing 152
sustainable architecture 185
Sweet's Catalogue of Building Construction 146
synaesthesia 95
synagogues 32–3

Takamatsu, Shin 148, *149*
Tarnier, Stéphane 124, *128*
Taut, Bruno
    Die Gläserne Kette group 107
    on expressionism 108
    Glashaus pavilion 96–7, *97*, *98*, 122
    Modern Architecture 78
    and Scheerbart 121
taxes 3–4
Teague, Walter Dorwin 137, 139, 140, 144
technological history 1–3
tempered glass 110, 151–2, 156
Terragni, Giuseppe 201–2

Théorie des Quatre Mouvements et des Destinées Générales (Fourier) 22
Theosophy 94, 96
thermal movement 110, 174–5
thermal performance 107, 142, 161–3, 162
Thermolux glass 111, 112
Thermopane 173, 174
Thought Forms (Besant and Leadbeater) 95
Tiffany, Charles L. 34, 96
Tiffany, Louis Comfort 34, 35–9
Tiffany Chapel 36, *37*
Tiffany Glass & Decorating Company 36–7, 38
tinted glass 112–14, 173–4, 184
tinted windows 174, 180, 181–2
Toledo Museum of Art Glass Pavilion 158–9, *159*
toughened glass. *See* tempered glass
Townshend Act, 1767 4
transparency metaphor 198–205
transparent luminescent solar concentrator 190
Tribune Tower competition 73
tropical modernism 161, 177–8
True Principles of Pointed or Christian Architecture (Pugin) 17, 29
Tschichold, Jan 194
Tschumi, Bernard 190
20 Fenchurch Street, London 188
twin-face facades. *See* double walled glass facades
Tzara, Tristan 20

ultraviolet coatings 189
ultraviolet light 134, 167
United Nations Secretariat building, New York 117, *118*, 174, 199
Universal Corporation 110
University Club, Chicago 39–41, *41*
University of California, Hallidie Building, San Francisco 102–5, *104*, 107

University of Oklahoma, Crystal
    Chapel (unbuilt) 143–4
University of Pennsylvania, Richards
    Medical Research Laboratories
    179–80
US Green Building Council (USGBC)
    185
utopia of glass 22–5

Vanderbilt, Cornelius 34
variable light transmission 184
Vari-Tran coating 184
vault lights 125, *126*
veiling reflectance 186
Venetian Building, Chicago 68–9
ventilation 85, 130, 162–3, 170, 172–3
vertical window 5, 87–8
verticality 70, 72, 73, 77, 78–9
Victorian stained glass 28
Villa Allegonda, Katwijk, The
    Netherlands 48
Villa La Roche 84, *84*, 86, 87
Vinoly, Rafael 188
Viollet-le-Duc, Eugene 94
Viracon 180
Vita glass 132–4
Vitrolite Company 135, *136*
Vitrolite glass 134, 135, *136*, 137, 138, 146
Vitrolux glass 138

Wainwright Building, St. Louis 77
Waldheim, Charles 62
Wallot, Paul 200, 202
wall-to-window ratio.
    See glazing ratio
Wasmuth Portfolio 48
water infiltration 110
Waukegan City Hall *204*, 205
WCAU tower, Philadelphia 148
weather responsive silicone
    membranes 190
Westin Bonaventure Hotel, Los
    Angeles 205–7, *206*

When the Cathedrals Were White (Le
    Corbusier) 169, 170
Wight, Peter 70
Wilfred, Thomas 95–6
Wilkinson Eyre 191
Williams, Owen 138, *139*
Willis, Faber & Dumas 157
Willis Faber & Dumas Building,
    Ipswich 152, *153*
Wils, Jan 48, 49
window glass 1, 100
window size 64
window tax 3
windowless stores 164–9
window-to-wall ratio. *See* glazing ratio
winter gardens 24
Wordsworth, William 28
World's Columbian Exposition, 1893,
    Chicago
    Falconnier bricks 129, 141
    Phoenix Pavilion 44
    supposed suppression of Chicago
        style 74
    Tiffany Chapel 36–7, *37*, 38
    Woman's Building triptych *37*
Wright, Frank Lloyd
    compositions for the Luxfer Prism
        Company 42–4, *43*
    endorsement of pro-UV glass 134
    glass as "curse of the classic" 16
    and Luxfer 82–3
    St. Mark's-in-the-Bowery, New
        York 134
    Research Tower, Racine,
        Wisconsin 144
    SC Johnson Administration
        Building 144, 179
    stained glass 42–7
    use of Pyrex glass tubes 144

Yang, Soo-in 190
Yost, J. W. 66

Zorlu Lantern, Istanbul 157, 169